THE SUPERIOR PENINSULA

Seasons in the Upper Peninsula of Michigan

Lon L. Emerick, Ph.D.

Cover Photograph by Scot Stewart
Drawings by Mary Frey

ISBN 0-9650577-5-5

Library of Congress Card Number 95-092859

Published by North Country

355 Heidtman Road, Skandia, MI 49885

Printed in the United States of America

First Edition 1996

10 9 8 7 6 5 4 3 2 1

PREFACE

The Superior Peninsula is a series of short essays describing a lay naturalist's abiding affection for a unique geographical region: the Upper Peninsula of Michigan. While the tales highlight very local and particular features, I believe (with James Joyce) that local explorations may have general, perhaps even planetary significance.

This book is not a travel guide for summer tourists (although vivid portraits of the land will guide the modern explorer); it is not a weighty treatise on the flora and fauna of the area (although plants, trees and wild creatures are featured in many of the essays); it is not a review of the colorful history of the Peninsula (although past and present are woven into the tales). It is a collection of 32 love letters which publicly affirm the author's devotion for the many exquisite facets of this portion of the north country. The material is arranged in four seasons with eight essays for each season.

The chapters comprising this book originated on woodland hiking trails, deserted beaches and other remote spots in the Peninsula. A number of good companions contributed generously of their impressions, insights and inspiration. In particular, Mary and John Argeropoulos, companions for all seasons, provided abundant fellowship and inexhaustible enthusiasm for every outdoor adventure. Dorothy Maywood Bird, distinguished lady of letters, offered the special brand of encouragement which only another writer can convey. Several of the tales appeared in slightly different form in the *Marquette Monthly* and *Michigan Out-of-Doors* and I acknowledge the interest and support of Pat O'Day and Kenneth Lowe.

Finally, my wife, Lynn and twin daughters, Mary and Lynn, helped create *The Superior Peninsula* in a thousand intricate ways but most of all by their unquestioning and abiding love.

Also by Lon Emerick

With Stick and String: Adventures with Bow and Arrow

That's Easy for You to Say: An Assault on Stuttering

CONTENTS

WINTER

SUMMER

SPRING

AUTUMN

To:

*The blue profound, Lake Superior, and
the flinty, forested land known as the
Upper Peninsula*

i quaeris peninsulam amoenum circumspice — ". . . if you seek a beautiful peninsula, look about you." A fitting motto for the State of Michigan. Except for one oversight: it should be plural. Most every schoolchild knows that Michigan is shaped like a mitten; what some people overlook, even professional cartographers, is that the State also has an Upper Peninsula. The adjective, "Upper," is, in the minds of those who live in this very special land, more than just a geographical reference. We believe it is the *Superior Peninsula*.

This magnificent part of the north country deserves the honorific title because it is superior in every way: Lake Superior, the largest, cleanest, roughest body of fresh water in the world guards the northern boundary; it has 1,100 miles of wild and rugged shoreline, thousands of miles of rushing rivers and over 140 waterfalls; acre upon acre of verdant forests, the deepest mine shafts in the world; the oldest community, Sault Ste. Marie, in the midwest; cool, pure, zingy air, and so much more. Now, if all that is not enough to justify the appellation, *Superior*, I would simply point out that *Paradise* is located in Michigan's Upper Peninsula (*Hell* is situated in the lower part of the state) . . . we visit the small community each summer.

I am being facetious, of course, but there is more than a little truth in the humor. The more than 300,000 residents of the Upper Peninsula display an intense feeling of pride in their unique homeland; the open spaces we enjoy seem to engender a well-developed sense of independence and self reliance. We resent intrusions from outsiders, particularly self-styled experts from the metropolitan areas of the Lower Peninsula of Michigan. Most probably, this truculence stems, to a certain extent, from the rejection and scorn the Superior Peninsula has endured over the years; it all started even before Michigan was admitted to the Union as a state.

In 1835, the governor and legislators of the Territory of Michigan would have gladly traded the Upper Peninsula for a much smaller strip of land (the Toledo Strip, 470 square miles) on the border with Ohio. In fact, it took a mini-war between the State of

Ohio and the Territory of Michigan to settle the matter. Both parties recruited motley armies to secure and hold the strip of land along the Maumee River; the land was desirable because it afforded a nice port on Lake Erie and the growing city of Toledo guarded a portion of a new canal between Erie and the Ohio River. The armies never met on the battlefield — it seems to have been planned that way — and the casualties were limited to one wounded Michigan deputy sheriff (he recovered from a stab wound), two horses killed (or one mule, the records are unclear), and the loss of a few pigs and chickens to the foraging armies. In the end, Washington imposed a solution: Ohio was awarded the Toledo Strip and Michigan received statehood and, as a consolation prize, 16,347 square miles north of the Mackinac Straits. Political solons and downstate newspapers cried a loud foul: Thanks, but no thanks, for "a region of perpetual snow, the *Ultima Thule*," said the Detroit Free Press in opposition to the compromise. A legislator was more graphic: "The Upper Peninsula," he stated, "is a sterile region on the shores of Lake Superior destined by soil and climate to remain forever a wilderness."

Fortunately for those of us addicted to wild places, much of the Superior Peninsula does remain relatively untamed; alas, however, there are many who are trying to convert the land to cash as swiftly as possible. Some individuals have accused me of also exploiting the region through my writing; the more new people attracted to the region, they argue, the greater the impact on the beaches, streams and forests. Their point is well taken. However, it is also possible that some readers may come to know and love the region and they, too, will have a vested interest in saving as well as savoring its many splendors. When a person does not know the Peninsula intimately, he is more willing to give it up to power plants, open pit mines and condominiums. Those who love the land will treat it gently.

As the reader will no doubt discern, my own affection for the Superior Peninsula is boundless. It is best to confess at the outset that I am a jealous lover; with a passion some detractors will judge too extreme, that I care not wisely but too abundantly. My answer, a paraphrase of an erstwhile presidential candidate's famous statement, is this challenge: *extremism in the love of the land is no vice; moderation in the pursuit of environmental goals is no virtue.*

As in all things which relate to human relationships with the land, Henry David Thoreau said it most eloquently; "I love my native valley; fit in it like an acorn in its cup."

PHOTO BY LON EMERICK

WINTER

Seasons in the Upper Peninsula of Michigan

"Suspended on a carpet of snow"

"The falls was frozen into huge daggers"

PHOTOS BY LON EMERICK

P ART   I

-- --·=--·--

W I N T E R

*I*t is altogether fitting and proper that these tales of affection for the Superior Peninsula commence with its longest season, winter. Just as the relentless glaciers molded and marked the landscape thousands of years ago, snow and ice still dominate the North Country. When winter is at its peak in our region, it is difficult to remember that it is merely one of four seasons — it seems as though we are stuck in one part of the annual cycle. In no other season can one witness so vividly the primitive, natural forces at work — awesome, beautiful, compelling.

Generally winter begins in mid-November and lingers until the end of April. But it is foolhardy to generalize about weather in the North Country for we have seen heavy snow storms obliterate the fall colors in September; more than once we have pushed our way through the drifts to reach a favorite fishing spot in early May. According to one year's weather diary, there was frost each month and a few snowflakes even fell during July and August. No matter what the date on the calendar, winter is never far away; it yields its grip slowly, grudgingly.

The character of the residents is influenced to a great extent by the lingering cold season. Although local people may complain ruefully that summer in the peninsula is merely six weeks of poor skiing, winter has built an individualism and independence, a toughness and a pride in surviving and thriving despite the deep snow and fierce cold. Indeed, when summer visitors ask with sly smirks about our winters, we sigh and nod in resignation — but after the tourist turmoil we look forward to the isolation and solitude of the longest season.

So, as fall wanes and days grow shorter, we wait expectantly for the first signs of approaching winter: a layer of sparkling hoarfrost decorating a platoon of cattails; flocks of snow buntings and longspurs swirling beside the roadways and in the open fields; scarlet morning skies over Lake Superior; pines and spruces intensely green against the stark grey branches of the deciduous trees; a soft white mantle of fresh snow clinging to a cold November dawn.

It is impossible to appreciate the impact of winter by simply coming north for a weekend of skiing. For residents of the peninsula, winter sports are not just a sometime diversion, they are a way of life. Snow and ice, rather than being irritations as they often are in urban areas, become sparkling vehicles for adventure and exploration. The longest season imprints vivid mental images.

Winter is for us an intense montage of outdoor memories. Here are just a few: long, dark nights with the stars hanging clear and close; the Northern lights performing an eerie pastel dance across the horizon; snow piled so high along the roads that drivers decorate their car antennas with bright orange balls to be seen at intersections; long hikes through the glittering brilliance of fresh snowfall in quiet woods; snowshoes propped in the snow beside a small fire; wood smoke gently perfuming the air so cold and pure you can almost drink it; the indescribably sensuous delight of warming cold hands and feet beside an open fireplace; waterfalls arrested in spectacular jumbles of sparkling stalactites; blue jays, evening grosbeaks and redpolls fluffed against the cold, cracking sunflower seeds at our bird feeders. And so many, many more.

Most of all there is the sound of silence. It descends like a blessing after all the cacophony of spring, the steady productive hum of summer and the clamor of the autumn harvest and migration. The snowscape simplifies by covering clutter and muffling the noises of the forest. It is a time of long shadows and long, long thoughts. It is a season of solitude, a time of quiescence, an opportunity for catching up and renewal.

THE WAY OF SNOWSHOES

e seemed to glide as if suspended on the vast unbroken white mantle of snow. Only the steady soft swish on the sparkling drifts underfoot, the slight creaking of the leather bindings and the faint click of the tails of our snowshoes reminded us that we were moving steadily along the old road and ever deeper into the wild area. Here, on the first day of a new year, we were seeking the margin of solitude which only a remote woodland in winter can provide. As we moved along the snow's bright surface in the same timeless way men did centuries before mechanization, we felt again the delightful lifting of the human spirit which comes when civilization, with all its busyness and pressures, is left behind.

Pausing briefly, I took in the panorama of winter trees, graceful lines now laid bare in gray silhouettes against the cerulean sky; ice crystals glinting from the alders beside the dark, frozen stream; delicate shadows tracing upon the shimmering snow. Most of all, the immense carpet of snow overwhelmed my senses and brought to mind a couplet by John Whittaker Watson:

> Oh! The snow, the beautiful snow,
> filling the sky and earth below.

Lynn stirred behind me — the temperature had hovered near ten degrees that morning and we were not yet warmed by the hike — and moved ahead to break trail. No human tracks preceded us as we made our way into the McCormick Tract toward the abandoned lodge by White Deer Lake. What more fitting way to celebrate New Year's Day, a new beginning, than a trek on a bright clean landscape into a pristine wild area?

We passed scores of weathered telephone poles beside the old road, tilted at crazy angles and trailing inert rusty wires. For many years, the wealthy and somewhat eccentric McCormick family maintained well-stocked and furnished facilities on White Deer

Lake, complete with resident caretakers, though they used the lodge only rarely. Three generations of McCormicks — descendants of Cyrus H. McCormick, inventor of the reaper — acquired a large tract of land astride Baraga and Marquette Counties in the central Upper Peninsula. In 1969, Gordon McCormick, last of the heirs, bequeathed the entire 17,000 acres to the U.S. Forest Service; it is now part of the Ottawa National Forest, one of two national forests in the peninsula.

The area is officially designated the Cyrus H. McCormick Experimental Forest,* a somewhat pedantic title for 27 square miles of Michigamme Highland — a region of dense forests, granite outcroppings, rushing streams and wilderness lakes. Trees and water dominate the tract. Last logged about 1910, the McCormick Forest is now covered by extensive stands of pine and hemlock. There are at least twenty lakes, including White Deer, Bulldog, Island and Margaret. Several famous rivers — the Yellow Dog, Huron, and Dead — originate or flow through the area, eventually dispatching their waters into Lake Superior.

It is a handsome, virile land. Access is limited and travel must be on foot or by canoe. Although the evidence of man's former presence in the McCormick Forest is abundant in the form of old tote roads, dams and stumps, people are encountered less frequently than deer and beaver. Now man comes as a visitor on Nature's terms. A very special portion of the forest in the northeast corner was set aside as a Research Natural Area for ecological investigation; this part was never logged and huge white pine and yellow birches stand beside the rapids and falls of the Yellow Dog River. Here, biologists study relatively undisturbed forest ecosystems to establish baselines for wildlife populations, data needed in order to chart human impact on the natural order of things. If humans need the tonic which flows from the untrammeled world of nature, and I firmly believe they do, then here is a spring from which to drink deeply.

Warmed now by the rhythmic pace, we stopped for a longer rest. Loosening our heavy parkas, we propped our snowshoes in a drift under a hemlock and used them as wicker seats while we sipped scalding tea from a thermos. As we sat there in the quiet winter forest, we felt as if we were one with the Chippewas and *coureurs de bois* who traversed this land — and perhaps this very spot — centuries before in search of game and furs..

*We took this snowshoe trek in 1970 just after the Forest Service acquired the property. The McCormick Tract is now a designated wilderness and the lodge, cabins and other signs of human activity have been removed.

The sport of snowshoeing is ancient, perhaps over four thousand years old. The first model was devised in Asia and probably consisted of simple planks, like small wide skis; migrants brought them across the land bridge from Siberia and adaptations appeared slowly in the New World. The Athabascans of Alaska shaped tough ash strips into large ovals and strung gut webbing across the frames. The tracks they left in the snow resembled those of the huge brown bears and hence the label bear paws. Another design, the Pickerel, is long and narrow, an excellent shape for open trail use. For all-around utility our Algonquin shoes — sometimes called Maine or Michigan — shaped like a long beaver tail, are ideal. All kinds of snowshoes provide a special way to move about in the winter world: simple, direct, self-propelled.

Snowshoeing on fresh, deep snow is like sinking into an airy white blanket; the fluffy covering acts as soundproofing and muffles movements and sounds. No motorized means of travel can provide the same experience; only by moving under your own power can you truly be a part of the quiet harmony of the winter woods. Snowshoeing is uncomplicated and unspoiled by modern gimmicks. Far from the madding crowd, there is no hustle, no falseness, only the traveler and the snowy woods. The silence, the snow, the almost magical aura evoked by the gliding motion stir ancient memories of our racial heritage. Each time I snowshoe I discover more about my place in the natural realm.

The pace and the simplicity of snowshoeing let the traveler really observe the winter world: lacy patterns of snow on an ancient hemlock stump; delicate tracery of ice crystals on the frozen surface of a small creek; the intricate drama of animal tracks written on the snow; the tightly folded buds of the deciduous trees, each one distinct and each a promise of spring.

Once we snowshoed along the shore of Lake Superior with several friends on a clear, cold night. As we paused near the tip of a wooded point, the moon rose slowly over the lake and cut a path of silver across the ice toward the spot where we stood. The group hushed into silence. At that moment — which is forever highlighted in my mind — we felt as if we were at the confluence of our beings and the creative forces of the universe. The Chippewas said it more simply: *Agimosse* — "I walk on snowshoes."

Now, as we neared White Deer Lake, a chickadee flew down to greet us with his happy chatter and a shy nuthatch yanked noisily from behind a dead spruce along the shoreline. Crossing over on the ice, now at least eighteen inches thick, we clambered up the rocks of a small island off-shore from the main lodge, and inspected the beautifully hand-crafted central cabin surrounded by several others nestled by granite knobs and tall pines. On a sunny, dry porch facing the south and out of the wind it was warm enough to shed our gloves and caps. Rummaging in our packs, we retrieved the lunch and leaned back against the warm boards to contemplate the wild shores of White Deer Lake.

Days spent in such remote environs are a bonus and should not be counted in a life span. We agreed that this wild place must remain as a remnant, a reminder of the natural order, of the way things were in the North Country. Thoreau said it better: "We need to witness our limits transgressed and some life pasturing freely where we never wander." There are precious few wilderness areas left, particularly in Michigan — parts of the Porcupine Mountains, the Huron Islands, small sections of the Ottawa and Hiawatha National Forests. In fact, just over 3% of publicly-owned land in the Superior Peninsula is now legally designated wilderness. A few strong voices crying out to save our remaining wild areas struck a respondent chord in many others and in 1964 Congress passed the Wilderness Act which set aside certain portions of the United States as " . . . an area where the earth and its community of life are untrammeled by man, where man himself is a visitor who does not remain." For purposes of legislation, a wilderness area was defined as 5000 contiguous acres of roadless area.

Yet wilderness is more than legislation and contiguous acres of roadless area. It is a way of thinking, a matter of human values. Wild, free growing areas are as much a part of our heritage and quality of life as libraries, art galleries and museums.

But, the "wise use" proponents argue, the McCormick Forest is just sitting there, not being used. And I reply for those who will listen: the sole criterion of usefulness cannot always be that of board feet, taconite, or tourist dollars. Wilderness, too, is "useful," measured not in profit terms but for its value as a setting where man is merely one member of the natural community which includes the pine, the eagle and all living creatures. The minority of self-propelled travelers ask only that a decent minority of the land be left in its natural state.

"What of the aged, the infirm, those disinclined to leave their vehicles?" the critics of wild places ask. Without roads and amenities, entry is limited only to those who are able to travel on foot. When I put this question recently to an eighty-nine-year-old trout fisherman, he snorted. "Why does every spot on earth need a macadam highway leading to it?" he asked rhetorically. "Sure, I'm sorry that I won't get to see the McCormick Forest," he continued, "But, look, there are hundreds of spots I *can* reach and have a comparable experience. And, you know, it comforts me to know that this same wild place will still be there for my great grandchildren to explore."

Some who oppose wildness seem to have an almost personal fear of its presence, linked to our pioneer experience. We once asked an old Finnish craftsman why he had removed all the trees around a cabin he was building on the shore of a remote lake. He looked at us for a long time, muttered something and finally dismissed the query as irrelevant; but before he turned back to his tools I caught the look in his eyes and I understood. It bespoke of a time when man hovered in a cave while awesome creatures stalked the land, of the ages when our ancestors lived in tiny clearings carved from miles of dark and foreboding forest. Now, we have awesome machines which can strip a wooded glade in minutes — and we must somehow exorcise those ancient fears and learn to live in harmony with our world.

We cannot, of course, really return to an earlier time; our world is too complicated for simplistic solutions. But we can cultivate our humility and rediscover facets of our humanity by doing something uncomplicated like abandoning ourselves to the magic of a winter forest.

As we made our way through the twilight back to the county road where our car was parked, we paused one last time and looked back at the darkened McCormick Forest. During our snowshoe adventure we had rediscovered and come to better understand what Thoreau meant when he observed that "in wildness is the preservation of the world."

P A S T Y   I N   M Y   P O C K E T

*T*he huge snow flakes fell slowly — drifting down through the aspens and striped maples almost like a sensual caress. The familiar path turned upward now toward Mount Marquette and even though I was less than a quarter mile from my home, the sounds of the town below were already muted. I could feel the warmth of the fresh pasty in my pocket as I topped the first rise and stopped on the trail to my special sanctuary, the Hidden Valley. Leaning on my walking stick I gazed at the expanse of white birches which crown the knoll and extend into the valley below. Although I have followed this path scores of times — it commences almost at our boundary line — the birches of the grove always surprise and exhilarate me by the way they light up the ridge and valley with their whiteness. I never get tired of watching birches and winter is the best time to get to know them. I like the way they grow gregariously in clumps, I admire their white parchment bark marked with black eyebrows raised as if in surprise, and the delicate tracery of their dark branches against the winter sky. Already the morning work-a-day hassles were dimming and I set off up the mountain with a new spring in my gait.

Everyone needs an Ephriam, a place to which he can flee and soothe his jangled nerve endings from the harsh assaults of modern living. There are times for everyone when the business of living doesn't meet expenses and our internal gyroscope needs to be re-set in line with what is important. A ramble in the woods has always been a tonic for me — up a hill or two until something takes over and the mind springs free — so now I sought the familiar solace of my special river valley.

This portion of the Carp River Valley makes a deep gash through terrain heavily forested with pine, spruce and hemlock. The Carp jumps and cascades over ancient granite ledges and eventually flows into Lake Superior just south of town. For centuries, bands of Chippewas camped at its mouth; in 1849, Robert Graveraet, one of the pioneers in the region, built the first primitive furnace for making "puddle iron" from the raw ore brought down a tote road from Negaunee ten miles away. For some time, the Valley was the main link between the iron mines and the port on the big lake.

Few people enter the Hidden Valley now. On the west it seems blocked by the high cliffs of a commercial ski hill; it is bounded on the east by Marquette Branch Prison, a formidable sandstone barrier complete with high walls and gun towers. In the decade that I have wandered the three-mile long Valley, I have encountered only a handful of people, usually fishermen who almost without exception are also seeking solitude. The signs of human impact are astonishingly few for a spot so close to civilization: old logging roads, now largely overgrown; ore test pits and some ancient mining adzes; the remains of a crude log cabin. Wildlife, though, is plentiful. During my frequent sojourns, I often see deer, an occasional black bear, raccoons, porcupines and other small animals; owls and hawks also find a quiet sanctuary in the Valley.

Although the land is officially owned by an iron mining company, I have come to think of this lovely spot as *my* valley. I do not mean this in the sense of ownership — men do not own land, they are merely stewards for a short time — but rather that so much of my psychic energy is invested in its hemlock groves, granite knobs and deep river pools that I belong to it, and it belongs to me. In fact, we have named several distinctive features in the area after particularly memorable visits. A high crag from which we can watch the nuances of Lake Superior is Lynn's Lookout; a long bench of granite where we spent a delightful winter afternoon baking bread strips rolled on green sticks is Sourdough Ridge; Summit Peak, with its expanse of rose-colored gneiss which we scaled one wet spring day, is the highest point in the area. Sometimes I am startled to find that others to whom I have shown the area do not see in the Hidden Valley what I have come to love and need. I suppose the valley is not as beautiful as many other spots in the Peninsula. But perhaps the famous Russian proverb about the child searching for his mother, the most beautiful woman in the world, is relevant. It is not simply that we love the land because it is beautiful, it is beautiful because we come to love it.

The snow fell faster now as I crossed over the last ridges and headed down a narrow gully to a favorite listening and watching point overlooking the river. With no breeze to guide them, the flakes ghosted down as if each crystal sought out just the right spot to land. Extending my hand, I caught several flakes and inspected their delicate, intricate patterns, marveling as children do, how each one could be different from the last. Remembering the remarkable photographs compiled over a lifetime by Wilson A. Bentley, who devoted his energy and resources to studying snow crystals, I looked more closely as the flakes fell on my dark mitten. Astonishingly, a small letter "H" nestled on my palm, then another and another. I lost track of time and, deep in reverie, recalled Thoreau's paean to a snowflake: "How full of the creative genius is the air in which they are generated. I should hardly admire more if real stars fell and lodged on my coat."

Hastening on in my eagerness, the tips of my snowshoes dug into a drift and sent me in an ungraceful glissade down the slope; a startled downy woodpecker flew undulating away, his shrill whinnying alarm call echoing across the stream. Brushing off the snow, I laughed, too, and hurried to find some dead pine branches for a small fire which would warm my soul as well as my lunch.

Although the pasty was still warm in its foil wrapping, I nestled it carefully near the edge of the crackling flames. If the Upper Peninsula has a regional dish, it most certainly is the delectable meal in a crust, the Cornish pasty ("pass-tee"): beef, sliced potatoes, onion, turnips, rutabagas — all placed in an crust and shaped like a half-moon. Regardless of their background or nationality, residents of the peninsula share an affinity for this savory dish.

Several nationalities have had a part in shaping the customs and character of the region. The Native Americans — whose language is preserved in the names of many towns: Escanaba, Ontonagon, Ahmeek — were here, of course, to greet the French explorers and priests — Radisson, Brule, Allouez, Marquette — who came in search of adventure, furs and souls. Germans, Swedes, Italians, Irish and Poles followed; they came to work the copper and iron mines, lumber the forests, or wrestle a precarious living farming the rocky soil.

Of all the ethnic groups which migrated to the Upper Peninsula, the Finnish probably had the greatest influence. There are more Finns in northern Michigan than in any other state. Finns identify closely with the land and this is reflected in family names: Aho means "field," Harju is "ridge," and Lahti translates "bay." They found in the peninsula a forest, soil, setting and climate much like their native Finland. These hardy settlers brought with them the traits of thrift, honesty, love of solitude and *"sisu"* which translates loosely into "courage." They also brought the sauna, or steam bath. The Finns are straightforward, open-faced people who look you in the eye and say what they mean; their native tongue with its characteristic cadence and lilt has left an indelible mark upon the speech of almost all residents of the region. But even Finnish cooks could not improve upon the Cornish pasty.

Despite their smaller numbers, the immigrants from Cornwall also had a significant impact upon the peninsula, particularly in terms of its economic development. Cornwall is a tiny, rocky peninsula at the southwest tip of England; it is famed as the land of the legends of King Arthur and as the staging ground for the Allied invasion of France. It is also a land of mines and miners — and the folklore abounds that wherever there is a hole in the ground, at the bottom of it will be a Cornish miner. When tin and copper mining waned in Cornwall at the middle of the 19th century, hundreds of skilled miners headed for the United States, and particularly to Upper Michigan where Douglass Houghton's geological survey had revealed the richest deposits of native copper in the world. Because of their experience, the Cornish were invariably made crew foremen or captains. In some cases, other workmen refused to enter a mine unless led and supervised by a "Cousin Jack," a label given to the miners from Cornwall because they always had another cousin back in the old country when additional workers were needed. A complex, hardworking, somewhat clannish and highly individualistic people of Celtic origin, they brought their distinctive foods with them — saffron bread and rolls, heavy cake, clotted cream. But their most famous culinary legacy is the pasty.

The pasty is a noble and venerable food; as early as 1390 it is mentioned by Jean Frossart and again appears in Shakespeare's *Merry Wives of Windsor* in 1600. The first pasty — called a "hoggan" — was simply a piece of meat, usually pork, wrapped in a lump of dough. The Cornish are accused of putting almost anything into a pie — kidney pies, eel pies, even "star-gazy" pies which consist of small fish which are aligned so that they stare upward at the diner! It is said that the Devil stays away from Cornwall for fear he will be put into a pasty. The pasty was designed as a hearty meal to be carried into the mine to sustain the men during the long shifts underground; at dinner-time it was simply heated on a shovel over a candle flame. My Cornish grandfather maintained, with just the hint of a twinkle in his eyes, that the pasties he carried underground were made with barley flour and were so hard they could be dropped down the main mine shaft without breaking!

There are many recipes for pasties but I have always liked this one, vouchsafed to me behind closed doors by Richard Allen, a slight Cornishman and master teacher in Tapiola on the Copper Range of the Upper Peninsula.

The Cornish Pasty

To make the crust for 5 pasties sift 3 level cups of flour and 1 tablespoon of salt. Cut in 1 cup suet or other shortening to the size of small peas. Add 1 cup cold water as needed until mixture sticks together. Cut into 5 portions.

Roll out dough on floured board to the size of a 9 inch pie tin.

Place two tablespoons of grated turnips or rutabagas on dough (optional). Add 3/4 cup potatoes cut into small pieces. Add 1/2 cup round steak, stew meat or other, cubed into small pieces.

Add salt and pepper to taste. Add minced onion to taste. Add about 2 more tablespoons potatoes and sprinkle with salt and pepper. Add small dash butter.

Fold over crust to make half circle and crinkle the edges to hold together, either at the far edge or on top of the pasty.

Put a knife slit in each pasty — bake at 400 degrees for one hour — and enjoy.

One pasty generally makes a meal, but as Mac Frimodig, writing in *Michigan Natural Resources* magazines says: "Keep in mind that a two-pasty man is the world's biggest compliment — or he's going to be."

It is good to remember our respective ethnic heritages with pride. We need roots. Just as surely, I thought as I sat drinking tea and contemplating the moods of the Carp River, we need ties also to our natural heritage. We need open spaces close to where we live, areas that are relatively untouched to which we can retreat for renewal. Wilderness doesn't necessarily have to be thousand-acre tracts in the great beyond.

We are so fortunate that urban sprawl has not yet metastasized to the Superior Peninsula. Perhaps it's on its way. There is something very persuasive about the idea that the good life must involve more, larger, faster. Is it possible that instead of fulfillment these dreams for a region contain elements of partial destruction? I worry that our native valley will become like every place else. What we have here now is good and we will lose a great deal of that goodness in the relentless pursuit of growth.

The snowfall had stopped and the woods were darkening when I finally stirred and carefully scattered the remains of my small fire. I had made contact and I felt rejuvenated in mind, body, spirit. I recalled John Muir's advice: "Climb the mountains and get their good tidings. Nature's peace will flow into you as sunshine flows into trees." I *know* what Muir meant but it takes repeated woodland experiences for me to *understand*. In his book, *The Walk of the Conscious Ants*, Taylor Morris makes a provocative distinction between *knowing* and *understanding*.

There is a difference. We may know, for example, that we are part of the web of life, but we do not understand it until we have experienced nature first hand. Knowledge alone is not enough. "The need is not for more brains," Loren Eiseley observed, "The need is now for a gentler, a more tolerant people that those who won for us against the ice, the tiger and the bear."

I thought again of those who had worked in and loved this peninsula, from the Chippewas to the Cornishmen. Theirs was physically a hard life with very few of the comforts their descendants call necessary. They would barely recognize the towns and cities that "progress" has changed but they understood completely their need for and dependence on the natural world.

Now, as I reached the granite crest which overlooks the town, I understood once again. The hillside where I paused was shrouded in twilight and deep blue shadows were creeping along the white mantle. Looking down upon the town I could see perpendicular plumes of blue smoke rising from the chimneys. The air was frosty, still. Far to the west, almost behind the flinty hills, a tiny patch of blue sky winked tantalizingly casting a faint glow on the snow, now covered with brilliants which squeaked underfoot. It was like beholding acres of diamonds. I savored the moment and then headed down the slope toward home.

T H E   N I G H T   O F   T H E   O W L

*E*arly one January dawn I shuffled into our darkened kitchen to start the morning coffee and glanced outside just in time to see a large bird fly up from the snow. Hastily, I fumbled for the 7x50 binoculars which always stand ready beside the large window overlooking our back yard. Although we reside in a suburban area near Marquette, our home is located on the edge of the Carp River Valley, a magnificent wild region of granite hills and thick forests. During the past decade we have seen a wide variety of wildlife in our backyard: rabbits, raccoons, skunks, deer and one spring morning, a huge black bear lumbering past. Last year a family of tree squirrels made a home in our bluebird nesting box; I discovered the naked babies when I attempted to perform the annual cleaning and hastily restored them to the nest of thin wood fibers. Once as I was chatting on the telephone with a university colleague and looking idly out the window, a short-tailed weasel catapulted from under our log pile and dashed across the backyard. He was solid white except for his eyes, nose and the jet black tip of his tail. The weasel undulated like a porpoise through the snow, first gliding on the surface and then burrowing under, his sinuous body moving in a restless frenzy. Our most frequent visitors, though, particularly in winter at our feeding stations, are the birds.

Now as I focused the binoculars I made out the unmistakable round-shouldered form of a barred owl perched uncertainly on the top bar of my children's swing set. Slowly he turned his head and seemed to stare toward the window. Owls have flat faces — facial discs bordered by tufted feathers — and their huge, light-gathering eyes are set rigidly in their sockets; in order to focus upon an object, they must turn their entire head. They have extremely flexible neck vertebrae and can swivel their heads almost three-fourths of a full circle. Suddenly, the owl shifted on the swing set, rose and drifted away into the dim woods. It was only then that I noticed the inert form of a cottontail rabbit in the snow near our bird feeder.

Several rabbits live under a jumble of old stumps and logs which the builder cleared when our home was constructed; the pile now adjoins a neighbor's yard at the far back edge of the property. A thick stand of young red maples decorates the shallow valley adjacent to the log pile and provides additional cover as well as a ready source of food. The cottontails prefer our cultivated fare, however, during the short growing season. Despite our determined efforts to fence them out, the bunnies make regular forays into our small garden each summer; the beans and peas are the price we pay for the hours of fun watching our furry neighbors frolic in our back yard.

Our human neighbor does not share our enthusiasm for watching rabbits play nor does he admire, as we do, their woodpile home. The woodpile, in particular, disturbs him; somehow it violates his values of order and neatness. At least once each week during the summer he makes a circuit of the jumbled logs and stumps in a futile effort to divine a solution. When I casually reminded him one day that downed and dead wood is part of nature, too, and that exquisitely colored fungi grow among the decaying logs, he turned away in despair and resumed raking his manicured Kentucky bluegrass.

Many homeowners, hungering for a relationship with the earth and perhaps feeling an ancient longing to till the soil, spend an inordinate amount of time maintaining their lawns. Every weekend they can be seen dethatching, raking, fertilizing, cutting, trimming and worrying over a monoculture of green grass. Although a relatively benign national obsession — except for the nutrients that get into the ground water and thence, in this area, into Lake Superior — it fosters the attitude that we can, and in fact must, improve upon more diversified natural ground covers.

No, I am not about to give up my woodpile. In fact, for the past few years I have abandoned mowing our backyard and allowed it to return to its natural wild state. I am very pleased with the results. Instead of a monotonous crop of green grass, there is now a progression of wildflowers: white and yellow violets in the spring; then orange hawkweed and escaped garden pinks during the summer; wild strawberries trailing in all directions; asters and goldenrod decorate our yard in early fall. Aspens and pin cherries have spread into the space and, to provide more cover for wildlife, we planted several small spruce and hemlock trees. Mosses grow under the trees and provide a soft green hue before the leaves emerge in spring. Even if our neighbors disapprove, the wild plants and animals flourish in our more natural surroundings.

Many more species of birds frequent our yard now — warblers and vireos search for insects in the aspens and cherries, flickers probe the ant hills in the moss and tiny, bellicose humming birds hover around the wildflowers. Our most spectacular avian visitor, a pileated woodpecker, rings a loud tattoo in search of grubs on a dead maple stump. One noon, our lunch forgotten, we watched the large black and white bird with its flaming crest as it chiseled oval holes in the decaying wood. But winter is our favorite time for watching birds. Then they come in scores to the feeders, their breeding season caution and secretiveness abandoned in their eagerness for food to sustain themselves against the cold. Blue jays dominate with their raucous calls and voracious appetites. Evening grosbeaks, a dozen at a time, flutter in, a shower of yellow, white and black. They eat more delicately than the jays, taking a sunflower seed in their heavy bills, nibbling lengthwise. By watching carefully, an observer can begin to identify individual birds; this past year, from December 27 until the last day of January, a female grosbeak with one blind eye visited our feeder. She always came alone. Later in the winter, purple finches (my children say the male looks as if he has been dipped in raspberry juice), goldfinches in their somber cold-weather garb, juncos and siskins compete for the millet and suet at our feeding stations.

After breakfast that cold January morning, we donned our snowshoes — the white mantle was over two feet deep — and traced out the story of the owl and the rabbit in the snow. A few crimson spots and bits of fur, a deep drag mark and the clear imprint of wing tips told the tale. The cottontail, only partly devoured, lay frozen in the snow. Hoping that the owl might return, we did not disturb his kill, although we thought we had seen the last of the successful night hunter.

Other feathered predators have visited our yard from time to time. Sometimes during an especially severe winter a snowy owl will be observed sitting solemnly on a telephone pole near the corner of our lot. A roving northern shrike may haunt the large sugar maple at the extreme rear of the property for a week or so. The most unusual hunter, though, was a rare peregrine falcon. One spring morning as I sat watching about a dozen cowbirds fight for spilled millet from winter bird feeding, a slate-gray form flashed down. The frightened birds scattered wildly but the falcon grasped a male and landed astride his prey near the back porch. The swift, endangered raptor was less then thirty feet from where I sat trans-fixed, torn between retrieving my camera and not wanting to miss even a moment of observation. The falcon spread his wings to cover the cowbird; a fierce wild look flashed from his dark eyes as he rocked his head slowly from side to side. The slanting rays of the morning sun lit up his white breast, barred belly and the distinctive black moustaches. When finally I did move slowly to get the camera, the falcon catapulted into the air and was gone. The north country, and all of us, will have lost something precious when the peregrine falcon no longer nests in its rocky eyrie. Determined to be ready this time should the barred owl return, I positioned my camera and placed a notebook and pencil nearby.

That evening at approximately the same light intensity at which it had flown away in the morning, the owl returned and landed beside the frozen rabbit. Owls are night hunters — "The owl, night's herald," said one of Shakespeare's characters in the *Rape of Lucrece* — and they are uniquely adapted for seeking out their prey in the dark. Their eyes are large and the retinas are more sensitive to the blue end of the spectrum, which dominates at night; their eyes also point forward, thus giving them binocular vision. Owls also have extraordinary hearing with which to detect the minute rustlings of mice, rats and other rodents. The flight of owls is incredibly silent due to the soft comb-like projections on the wing feathers — they can literally float like a shadow through the forest.

Now we could easily make out the dark brown eyes, the dark horizontal bars on its light breast and collar, the dark vertical streaks on its belly. The barred owl *(Strix varia)* is the most common owl in the peninsula; their favorite habitat is deciduous or conifer woodlands, particularly river bottoms. Often the barred owl is called a "hoot owl" because of his characteristic call. I remember vividly listening to its ethereal eight-hooted voice while lying awake late at night at Boy Scout camp. "Who cooks for you, who cooks for you-all," he seems to say with distinct downward drawl on the last word.

Owls have always fascinated me. Once, during a particularly low point in my life as a student at a large midwestern university, I anxiously roamed the campus early one morning. As I neared a small wooded area beside the carillon tower, a screech owl poked its head out from a hole in an oak tree, uttered a single mournful whinny and then seemed to wink puckishly. The incident amused me so that I temporarily forgot my woes and began to think more constructively about my problems. Another time early one foggy October morning I was attacked by an owl while deer hunting. I had seen six deer in the area and I was being especially careful to reach my stand with as little noise as possible. It was still dark and the woods were eerie and foreboding. Suddenly a whoosh filled my ears, and with a solid thump my cap left my head! My assailant was a great horned owl soaring in a tight circle around me before I shouted and frightened it away. Now I know how a rabbit feels.

As our backyard grew darker, the owl seized the rabbit with its talons and started to pull and tug with its hooked beak, but the rabbit appeared frozen and unyielding. Fascinated, we watched the bird sit astride the cottontail and fluff out its feathers in what seemed to be an incubating gesture. Perhaps it was simply some strigidean ritual. All that night, as I checked hourly, the barred owl sat upon its prey apparently thawing the meat; from time to time, it would pull off chunks and devour them.

Finally, at dawn and about the same illumination as before, the barred owl flew away with the last scrap of the rabbit in its talons. Again we checked the spot where the owl had fed during the night; only a few fragments of fur were scattered in the snow.

Stimulated by the wildlife drama which unfolded in the backyard, my children studied owls for several days. We drew pictures, colored them and talked about the role of predators in the natural order of things. We learned that owls play a vital role — as do other predators — in maintaining the vigor and harmony of any wildlife community. They do their prey a service by pruning the population and keeping the numbers in line with the food supply and cover. The girls took to watching birds with a new delight.

Bird watchers — most of whom now call themselves "birders" — are favorite targets of cartoonists. Some local legislators and industrial leaders use less humor and more derision. "Who are you for," they ask rhetorically when issues of the environment arise, "people or birds?" It's not really a matter of choice — we all should be looking out for birds.

My grandfather, a Cornish copper miner, was an avid bird watcher. In fact, he carried a canary down into the mine shaft with him. Birds are very sensitive indicators of air conditions and miners knew that if the canary died or even fluttered about in its cage, they had better exit the mine in a hurry. Those early miners were smarter than we seem to be; they were serious about bird watching.

Birds still have a lot to tell us about the health of our planet. We know that the most important factor in the health and survival of birds — of all creatures — is a place to live, a place which provides food, water and cover. Everyone needs a home and when our home cannot support the loon, the osprey, or the wood thrush, then perhaps humans too are in peril. Maybe it is time that we all got serious about bird watching.

Our family will not soon forget the night of the owl. We learned that it is possible in small but important way to experience wilderness in your own backyard. Even more importantly, we understood better the interconnected web of life, all life, and our place in the web.

WINTER   WATERFALLS

The best places to witness the primitive forces of winter at work in the Peninsula are the many swift and impatient rivers which course its flinty hills. Fortunately for watchers of waterfalls, this region features a multitude of rocky ledges and canyons over which the more than twelve thousand miles of rivers, streams and creeks cascade toward the icy embrace of Lakes Superior, Michigan and Huron. Long before even the Native Americans took up residence in what is now the Upper Peninsula, the ancient Laurentian Mountains yielded to the slow but irresistible forces of erosion and gradually sank beneath the warm waters of huge inland Paleozoic seas. Sandstone was then laid down in horizontal strata overlying the Precambrian granite. Vast ice sheets — as much as a mile thick — scoured the area and finally withdrew, forming torrential rivers and the forerunners of the present Great Lakes.

Herman Melville wrote that meditation and water are wedded forever and I have always found that the best places for thinking — even simply thinking that it's nice not to be thinking of anything — are close to flowing water. For more than three decades now I have been self-appointed inspector of the region's waterfalls. According to the tourist council, which likes to keep track of such things, there are over 140 falls, ranging from small leaps to the thundering Tahquamenon. So, happily, my labors are never-ending. During my short tenure as unpaid inspector, I have tried to see each fall in every season.

Waterfalls cast a very special spell: Who can resist the sound of water plummeting down, glistening like liquid silver as it tumbles over rocky ledges and sprays the viewer with its subtle, fragrant breath? In spring, fed by melting snow, the falls are brawling, lusty infants in full, impatient cry. In summer they are more sedate — cool, green and shady places where shy brook trout linger in deep pools. Resplendent in yellow, orange and red backdrop, autumn waterfalls are often slowed to a quiet trickle, yet speak clearly to those who listen. One autumn while returning to our home from Lower Michigan where I had just completed my doctoral studies, we paused for a family picnic beside Wagner Falls near Munising. It had been a week filled with tension, confusion and celebration; we seemed to visibly unwind as we sat quietly beside the small waterfall watching brilliantly colored leaves swirl gently in a small pool. My daughter Mary, then just three years old, placed her hand in mine and said softly, "Daddy, it's singing to me." Squeezing her hand gently, I glanced over at her twin sister, Lynn — whose name, incidentally, is Gaelic for "waterfall" — noticed that her eyes were glistening; she, too, was listening to the music of nature, the pipes of Pan which Sigurd Olson described so poignantly in *Open Horizons*, his autobiography-in-nature. Autumn is indeed a special time for waterfall watching.

But my favorite season for inspecting waterfalls is winter. Since the fair weather visitors are far away, my self-imposed duties increase. Not snow, nor sleet or winter gloom stay me from my appointed rounds to hear the muted voices of water held captive under the ice. Now they sing solely for me. When I view a frozen waterfall I imagine that the dashing spirit of the foaming water has been caught in an enchanted, spellbound pause. The perpetual motion is now arrested in shimmering spangles of stalactites and stalagmites; the restless water is transformed, it is caught and held suspended in glittering ice caps, long spires and lacy filigree. My reconnaissance of frozen waterfalls was noted in three recent journal entries:

January 29.

Let's hear it for the Wilderness Act! The ice caves north of Eben in Alger County are now officially within the Rock River Canyon Wilderness. Now one must snowshoe or ski into the caves; no more noisy snowmobiles. This spectacular display should be approached quietly, even reverently. The ice formations are especially spectacular this year: Long fluted columns of pale green; thick Byzantine pillars in amber and ivory. I crawled in behind the formations and was delighted to find a forest of crystal-clear icicles. When I accidentally bumped several icicles they fell and shattered on the icy floor, setting off an enchanting musical tinkling.

February 18.

High noon at Miners Falls in the Pictured Rocks National Lakeshore. The Miners River has cut a deep gorge in the sandstone over the centuries; the foaming water, now almost hidden by a thick carapace of ice, leaps about 20 feet. Icicles at least ten feet long, colored a soft aquamarine, hang from the ledges to the left of the main falls. One or two smaller stalactites have an amber hue. As we ate lunch, snow began falling heavily, not in flakes but in large clumps. The river is almost all snowbound; in spots downstream we could make out the dark water, a black gash against the white surroundings. Spruces and hemlocks stand as dark green sentinels with snow on their shoulders.

March 9.

Alder Falls is completely frozen over and covered with layers of snow. Down river the water is open; I crossed on a snow and ice bridge and bent down to examine the delicate ice crystals. The sun came out and now the open water looks like a silver serpent winding its way through the snowy woods. Rocks capped with snow appear to be riding on the "river-snake." Whose woods are these near Big Bay? I don't care, for it is very, very quiet and the sparkling white coverlet of snow extends as far as I can see in all directions.

It is very difficult to identify my favorite winter waterfall for they are all gentle on my mind. Because it is quite close to home, I return again and again to Morgan Falls. It is small, barely a ten foot drop but it often wears a delicate fairy cap of glittering ice; the white cedars which hover around it are coated in sheer frozen layers by the mist. Each winter I try to spend a day paying my respects to Canyon Falls near L'Anse; it features a succession of rapids and cascades which plunge rampant through a narrow granite gorge. Spectacular Laughing Whitefish Falls with its long staircase drop and sandstone caves ranks high on my list of favorite frozen falls. The latest rival for my affections is Douglass Houghton Falls near Lake Linden in the Copper Country; its winter garment is a tall amber and blue ice column.

Probably the most spectacular waterfall in Michigan — and with its 40 foot drop certainly the highest — is the Tahquamenon (rhymes with phenomenon and means "great amber waters"). The largest falls east of the Mississippi after Niagara, the Tahquamenon is located near Newberry in northern Luce County. According to Longfellow's epic saga, which was based largely on a collection of Indian legends compiled by Henry Schoolcraft, the brave Hiawatha built his birch bark canoe on the banks of the mighty Tahquamenon River. In winter, the Falls become a glittering display of immense exquisitely colored ice columns.

During one particularly cold February recently, my family and I spent an entire day inspecting the many charms of Tahquamenon Falls. Parking our car in the lot built for summer crowds, we followed the narrow path through the dense forest. The winter woods were hushed — all we could hear when we stopped and strained to hear were the muted voice of the Falls and an occasional guttural croak of a circling raven. We stopped on the path where it first overlooks the Falls: nothing had prepared us for the overwhelming beauty of the dark red-brown water, the many ice columns, the sparkling carpet of snow, the azure sky — all framed by the dark bulk of huge hemlocks beside the trail.

Sliding down a long series of steps, now cushioned by snow, we watched the thundering waters at close range. The river at this point is over 100 feet wide; all but the very central portion of the Falls was frozen into huge daggers. Below the Falls the river was completely frozen and covered with a fresh layer of snow. The waters — stained amber due to decaying vegetation in the swamps which it drains — drop forty feet over ledges of Cambrian sandstone.

The colors at this close range were breathtaking. Although the amber-stained ice columns predominated, we could see pale greens and blues and even a subtle rose where the water had oozed out between the layers of sandstone. Seeking an even closer inspection point, we descended the steep wooded banks beside the Falls and edged our way carefully toward the jumbles of beautifully hued ice. We moved up close beside the falling waters, stopping barely a yard away from the frothing foot of the falls. It was like being in a crystalline fantasy land, but far better to me than the Disney artifacts. This one was real, not a plastic and painted replica. On hands and knees we crept slowly through and among the gigantic columns, our minds boggled by the power and immensity of the scene. I whispered thanks to Ben East, distinguished outdoor writer from Michigan, who with several companions made a winter visit to the Falls in 1929. At that time there were no winter roads to the Tahquamenon and the adventurers trekked overland on snowshoes for several days to photograph the Falls in its winter setting. Mr. East's efforts helped to bring recognition to this lovely natural spot and several years later it was dedicated as a state park. The park now encompasses both the main or Upper Falls and, four miles downstream, a series of smaller drops, the Lower Falls. A well-maintained trail connects the two waterfalls on the river so we donned our snowshoes and walked down to pay our respects to the Lower Falls. Inspecting winter waterfalls can become habit forming.

Fortunately, my addiction for watching winter waterfalls can be satisfied quite easily in the Upper Peninsula. I've found, however, I must be careful to time my visits to avoid the multiplying motorized snow traveler.

On a Sunday afternoon I snowshoed into the Falls on the Little Garlic River just ten miles north of town. I had walked over a series of heavily wooded ridges, across frozen Lake Blemhuber and along the winding course of the river to the spot where it races down a rocky defile. The falls were frozen in several large white spires. Bending closely and listening carefully I could detect the deep murmur of the water under the thick mantle of ice and snow. As I sat there communing with the Little Garlic Falls in lonely splendor, a visitor on an abominable snowmobile hove into view and roared up to the very spot where I meditated.

"Pretty, huh?" the portly driver said brightly, removing his goggles. "I really like to get back here in the woods where it's quiet in the winter." I looked at him for a long moment and resumed my scrutiny of the frozen waterfall hoping thereby to exclude the assault on my previously quiet winter forest. He blinked and shifted his bulk on the seat of the yellow snow machine.

"Say, where is your machine?" he asked, looking about. Snowmobile enthusiasts always call their motorized craft 'machines'; the verb describing what you do on these machines is 'riding'.

"I don't have one . . . I came in on snowshoes," I answered.

"You what?" he exploded. "But that's three miles. You ought to get yourself one of these here machines. Sure beats walking."

I could stand it no longer. "Look," I said, using my most reasonable tone. "I walked back here because I wanted to savor the experience, not use it up. At least two dozen others like me — cross country skiers, walkers on snowshoes — could be in this same area and no one would know it. But just one snowmobile like yours, or one trail bike in the summer — and the impact of the noise spreads a zone of influence for a least a half-mile . . ." I ran down.

"Well, I dunno . . . you can see so much more country riding," he responded. Now I warmed again to the topic.

"You mean you pass *through* much more country but I bet you *see* less. In fact, a person on snowshoes can see more in one mile than you do riding all day. How can you have a natural experience on a snowmobile: coveralled, helmeted, goggled, staring straight ahead at the tailpipe of the next machine as you speed along in a noisy parade? Is there some prize for how much territory a person can cover in a day?"

The snowmobiler stared at me, his features set in lines of disgust. Finally he said, "It's still a free country, fella!" With that he started his machine, raced the motor three times and churned off with an ear-splitting roar trailing a haze of oily red breath.

It was a long time before my ears adjusted to the silence and even longer until I could detect again the faint murmur of the water under the ice. I heard also the echoes of the testy exchange with the snowmobiler. Surely we had talked past, not to, each other. Perhaps we could have reached consensus on at least one thing: It is better to be outside enjoying the winter clime than sitting on a couch in an overheated house. At any rate, now the forest was quiet and I could resume my solitary musing by the frozen waterfall.

Loren Eiseley suggests that if there is magic on this planet, it is contained in water. That water which flew by so swiftly, ever changingly in all other seasons is captured and held in winter in myriads of patterns and shapes for me to contemplate at my leisure. That, surely, is a form of magic — and the granite cliffs and ledges of this lovely land offer it in abundance.

A W I N T E R   S I W A S H

The carefully arranged pile of birch bark and dry twigs glowed briefly, sputtered and went out. My fingers numbed quickly in the cold as I again fumbled with the matches. This time the fire flared brightly, illuminating the dark snowy cove, my blanket shelter and my snowshoes propped in the drift nearby. Remembering Jack London's magnificent short story, "To Build A Fire," I glanced uneasily up at the branches over my head. Sighing in relief — they offered no threat — I placed my small teabilly on a stick over the flames and sat back to enjoy the delicate warmth of the small fire.

Cold weather camping is becoming even more popular among those who cannot resist the insistent call of the winter wilderness. Deer hunters in northern climes have been tenting in snow drifts for years. But now advocates of ski touring, snowshoeing and year-round hiking are discovering the quiet delights of the winter season. Yet few modern campers have experienced the simple joys of *siwashing*, and fewer still have tried a winter *siwash*.

"Siwash" is an Native American word that means traveling cross country and living off the land as you go. The Chippewa and Cree ranged far and wide in search of game and fur bearing animals with only a gun, an axe, a blanket and the ever-present teabilly (a pot for boiling water). Sometimes they would also carry a supply of pemmican — a lean meat, dried and pounded fine and packed in hide sacks. That is really traveling light! Siwashing calls for the essentials and nothing more.

I cheated a little on my winter siwash. In addition to a supply of pemmican, I took a small box of dried fruit and a little old-fashioned hardtack bread. Instead of a gun, I carried a camera and a tripod lashed to the pack. In my pack sack were a wool blanket, a small axe, a teabilly, a candle and book, and a scratch pad for making notes. The three basic items I carry on every hike — compass, knife and match safe — were in my coat pockets.

One Friday afternoon in late January, I tightened the straps on my snowshoes, shouldered my small pack and headed back into the timber. The snow crunched metallically underfoot as I threaded my way between the jack pines and skirted around windfalls. I did not have far to go to find my first campsite. Topping a small rise, I chanced upon a deep ravine bordered on two sides by dense stands of cedar and hemlock. In the center, well out of the chilly breeze, I found an old windfall with plenty of dead firewood. I dubbed this discovery "Emerick's Cove."

Clearing the snow away carefully (in winter camping, the most vital concern is to keep dry), I draped my thick wool blanket over three small branches forming an inverted V. It made a small snug shelter with a huge pine log at the rear. Cutting a large supply of dead firewood, I built the tiny fire before my makeshift shelter. There simply are too many people now using the forests to permit shelter building with live materials, or, for that matter, building shelters at all. It is not fair for the next visitor seeking a wilderness experience to have to see lean-to structures in various states of disrepair. Neither can we, in good conscience, cut live trees for firewood except in an emergency situation. In a short while the blackened teabilly was simmering with snow-melted water and my bivouac was complete. Only a faint glow showed in the western sky and then darkness embraced the small cove.

The splendid solitude of that first night was a delightful experience. I do not go to the woods to "rough it"; things are already rough enough in the clamor and confusion of our world. I go to "smooth it," to plane off the layers of civilization and get past the veneer and down to the essentials. How simple everything seems with your back against a sturdy log; how soothing to be doing simple timeless things. Thoreau made a stirring appeal when he wrote that we should drive life into a corner and reduce it to its simplest terms. Surely few of us can do this as dramatically as did Thoreau when he built his cabin on the shore of Walden Pond. But one can for a time flee the concrete and confusion; we can abandon the schedules of the city and suburb and free ourselves from the stultifying ticky-tacky of our highly "civilized" world. I had camped before in winter (and still do) but always with shelter, sleeping bag and full rations. This was to be a more primitive experience: I wanted to feel the full impact of the wilderness with as few modern trappings as possible. Spending two January nights in the Michigan woods with only a blanket for shelter is one way to reduce life to its simplest form.

For a long time I sat pondering, drinking cups of steaming tea and listening to the soft crackling of the fire. Even a small flame mesmerizes us, a remnant perhaps of our former intimacy with the magic of fire; the Swahili call it "dreaming the fire." Lighting my old corncob pipe, I stood and moved away from the fire; I tried to identify the constellations that hung close in the inky sky.

Finally I dozed — in a fugue state the Eskimos term "koviashuttok," a state of well being, joyful, fully and pleasantly in the present — and woke somewhat startled to discover the sun heralding a new day.

In less than three minutes after breakfast, dried apricots and hardtack washed down with scalding black tea, I had donned my snowshoes and headed for the dense cover along the river. This is the beauty of the siwash: when you leave behind the so-called conveniences of modern living you also avoid the responsibilities and encumbrances of the more complex life.

It was bitterly cold but I was warmly dressed. Both my coat and pants were of heavy wool. I wore down insulated underwear and a pair of army surplus insulated boots — not quite the basic clothing of the original siwashes. Even the "sundogs," those pulsating strips of pale blue, yellow and white on either side of the morning sun, could not frighten me from stalking in the thickets beside the river. Winter shadows are long, though, and the warming rays of the sun never quite overcome the cold.

Although I failed in my camera quest for game, I did make the acquaintance of one woodland creature on this frosty morning. As I stood beside the river, a movement caught my eye. A coal-black fox, the first and last I have ever seen, emerged stealthily from a thicket, nose to the snow, intent upon the track of his prey. On an impulse I pursed my lips and made a low kissing sound. The fox stopped in mid stride, scanned the area then, in one flowing movement, he bounded toward me! A few feet away, he stopped abruptly, sat on his haunches and turned his head sideways giving me a distinctly quizzical stare. We watched each other intently for perhaps a minute. What an intelligent expression gleamed from those dark eyes! Then with great dignity, he slowly turned and trotted down into a ravine. Only then did I think of my camera snug inside my coat.

When the sun was at its highest arc, I stopped to make my lunch and met more residents of the area. While I busied myself building a small fire to melt snow for tea, a pair of fluffy black-capped chickadees dropped down to a low branch and chattered a friendly welcome. Then as if to remind me that winter is after all a harbinger of spring, one tilted back its head and proudly gave forth its plaintive two-noted whistle. So moved was I that I gave them the last of my hardtack as a reward.

The second night of my siwash I made camp in a shallow cave under the roots of a giant oak tree high up on the river bank. The high white waters of spring had cut a small but comfortable niche under the huge roots. I built a fire, laid in a supply of firewood and wrapped myself in the blanket, nibbling on the last of the pemmican and drinking cups of strong tea. Later I took a candle from my pack sack, propped it up on the tripod and read from Sigurd Olson's magnificent book *The Singing Wilderness*. Long a guide in the famous canoe country of northeast Minnesota, Olson conveys vividly the sounds, smells and sights of the out-of-doors. He also maintains that much of our modern malaise stems from our rapid technological and sociological shift from a creature of nature to one forced into a civilized mold. Although we have made some remarkable accomplishments, we cannot escape our link with nature and its basic rhythms; even though our surroundings and way of life have changed profoundly, our biologic nature remains much the same. We still carry in our collective racial unconscious the remembrance of water, the passage of the seasons, an intimacy with natural sounds and smells.

How did so many humans lose their ties with the natural realm? I wondered as I sat there listening to the soft guttering of the fire and reflecting on Sig Olson's words. Why have we forgotten that the earth is our mother, not simply a ready source of raw materials to support an ever-faster and more wasteful form of living? Retrieving a small pencil stub I scribbled my thoughts that poured forth on that clear winter night:

Aldo Leopold wrote several decades ago that we abuse the land because we regard it as a commodity which belongs to us instead of a community to which we belong. We set ourselves apart, above nature. We speak of salamanders, timber wolves and white pines as separate and apart from us, as entities over which we have dominion. Perhaps I'm intoxicated on the clear air here, but sometimes it seems as if we are treating the land like a conquering army.

Science and technology are clearly not the answers to our environmental woes. In fact, science, especially science wedded to technology, has exacerbated our problems. We have come to worship the new gods of technology and technique; whatever or whomever gets in the way of their progress must be sacrificed at the altar. Science separates itself from humanity; it promulgates, as Archibald McLeish points out, not the law of the good, the human, the decent, but the law of the possible. Whatever *can* be done somehow takes on an imperative and *must* be done.

What we need now is love for the land. We need to be like the Navajo who reminds himself each morning to walk gently on and in harmony with Mother Earth. Let us acknowledge it: The only lasting, proven design of life, a design in which every event occurs according an integrated plan, is the system of nature. Not only must we come to an understanding of nature's laws, but, more important, acknowledge and accept our interdependence on them.

A soft silent snow fell steadily that night and by morning my snowshoes and pack sack were only white mounds. In the morning I wandered in a wide arc back to my car. Once, as I rounded a sharp bend near the edge of a brushy marsh, four whitetail deer leaped to their feet, hesitated a moment and then bounded gracefully up the far hillside. I found their beds, warm deep ovals in the snow. I traced the tracks of a mink near the rapids where the river never freezes. Tracks in the snow indicate that life goes on despite the cold of winter. Several times I heard the throbbing drum of a pileated woodpecker, but I could never catch sight of his flashy colors among the trees.

Soon I reached the old logging trail and my parked car. Although tired and hungry, my head was clear and my senses bright and clean. For a time I had lived close to nature satisfying a need that every human being carries deep within: the need to return periodically to the simple refreshment and renewal that only the woods and waters, only the singing of the wilderness can satisfy.

John Muir once wrote that most people are *on* the world, not *in* it. We must remember that we live *within* the environment. I paused at the car and looked back at the quiet forest. I had for a time lived simply and now I would truly appreciate more conventional camping adventures. It had been a good *siwash* and now I was returning home.

T H E   C A B I N

*H*e calls it "The Shack" and viewed objectively, it probably is just an old woods shack. Wind, often carrying a fine dusting of snow crystals, sneaks in around the ill-fitting windows and the gap under the door. The tarpaper roof leaks, the stove pipe drips creosote and the crude floor pitches sharply toward one corner. But the hand-hewn square-beamed old logs fit together snugly and even at zero degrees outside it is cozy and warm beside the barrel stove. The gently flickering light of two oil lamps glints gently from the chinking and reflects mellow highlights of pale brown and silver in the weathered wood. The smells are virile and organic: wood smoke, sourdough sponge rising on the warming shelf, wool garments drying, freshly split maple stacked in the corner, the aromatic coffee pot hissing softly on the stove. Leaning back, I feel and admire the substantial texture of the grain in the old logs — unlike the garish reflections from incandescent lighting, the lantern illumination seems to soak into the wood — and I relax even more fully.

The simple life possible in Bill's old cabin is appealing to more and more persons. Many individuals I know hunger for such an escape, some small spot where it is possible to turn away from the complications of our present civilization. For most it is corrective, not a substitute. However, quite a few moderns, not just the over-stereotyped young persons in communes but people from all levels of society, are returning to more simple ways of living. Many states report a trend back to farms and rural areas. We are making a belated discovery that possessions alone are not enough, that quality of life is more important than quantity and that our human psychic needs are somehow linked to more primitive life styles.

This is the story of one person — student, friend and fellow-explorer — who chose the path less traveled and it made all the difference in his life. Harassed by capricious academic barriers of graduate school, he decided to adopt for a time an extremely simple form of life in a ramshackle abandoned log cabin. Perhaps in his actions, by inspecting why he made this primitive sojourn and how he lived, we can in some small way identify how we, too, can achieve the surcease that comes with simplicity. For, as Welshman Alwyn Rhys once observed, "When you are at the brink of an abyss, the only progressive move you can make is a step backward."

I have known Bill for more than 30 years, ever since he enrolled as an undergraduate in courses which I taught. Despite the demands of college, he retained and cultivated his need for a personal relationship with the out-of-doors. Then came a three-year interruption while he served in the military including a tour of duty as a medic in the jungles of Viet Nam. His nerve endings were jangled when he returned from the service; graduate school, with all the posturing and academic game-playing, did little to soothe his psyche. Advanced education can be a trail of tears and frustration, particularly for the independent student who cannot or will not tolerate the intellectual hazing. Feeling demeaned and used up, Bill decided to regain a feel for what is important by following the formula of Thoreau: "When a mathematician would solve a difficult problem, he first frees the equation of all incumbrances and reduces it to its simplest terms. So simplify the problem of life."

Bill remembered the old cabin in the woods near his parents' farm. Here, he thought, was the ideal spot to put his internal systems in order. Here he could sort out his values and again gain a measure of control over his own life. His new life style would be guided by three principles: simplicity, solitude and self-reliance. Thus, Bill set about reestablishing his independence by moving to the old cabin and with his own skills and a few tools, putting the place in order.

The cabin sits on a knoll close to the edge of a dense woodlot of mixed northern hardwoods. It faces westward overlooking an old pasture which is now dotted with stubby hawthorn and gooseberry bushes. Several large cottonwood trees stand guard near the north wall and an ancient outhouse, tilting precariously, can be seen just beyond the trees.

No one is certain just when the cabin was built but the best guess is that is served as a bunk house or office for a lumber company about the turn of the century. In the early forties, an old friend of Bill's family, affectionately known only as "Old Matt," brought the structure to its present location log by log. Old Matt lived in the cabin until his death in 1952; then it was abandoned to weather and wild creatures.

The mansard roof had fallen in and the dirt floor was littered with shredded paper and wood chips left behind by the woodchuck family when Bill started work on the cabin

ILLUSTRATION BY LON EMERICK

one late spring day. The square logs were sound, though, and fit together snugly where they dove-tailed at the corners. After cleaning up, Bill built a crude plank floor and installed balsam poles as rafters; an old barrel was fashioned into a stove and set on flat rocks near the center of the one room. The roof was repaired and patched and a chimney-pipe erected. When weather permitted, he planted a small garden and cut wood for the long winter season. An army cot, a packing box for storage, a simple table and chairs and a few personal items were moved in and Bill commenced his year-long residence in the old cabin.

There is nothing like a log cabin for its quiet, warm and homey charm. Perhaps the sturdy cedar or pine logs create a sense of permanence, strength and simplicity which stirs old memories of when life was physically harder but less complicated. The memories of my Grandfather's cabin are crystal clear: braided rugs on the simple pine floor, over-stuffed chairs, a stone fireplace, smells of food cooking on a wood range. The room seemed to embrace and welcome the visitor, encouraged him to linger, to relax and shed the complications and compulsions of modern life. A log cabin, even an old one like Bill's, floods the visitor with all the nostalgia of frontier existence — and we sense deeply that happiness has something to do with simplicity.

During the winter of Bill's year in the primitive woodland cabin, I was invited to visit and share his life for a day. On a subzero morning in late February, I strapped on snowshoes and tramped through the frozen woodlot toward the cabin. The sun rose slowly, agonizingly slowly it always seems on northern winter mornings, but the first rays lit up the hoarfrost coating the maples and the sparkles extended as far as I could see. Even before I saw the cabin through the trees, the rich aroma of wood smoke and fresh coffee quickened my pace. Soon I was warming my hands beside the barrel stove while Bill prepared the sourdough for pancakes.

Breakfast that morning, steaming black coffee and pancakes sprinkled with brown sugar, was fit for royalty. I noticed almost immediately that Bill seemed very relaxed, almost serene. He parried my indirect inquiries about himself by suggesting that we make an inspection of the winter morning. Stoking the stove with several stout logs, we donned our heavy parkas and set forth.

We stalked through the maple woodlot where Bill planned to tap trees for syrup in early spring. Pausing often, we admired the delicate blue shadows traced on the snow by tree branches and tried to unravel a maze of snowshoe hare tracks. Crossing a stream, now frozen and covered with deep snow drifts, we made our way through a dense cedar swamp to pay our respects to a family of beaver which lived on the edge of a small slough. The beaver declined to make an appearance but we found a set of fresh coyote tracks and were startled when a grouse suddenly took wing from deep in a snowbank where it had burrowed to escape the cold. We made a large circle over several ridges, down a long-abandoned railroad spur and headed back through the spruces to the old cabin.

The winter air had made us both hungry and Bill suggested that we eat a simple homemade meal. Some meal! Some eating! Imagine a woodland feast in a warm cabin after a long tramp through the snow-covered forest: smoked venison steaks from a deer he had taken himself, soup made with wild leeks dug in the spring and hung to dry from the rafters, parched corn from his garden, and, for dessert, sourdough pancakes made with wild blueberries. Later, Bill pulled a chair up beside the barrel stove, lit his pipe and slowly began to talk of his life in the old cabin. I listened carefully, took some notes, and as far as I can remember this is what he said on that cold winter afternoon:

> *"When I first moved into the old shack, I was a little bit apprehensive about being alone — I was afraid that by looking so closely at myself, I might not like what I found. Or, worse yet, that there was simply nothing there to find. But as I grew accustomed to the quiet and the slower pace, my mind seemed to spring free from the morbid concern with graduate school; the problems of classes, term papers and pleasing professors don't seem important in this old place. I think*

I rediscovered an idea that is very old and very true: that the basis of any real education is not a knowledge of chemistry, literature or even speech pathology, but a knowledge of yourself. How can I work with people and help them redirect their lives without knowing who I am and what I value? I read somewhere that we travel down life's highway basically with ourselves and we had better make sure we have a good companion.

I relearned another basic truth: there is a difference between being alone and being by yourself. I have never felt so alone as in a crowded airport or bus terminal; scores of people but no human contact. In these days and nights by myself I have had the greatest moments of clarity — that life is not complicated, we complicate it.

Let me cite an example: there is no place in this cabin for unnecessary items; I am forced to simplify. I must, for instance, sort out what is need and what is want. I need firewood. In fact, the woodpile teaches a plain lesson: the heat you have is dependent on your own strength. I may want a cheeseburger or a Corvette but in order to get them, I cannot simply depend upon myself — I must more or less sell my independence. It is too easy to let your wants become your needs until gradually things are controlling you. And there is a sense of personal pride in being self reliant; there is a simple and yet very fulfilling feeling in seeing something through and then standing back and admiring it as your own accomplishment. But there is a better way to summarize what I am saying: how far are a person's daily activities from their ultimate purpose or outcome? Many people commute to the city and spend their day phoning, meeting or reading memos to earn dollars to pay for a potato or a fish — compare all that activity to farming or fishing for a living.

Sure, sometimes I miss the hectic pace, the adrenaline rush of life in the fast track. But, lots of activity, too much experience that is not carefully probed and understood, leads to overload — and rejection of everything. It's like trying to digest too much food — the body rejects it. I have learned patience out here in the woods. When I first moved in I thought I had to do everything at once — the chinking, the garden, getting up the firewood, controlling the mice which were eating me out of house and home. Nature will not be rushed, nor does she care that I survive any more than that grouse we flushed should make it through the winter. Living like this forces a slower pace, it is soothing and my tension and edginess have given way to quiescence. Like this old cabin, I am a part of the forest community; a small part, but a part nonetheless. How can anyone live so close to the natural world and refuse to participate?

   I am not sure that just anyone can live like this. Nor can some-one simply come out here and spend a day or two and derive the same benefits. I agree with Billie Wright in her book Four Seasons North, when she wrote that there is a difference between having wilderness experiences and experiencing wilderness. This is my way of life — at least for now — not a short vacation or weekend diversion.

   At any rate, I found for me the missing ingredients in my life. It had to do with intensity, vividness — in short, quality. Like Thoreau, "I went to the woods because I wished to live deliberately, to confront only the essential facts of life, and see if I could learn what it had to teach, and not, when I came to die, discover that I had not lived."

A powerful message and I pondered on it all the next week as I chafed under a heavy schedule of urgent, but not important, meetings and other academic folderol. I conclud-ed that it is highly unlikely that many modern persons can return to nature completely the way Bill was able to do. Most of us are products of our times and we cannot *substi-tute* a primitive life style for the form of contemporary existence into which we were born and reared. But we can, as Colin Fletcher points out, use experiences in natural settings as a *corrective*, as a way of simplifying and smoothing out the wrinkles the present civi-lization irons into our psyches. There are two ways we can make it work.

First, we can introduce more of the simplicities into our daily life — planting a gar-den, cutting firewood by hand, gathering wild fruits in season. Secondly, and even more importantly, we can be especially careful of not letting complexities slip into our "correc-tive" experiences. Keep your camping and hiking adventures as free from the trappings of civilization as possible — no electric blankets, alarm clocks, portable radios. Use a canoe instead of a motor boat, let the forest floor grow instead of grass, eschew the obses-sion with camp improvement projects, take time to smell the wild flowers.

It also helps to store up memories. One morning three weeks after my visit to the old cabin, I happened to pull out the wool shirt I had worn at Bill's fireside chat. The acrid odor of wood smoke filled my senses and instantly I was flooded with images of the cabin brooding in the clearing, of the snowshoe hike through the winter woods, of venison steaks and sourdough pancakes, of the compelling story I had heard. I wore the shirt and smiled inwardly all day.

L I T T L E   P R E S Q U E   I S L E

*T*he sleepy passengers perked up and looked around when I stopped the truck and backed into a snowy alcove just off the Big Bay Road.

"Are we there yet?" teased Jason, sitting up straight and stroking his red beard. The other four students chuckled at his parody of an impatient child and started to collect their gear for the early morning cross-country ski trek.

We were playing hooky from the university, stealing some time from our academic and clinical duties for a short ski and psychic cleansing. The students called these biweekly outings "mental hygiene respites," and we all rationalized that, as laborers in the vineyards of speech therapy, we must keep ourselves in better psychological health than our clients.

"What *is* this place, anyway" asked Peta, admiring the morning sun glinting on the snow.

"This is Little Presque Isle, a very special spot in the U.P. You will get to see — even walk on — one of the last islets of the south shore of Lake Superior. And, best of all, the entire 2500 acres now belongs to you."

"Alright, let's do it!" shouted Jim, impatiently gliding toward Granite Point.

The feeble pink rays of the sunrise traced delicate patterns on the snow-covered pines lining the narrow trail. Moving swiftly, we approached the Point and looked out at the small island, snow-laden and spangled with icicles but rising boldly from the frigid embrace of Lake Superior.

"Hey, let's go over to the island," insisted Marie.

"We will," I said, "but first let's look around on the mainland."

With its blend of water, beach, rock outcroppings and thick forest, the Little Presque Isle area is the quintessence of the lovely landscape of the Superior Peninsula. On the south side of the Point, a series of small coves and cliffs as high as 50 feet have formed, creating in miniature the layered and fluted formations found at Pictured Rocks National Lakeshore, 50 miles to the east. North of the Point extends a sweep of sand beach punctuated only by Harlow Creek; each year the creek alters its winding course as it empties into Lake Superior. Back from the rock and sand beaches is a dense covering of tall red pines; shadbush and blueberry form the under story. The old beach lines can be seen as a series of low ridges further inland.

The brief tour of the mainland was finished. "So, wouldn't this be a great place for a power plant?" I asked. "A what?" the students said, almost in unison.

"Seriously, that's what almost happened here in 1968," I said and then traced the history of this place for them.

In late 1968, an electrical power generating company proposed building a multi-million dollar coal-fired power plant at Little Presque Isle. Just imagine it: a giant power plant where the red pine groves had been; huge smoke stacks looming along the shoreline; an ugly metal dock jutting out into the clear waters of the lake; monstrous coal piles; slurry pipes leading back to dump sites in low areas — all plans described as "improvement" by representatives of the power company. The land had been promptly rezoned and the project was on a fast-forward track.

"What happened?" asked Jason.

"Well, the story is a good example of the environmental slogan, 'Think globally, act locally'. There are so many fights to protect the land, you have to learn when to pick 'em. But, let's cross over now . . . I want to show you this unique island and we can have some hot chocolate and an ethnic treat."

Propping our skis in a drift near the top of Granite Point, we cautiously made our way across a large ridge of ice linking the island to the mainland. In summer, the waves dance over the sand bar and rock shelf, but now the thick ice provided a convenient bridge. We paused to inspect piles of blue ice uplifted in thin sheets and arrayed in jumbled rows; some were a delicate pastel, others a rich aquamarine. All resembled shards of blue glass thrown about in casual heaps by some mighty celestial force.

At one time the Island was connected to the point by a narrow rocky peninsula. Charles W. Penny, who accompanied Douglass Houghton on a geological survey of the Lake Superior country in the summer of 1840, camped in the area and recorded this comment in his journal: (Little Presque Isle) "is a knob of granite about thirty feet high connected with the land by red sandstone. It is almost an island as the strip of sandstone is not over four rods in width."

On the south side of the Island, we found a dry spot under a large pine where the sun had melted the snow and the ancient bed of needles lay open and warm. We sat on the thick carpet, leaned back against the trees and watched ice floes riding the waves far out in Lake Superior. It was difficult to believe we were only seven miles from town; the world seems far less complicated with your back against a red pine trunk. As the student relaxed with steaming mugs of hot chocolate, I traced the history of the struggle to save this marvelous spot.

The fight for this one beauty spot, Little Presque Isle, began in December, 1968, when a letter in the local newspaper, from an editor of a weekly paper in another Upper Peninsula town, shocked those who know the area well and sparked the interest of others.

> *"To the Editor:*
>
> *Build a power plant at Little Presque Isle? Why not start a garbage dump on the steps of the Lincoln Memorial, convert the Taj Mahal to a root beer stand or make the Brockway Mountain Drive an International Speedway?*
>
> *Go ahead, tell me I'm reactionary, opposed to progress, a pebble in the path of industrial development, more jobs and more prosperity. At the same time try and convince me that a multi-million dollar plant located along that piney, rocky shoreline won't be a nuisance and an eyesore that will blotch the Lake Superior woods and waters for miles in each direction.*
>
> *I will concede the need for power, and for new power plants. I accept the fact that industrial growth is a necessary thing in our Upper Peninsula, and I applaud those people willing to invest their money and energy in promoting such growth. I am not convinced, however, that such growth and progress must be made at the expense of our heritage of beauty, tranquillity and unspoiled shorelines.*
>
> *Some time take a day and go up to Sugar Loaf Mountain on the Big Bay Road north of Marquette. Climb to the summit and Si Quaeris Peninsulam Amoenam Circumspice — if you seek a pleasant peninsula, look about you.*
>
> *If the day is clear enough, far to the east you can see the pastel smudges of the Pictured Rocks and northward to the misty shores of*

the Huron Islands. Inland are the rolling ridges of pine and hardwood, the double hump of Hogsback Mountain, the far horizons of the Huron Mountains, the marshes, valleys and rock outcroppings of an untamed land. Just east is Presque Isle, just west is Little Presque Isle and Harlow Creek. And now they want to build a power plant right in the midst of all that beauty and grandeur.

Call it progress if you like, when you speak of building a gener- ating plant along those shores. I call it a disaster and a sad reflection that we prize material things and the glittering lure of progress and prosperity far more than we value the intangibles of beauty and serenity.

Perhaps it is unreasonable to ask if no other site is available; perhaps it is foolish to feel so strongly about this small corner of a busy, bustling world; perhaps I am naive to even raise the question of what are true values and assets in the face of grandiose plans of industrial giants like Cleveland-Cliffs and U.P. Power, but a small part of me will die along with that small part of the world, and protest I must, or my conscience will give me no peace.

Dave Rood
Manistique

Dorothy Maywood Bird, a distinguished author and educator who had lived in Marquette as a small girl and returned after many years in the capital city of Lansing, called a group together in her living room. More and larger meetings followed and a new group, Citizens to Save the Superior Shoreline, was formed to protest the use of this beautiful rock and sand dune shoreline as an industrial site. The land was privately owned, rezoned by the township board and now under option to the power company. Every objection was met with engineering studies showing the cheaper cost of using this site — studies too costly for the volunteer group to duplicate or confirm.

The only recourse for the new group and its supporters was persuasion and pres- sure on the companies and the persons involved in the decision — and many avenues were opened. Major newspapers from Chicago, Milwaukee and Detroit ran weekend fea- tures and photo articles on the conflict; petitions opposing the plans were circulated and 9,000 signatures were presented to company officials; radio and television outlets picked up the story.

The citizens' group grew, with financial and moral support coming from all over Michigan and many other states. The web of persons across the country who knew of and

loved the area was a source of surprise and encouragement to the local group. Little actual communication between the opposing sides took place during the nearly two years the
conflict continued. Then one August day the announcement came: the power company
had dropped its option on the Little Presque Isle shoreline and Harlow Lake site. It would
expand its current power generating plant in the city limits of Marquette.

Not everyone was pleased with the decision to expand in the city; the additional
smoke, noise and visual impact were undesirable. But Little Presque Isle had been saved
from one threat — and the small living room group which had metamorphosed into a
strong force in the community was delighted. The group members went on to work for
and against many other issues affecting the quality of the environment; growth of the
region, wilderness areas and shoreline use, while keeping a wary eye on the Little Presque
Isle area, still undeveloped but still zoned for industrial use.

For five years, nothing changed outwardly. Then in 1975, the largest mining company in the Upper Peninsula announced its desire to acquire 8,000 acres of state forest
land for a new iron ore mining project through a swap for lands which the state might
wish to own for public use. The state proposed receiving Little Presque Isle and Wetmore
Landing shorelands, over three miles long, and the inland area of Harlow Lake — a total
of 2,500 acres of prime recreational land.

After the land swap, years went by at Little Presque Isle. Swimmers, picnickers,
kayakers and beach walkers came, marveled and left refreshed. Cleanup of trash left by
thoughtless visitors was needed periodically; otherwise the land was magnificent,
unchanged and undeveloped.

In 1991, the Department of Natural Resources, using a grant from the Michigan
Land Trust, proposed development of a recreational vehicle campground on the shoreline
of Little Presque Isle. Roads, pads and spaces for 27 camping vehicles were part of the
plan. As if 20 years had not elapsed, the protests rose again. Photos, slide shows and
DNR internal documents outlining staff and consultant recommendations against development on the shorelines convinced the Michigan Natural Resources Council in June,
1993 to reconsider the plan. A Citizens Advisory Committee to review all issues related
to the 2,500 acre tract was created; for 21 difficult and contentious meetings, the
Committee struggled to reach a new plan for the area.

"And so, my children," I concluded as they finished the last of the hot chocolate and
the remaining crumbs of Cornish heavy cake, "the island on which you sit will be protected as a wilderness site and most of the shoreline you explored earlier this morning
will be designated a natural area. There will be no new roads or development on the Lake

Superior shoreline and a few carefully planned facilities in the wooded areas around Harlow Lake. Now that you have seen this, what do you think of the ending of the story?"

"It's hard to add anything to that," said Amanda, as she stood and turned full circle to look at the Island, the lake and the shoreline. "But it makes me believe that enough people who care enough really can make a difference."

—◆—

T H E   M O O N   O F   T H E
S N O W C R U S T

*I*n late March when it seems as if winter will never end, when the sun shines feebly with little real warmth, when senses become jaded with the monochromatic snowscape, there arrives a very special interlude. We call it the Moon of the Snowcrust. Although it is a comparatively brief period — anywhere from three days to three weeks — we await it each year with keen anticipation.

Warmed slightly by the sunshine which lingers longer each day, the top layer of exposed snow crystals melts slowly and water inches down through the interstices of the settling mass of snow; during the cold nights the surface freezes again and again, forming a crust strong enough to support a hiker's weight. Now, after long months of pushing our way through heavy drifts, we can roam at will through the forests; and the new freedom of walking on *top* of an expanse of frozen snow often elicits an unabashed and joyful winter frolic.

It was the first week of April when John, a hiking companion for all seasons, suggested we cure our late winter malaise with a final snowshoe trek into the Carp River Valley. The north face of Summit Peak, a high pinnacle of rose quartz decorated with jack pine, would be our objective. We set forth from my home on snowshoes but realized immediately that we could literally skate on the hard crust; the webs were quickly cached under the low spreading branches of a spruce and, our mood already lightened, we set off on the familiar path.

Up we went: past the knoll where the white birches brighten the ridges, over the steep ascent to Mount Marquette, across to the overlook into the Hidden Valley. Our frolic began in earnest when we made our descent toward the Carp River; aided by a thin layer of fresh powder snow on the hard crust, we rapidly discovered we could skim down the hillsides, slipping and sliding on feet, knees and backs in a shower of white fluff. The winter blahs forgotten, we glissaded swiftly down the slopes with wild shouts, swinging around trees to pick up speed. On the hillside where the valley makes its final precipitous descent to the river, I swept down the steep bank at top speed. An unseen stump, covered with a deep drift, launched me out into space like a ski jumper and I landed spread-eagled in the soft snow beside the river where the rays of the sun seldom reach. After checking to make sure I was not injured, John collapsed in a helpless fit of laughter beside me in the snow drifts.

An immersion in nature often elicits such childlike abandonment in those persons responsive to the joy of woods, lakes and mountains. There is untold exhilaration in shaking free from the tendency to maintain rigid, rational control over our expressions, to let oneself go in the sheer joy of being — without critical analysis or objective examination. After holding the damp hand of anxiety and despair in the speech clinic for three decades, I am convinced that we need these times of childlike innocence to maintain our mental hygiene, perhaps even to preserve our humanity. In his book, *The Decline of Pleasure,* Walter Kerr argues that much of our personal and social trouble stems from the fact that our lives lack spontaneous pleasure. We have come to look at everything in terms of utility — will it buy a tank of gas or bring us closer to a cure for cancer? How much is it worth? The habit of analysis — sticking to the facts, Ma'am — wears away our feelings and denies our emotionality. Responding to nature, losing ourselves in a relationship with the earth, creates a regenerative power that fills us with fresh life, it creates a new delight in ourselves, not in shows or entertainments which are designed to offer temporary pleasure or diversion.

Persons who love nature are not self-conscious about their affection. "Innocence," Annie Dillard writes in her hauntingly beautiful book, *Pilgrim at Tinker Creek,* "is the spirit's unself-conscious state at any moment of pure devotion to any object." Who can forget the tale of John Muir clinging to the top of a huge pine in a Sierra windstorm, swinging to and fro like a bobolink on a stalk of wheat; spending an enchanted sleepless night close beside a waterfall in Yosemite; or, upon feeling tremors, rushing out of his makeshift mountain shelter shouting. "A noble earthquake!"

Some of my own most fulfilling experiences — none as dramatic as John Muir's — have occurred when I simply followed an impulse of abandonment. One wintertime when as a youth I lived in a suburb of Detroit, an unseasonable rain coated a five inch layer of snow with a thick lamination of ice. The surface was frozen solid, the area had become a huge skating rink. The city came to an abrupt standstill; traffic was virtually nonexistent.

Schools were cancelled and hastily at dawn I pulled on my skates and glided about in a crystalline fantasy world. The freedom to go wherever I wished — across yards, down driveways, along streets — released some hooded passion deep within me. I could not get enough skating. Over the shiny surface I sailed, the wind in my face, my feet flying, my spirits soaring even as the skate blades dashing along the ice. In an instant I became Hans Brinker speeding down a frozen canal in Holland to win the silver skates; then I was a speed skater gliding around a long oval rink in powerful rhythmic strides; finally I was an all star hockey player, bent low, feinting my opponents out of position and then flashing in on the net to score the winning goal in the last ten seconds.

Another time during one of the summers I spent on my Grandfather's hardscrabble farm in the north country, I lost myself in a summer rain shower. A small crew of lumberjacks were selectively cutting the back part of grandfather's forty acres of pine and popple woods; my brother and I had the job of bringing the men cold well water twice each day. One muggy August afternoon just as we were finishing our rounds, it began to rain, softly at first and then turning into a torrential downpour. My brother, grandfather and one of the workmen burrowed under a thick umbrella of downed pine branches where they stayed warm and dry. But what they missed! I headed back toward the log cabin a half mile distant, first running and then slowing to a walk. In my eleven years I had never been out in the woods in a heavy rainfall. All my senses seemed to come alive. I saw water bouncing off ferns, cascading down beech leaves, felt it beating on my shoulders and outstretched palms. Pungent odors emanated upward from the forest floor, rich, musky, primeval. Stopping in a small clearing, I stretched my arms upward and let the moisture envelop me; looking skyward my eyes filled with rain and the trees became a misty green blur — and I felt as one with the wet woods. My grandmother scolded me severely when I appeared, drenched, at the cabin door, but I had followed a different path and it had made all the difference.

Much of what we call our civilized life — the marketplace and established social order where we sell a part of ourselves to obtain "comfort" and "security" — requires a degree of conformity or "sophistication." We learn at all too young an age to be aware of self, to be glancing always over our shoulder to see who may be looking and evaluating. We learn to hood our passions, deny our impulses, conceal our joys. We learn to pretend to be detached, non-involved, unaffected, unemotional — in short, to surrender to the great American disorder, being "cool." In fact we do this so well that we become, to some extent, prisoners cloaked in societal inhibition, wrapped tight in our skin envelopes, wanting to reach out to each other (as well as to nature) but not wanting to appear childish. Thus we come to act upon someone else's concept of taste — what is the current "in" thing to do, wear or say — not some joyous choice of our own. Have I overstated the issue? I think not. Despite unprecedented prosperity and control of the environment, people feel more destitute and unfree than ever before. We are victims of "deficit living" as well as deficit spending. In my view the solution, as with many central aspects of life, is paradoxical: to find ourself, we must lose ourself. Lose ourselves, perhaps, on a snow-covered hillside.

Now John and I toiled up the steep, slippery northern slope of Summit Peak. Progress was slow. We gained three steps only to slide back two on the hard surface. Skirting the rocky overhang near the top — in summer we would wedge our way up this route — we crawled the last few yards to the highest point. The view in all directions was breathtaking: to the east Lake Superior, today a deep, almost purple-blue, extended as far as we could see; heavily wooded hills and granite knobs rolled away to the south and west; far down the slope to the north we could make out the deep green gash where the Carp River, now frozen and snow-covered, made its way down the valley. We felt as if we were at the summit of the universe.

Below the peak on the south side we found an open warm spot among wintergreen and old needles beneath the jack pines. We built a small fire, more to celebrate and prolong our experience than for warmth, and sat quietly with our backs against a tree. John produced a treat, a bar of maple sugar candy. Nothing could have been a more fitting feast to fete the Moon of the Snowcrust.

The Moon of the Snowcrust is the time for gathering and rendering maple syrup in the north country. In order for the sap to flow in sufficient quantities for making syrup, there must be warming days (over 40 degrees) with sunshine and cool clear nights (between 20-30 degrees); huge amounts are needed for it takes 40 to 50 gallons of sap to make one gallon of syrup. No one knows who first discovered the delectable sweet but it is indigenous to North America, particularly four northern states, Vermont, New York, Michigan and Wisconsin. Native Americans knew the source of maple sugar and used it long before the colonists arrived; an Iroquois legend has it that the source of sweet was found by accident:

> *Early one spring morning Woksis, an Iroquois chief, pulled his tomahawk from a maple tree where he had left it and went hunting. Later that same day, the chief's squaw noticed what seemed to be water dripping from the gash in the tree; instead of going all the way to the river for water, she collected a basket of the sap and used it to*

cook the venison stew for supper. The heavy pot bubbled over a small fire all day. By the time Woksis returned from his day of hunting, the odor of sweet syrup permeated his tepee. When he tested the meal, the chief was delighted and the gathering of maple sap became a yearly ritual.

Recently I spent a day and night assisting a local farmer in the sugarbush. We emptied the buckets hung on spiles — metal tubes inserted into holes bored in the tree trunks — and cut a supply of firewood for the night-long rendering. The hours passed quickly in the old shack; we fed the fire, stirred the sap in the large shallow vat and chatted quietly. He told me that he taps both red and sugar maples but that the latter, *Acer saccarum*, yields the best quality sap — as much as 12 gallons from the mature tree. Despite the sleepless night I was not tired when at dawn the batch was

finally ready and we emerged from the dark sugar house to pour a ladle of the hot syrup in the snow. It tasted of sunshine and of the sweet promise of spring.

A flock of redpolls swept into the branches of the jack pines directly over John's head, disturbing my reverie. Before they fluttered away, we identified one smaller frostier looking bird as a hoary redpoll; when it flew I could see the clear white rump. We explored for evidence of other wild creatures on Summit Peak. Deer had been here earlier in the winter; we found pellets and saw where they had browsed the small aspens on the east slope of the peak. Whitetail deer have difficulty moving about during the time of the late winter snowcrust. Their small sharp hooves break through the snowcrust and much energy is expended at a time when reserves are low; yet predators (the major one here in the Upper Peninsula is the pack of free-running family dogs) can race along the snow surface.

We discovered a porcupine trail, a packed-down path leading from tree to tree under the pines. Glancing up we saw where a porky had completely denuded the top branches of a white pine with its sharp teeth. Once during a survival weekend I killed a large porcupine and broiled it on a spit over an open fire. It tasted exactly like a bunch of white pine needles and I vowed never to kill another of the slow-witted creatures; better to eat boiled rock tripe or even the inner bark of aspens. My distaste, however, now that I think back upon it, may have been the result of my veterinarian companion's graphic post mortem — each of the porcupine's many parasites was described and delineated in Latin nomenclature as we dressed out the creature for cooking!

We stood silently and watched the shadows begin to lengthen in the valley far below. A somber black raven soared effortlessly among the tallest pines and then merged with the shadows; a single hoarse croak drifted up on the slight breeze. I recalled a line from William Davies' poem called *Leisure:*

> *A poor life this if, full of care*
> *We have no time to stand and stare.*

Returning to our small fire, now just a few glowing coals, we savored the last fragments of John's maple candy. Sitting in the sunshine on the south side of the peak, spring time seemed somehow closer. Soon the sun and rains would erode and wash away the white blanket which had for so many months covered the forests and the hills, soon the ice in tiny Lake Buschell which lay hidden a few hundred yards below the peak would turn black, and soon the willows and aspens would begin to show the first blush of green.

Still, it was difficult to believe that beneath those feet of snow are ferns, wildflowers and other woodland plants ready to germinate each in its own time, each according to some predetermined sequence. And each year we know they will — and that the ending of winter is, for all creatures, a reassurance of familiar cycles, of things that do not change.

But for now we would enjoy the season at hand: the Moon of the Snowcrust. Scattering the remains of the fire, we headed down the slopes and were soon lost in the wild abandonment of snowy glissades.

S PRING

Seasons in the Upper Peninsula of Michigan

"Miners Castle"

"Yellow lady's slippers"

PHOTOS BY LON EMERICK

S P R I N G

Late one April morning as I leaned back and surveyed my desk piled high with paper work, a wave of weariness and boredom swept over me. All at once I was jaded with my scholarly winter projects, surfeited with memos and faculty committees, tired of spending long days in an overheated and under-ventilated office. The symptoms were readily identifiable for denizens of the North Country — an advanced case of cabin fever. The prescription was obvious.

Abandoning my work — it would still be there when I returned, I rationalized — I went forth to seek signs of spring. Suddenly it was terribly important that I find some evidence of new life, of greenness, after the long monochromatic dormancy of winter. A line from a poem by James Thomson ran through my mind —

> *"Come, gentle spring*
> *ethereal mildness, come."*

Following an old railroad right-of-way north of town, I looked for a spot where April sun might have had its way with the drifts. On a hillside facing southwest, I found a dry patch among the crinkly brown leaves of the past autumn; leaning back against a large oak, I contemplated my surroundings. On the forest floor, only two plants showed the greening of spring, a bed of moss and a small patch of wintergreen. I picked a few glistening leaves of the latter for a tea time which would taste of the woods slowly coming to life. As I sat there reveling in the sunshine, a Mourning Cloak butterfly fluttered past and landed on a nearby maple; it opened its fragile wings slowly as if it too savored the warm rays.

I lay back in the dry leaves and gazed up at the clear blue sky. High overhead several snow white herring gulls flashed in the sun; I could just discern their peevish calls and I was flooded with memories of Lake Superior's foaming waves, camping and summer fun. As I rose to leave the hillside, my foot brushed away a clump of leaves exposing the familiar thick oblong leaves of the trailing arbutus. Carefully, I lifted a vine and looked closely for the blossom. There it was, one pink bud, half-opened. On bended knee, reverently, I sniffed the delicate vanilla fragrance.

Further down the old railroad bed I found a clump of willows sporting a new tiara of soft pearly grey buds. Nearby a small creek, now swollen with melting snow, threatened to flood a cattail marsh. When I stopped to listen to the music of flowing water, a pair of mallards flushed in a spray of droplets, their blue wing speculums shining iridescent in the slanting rays of the sun.

My steps were now jaunty as I returned along the old railway; the lines of boredom and depression were erased from my face. The warmth of the sunshine on my shoulders made me smile and I mused aloud, "The April sun brings a warming to the spirit as well as to the land."

A   N o r t h e r n   S p r i n g

Our twin daughters, Mary and Lynn, scampered ahead with youthful energy through the woods exploring each new clump of wildflowers along the path. Free at last from our heavy winter wraps and cumbersome boots, my wife and I felt like skipping, too, as the forest trail beckoned us toward Laughing Whitefish Falls. The fragrance of thousands of opening tree buds perfumed the air; the earth was warming and the musty pungence of leaf mold drifted upward at every step. Wildflowers in bloom — trout lily, spring beauty and violets — extended through the forest like a multi-colored fantasy carpet as far as we could see. From a nearby glade came the incessant wheezy call of a phoebe, while overhead a chorus of lisping myrtle warblers flitted about in the maples. Another Northern Spring!

For those who live in a warmer climate, it is difficult to understand why spring is a major, almost magical event in the Superior Peninsula. You cannot truly appreciate the overwhelming joy of open water, a bare sun-warmed hillside or the first wildflower simply by coming north for the spring season. Only after you have lived through a northern winter, only after you have endured the many storms, the short twilight days, the weeks of frigid arctic air, can you begin to understand the longing of the natives for the soft greenness of spring. It is like eating jam made from wild strawberries; only those who have picked the tiny, elusive fruit can really appreciate the preserves.

How we love to watch the transformations of spring! When we first wander about in the forest after the spring melting occurs, the carpet of dead leaves pressed down by layers of heavy snow seem barren and inert. Then, as if by some magical signal, the green tips of wildflowers emerge pushing aside the matted leaves as they reach for the sun. Almost before our eyes the dull grays and browns give way to the harlequin hues of blooming wildflowers. Nature seems to realize that time is very short in the north country and that much of the colorful bounty must unfold swiftly. Every hour of sunshine is

precious. There is no time to linger. Hues are most vibrant, aromas more intense, sounds more compelling in a northern spring. Even though I have been an especially attentive lover of seasonal change, I will probably never completely know all the facets of spring — like an independent young girl she is fickle, mercurial, ephemeral. Yet each small initial sign of life awakening brings a flood of memories: the annual parade of wildflowers, aspen hillsides brushed with pale green, geese flying north again, the sound of water flowing among moss-covered rocks. And I know that I, too, in my very blood, am responding to the call of spring.

I have never been able to resist the invitation of spring. "I have an appointment with Spring," Thoreau wrote, "She comes to my window to wake me, and I go forth an hour or two earlier than usual." There has always been one day each spring that epitomizes the season for me, one day in which the forces emerge and blend in a unique essence of change and a new beginning. My memories of two such days are especially vivid. One chilly April morning as I delivered Sunday papers as a youth, I beheld a ragged checkmark of Canada geese flying so low that I could easily make out their white chin straps. They seemed to be struggling in the air. As I watched, the formation broke up and they flapped about in confusion directly overhead. Then suddenly a goose perceptibly larger that the rest honked loudly as if exhorting the others to follow him and set off toward the north; the flock fell in behind the leader in a tight V. I watched until they were out of sight. My hands were cold and the paper bag still hung heavily across my shoulders but now my mood was changed and I knew the long days of summer were soon to follow.

Another time, while attending a large midwestern university, I abandoned classes to greet scores of migrating birds arriving on the front edge of a May morning isotherm. A gentle misty rain fell and I had the campus woodlot to myself. In a single red maple I beheld three members of the thrush family, a bluebird, a veery and a wood thrush. The first and only prothonotary warbler I have ever seen flitted about in the budding witch hazel beneath the thrushes. Spring is a season of cameo experiences. Here in the north the essence of spring for our family is an annual hike to catalog the wildflowers along the path to the falls on the Laughing Whitefish River.

Laughing Whitefish Falls Scenic Site is located southeast of Marquette near the small farming community of Sundell. Several years ago the Michigan Department of Natural Resources traded lands with a lumber company in order to set aside this unique Upper Peninsula area in the public trust.

Our annual appointment with spring takes place near this river because it is here that a profusion of wildflowers blooms about the second weekend in May each year. The path leading from the parking area to the falls follows an old logging railroad spur; large holes were dug years before to obtain fill to build up the railroad bed and at this season they are filled with water from melted snow. I knelt down beside one of these vernal ponds and looked closely. Two water striders edged away and a small green frog eyed me warily from the far bank. Several mosquito larvae jiggled near the surface reminding me that soon I must purchase our annual supply of insect repellent. Cupping some of the water in my hands, I thought of the hundreds of tiny organisms eking out a brief but fecund existence.

As we hiked slowly along the path we listed the wildflowers in bloom. The delicate white pink-veined blossoms of the Carolina spring beauty shone everywhere in profusion. Mixed in with the spring beauty we found another flower with four to eight blossoms tipped with yellow on a stem; each blossom looked like a pair of inverted Dutch pantaloons. Appropriately named Dutchman's breeches, it often grows with a close relative, squirrel corn. Clumps of violets — white, yellow and purple — contrasted with the spring beauty and Dutchman's breeches. On the drier hillsides, we found the delicate Canada mayflower, both false and "real" Solomon's seal and the small bright anemone.

A chipmunk, thin and gaunt from his long winter underground, chattered loudly and dashed across the path toward an old stump while we paused to record the first entries in our record of spring flowers. Close beside the decaying stump we discovered three blossoming bloodroots. This member of the poppy family sports a single pale, lobed leaf which embraces a stalk topped by a white flower with eight to ten petals. The root exudes a blood red juice which the Native Americans used for making war paint.

Where the forest path turns abruptly away from the old railroad spur, I was delighted to discover again several decaying logs covered with light green moss. I confess that I am a fan of old mossy logs. I tend to ignore them during the summer when everything is green in the forest but in spring, against the backdrop of dead leaves they have a special appeal. I like to sit beside them in the spring woods and lose myself in the soft greenness. Now, on the small hillside beside us, a particularly large fallen log provided a backdrop for a colony of trillium; a portion of the mossy trunk seemed to make a green velvet proscenium for a cluster of four particularly lovely flowers nodding in the gentle breeze.

Each wildflower has a spirit all its own, an elan that is characteristic. One of our favorites, the trillium, is described in plant taxonomy texts as a liliaceous herb having a whorl of three leaves out of which rises a single three-petaled flower. And we add: out of which rises our own spirits. Emerson wrote that the earth laughs in flowers and certainly one of the most infectious and merry chuckles comes from the trillium.

We paused a moment to rest beside a small creek which eventually flows into the Laughing Whitefish River. Close beside its banks in the damp spots were clusters of marsh marigolds; their bright yellow blossoms gleamed in the sunlight. Following the creek for a short way we came upon a single Jack-in-the-Pulpit; it stood bravely beside the water, its striped hood forming a canopied pulpit for a tiny upright figure. My children bent close and listened carefully for a woodland sermon but heard only the soft chuckling of water flowing in the tiny stream. What Jack might say if we but knew flower language is: "Don't pick wildflowers — most are protected by law and look so much better gracing the forest floor than they do wilting on a dinner table." Selah!

Now the path ended at the brink of the falls and the roaring water filled our ears; the spray made shimmering prisms in the bright noon sunlight and filled the gorge with mist. We spread out a blanket on the soft moss and ate our lunch beside the tumbling waters.

The Laughing Whitefish River cuts through dense wilderness near the center of the Upper Peninsula and eventually flows into Lake Superior. Above the falls, the river is shallow and only about fifty feet wide. It drops down into a deep gorge over a gradual staircase of sandstone palisades; the snow- and spring-fed waters cascade over the rocks creating a lacy bridal veil. The rims on both sides of the gorge are heavily timbered with hemlock, white pine and mixed hardwoods.

We clambered down the stairway built against the cliff for a closer look at the rushing water and the steep walls of the gorge. Close beside the falls itself we found a favorite spot: a deep cave cut into the layers of multicolored sandstone which form the sides of the river chasm. We sat close together and listened to the roar. We felt a need to capture and hold this beauty that we had waited for through the long winter, to fill our senses with this gay bubbling song of spring.

Returning to the rim we followed a faint trail along the west ridge of the gorge. It led along the narrow crest through a grove of huge hemlock and white pine trees, most of which appeared to be remnants of the virgin forest which covered this region. Apparently this small grove at the top of the gorge was not accessible to the early loggers. We saw other large pines further along and followed the crest for almost a mile. Where the ridge descended to the floor of the valley, we made an exciting discovery: here grew a triad of truly huge white pines, three giants that towered well over 150 feet and exceeded five feet in diameter through the trunk. Quietly, almost reverently, we sat on the thick duff of yellow pine needles and contemplated these magnificent trees. As we rested silently among the huge boles, a nearby winter wren sang his tinkling refrain again and again. We stayed a long time and all the while our daughter Mary had been covering pages of paper with lines of poetry. She and her sister write constantly, so we were not surprised when she announced she had finished a poem about the white pines, but we were impressed at her understanding and her appreciation of all we had been seeing.

The Majestic White Pine

The white pine like a statue stands there
As if a reminder to when it was everywhere.
It stands by Lake Superior
Different from the other trees, but not inferior.
Standing unmoving, sheltering small animals of the wood.
If it could speak,
It would.
It would tell tales of fire raging through the grass,
Making it so black nobody could pass.
It would tell
Tales of loggers who would fell
Many white pines; for them no bells would knell.

The subtle fragrance and colorful beauty of the wildflowers we had seen along the path, the roar of the falls, the immense white pines and the ethereal refrain of the winter wren were in our thoughts as we turned the car toward the highway and home. No one wanted to speak lest somehow we break the spell of spring. It was then I noted the clouds building up toward the northeast. Soon the rain spattered the windshield and before we were halfway home it turned to heavy wet snow. By morning two inches of snow covered the ground.

As I looked out at our snowy back yard the next morning, a fluffed up robin skidded to a landing on the porch and regarded me with an irritated expression. He looked so comically exasperated that I laughed out loud. Hurriedly I donned boots and warm clothes and went forth to survey the wildflowers growing on the slopes near our home. An extensive bed of adder's tongue leaves were flattened under the wet snow; the plants looked hopelessly frozen. But then I saw something that lifted my spirits and renewed the promise of spring: there under the snow, and showing bravely through, was a single blossom flashing yellow against the white mantle. The Northern Spring was not gone, merely postponed and its signs were still there for those who searched.

LONG SHIPS ON THE HORIZON

*I*t was very late on a wet gloomy night in April as I made my way wearily home from the university. Turning down the shoreline drive, I was thrilled to see a long row of lights moving slowly into the harbor — the first ore boat of the season was arriving! Many years ago, before modern land and air travel, the Peninsula was isolated for many months during the long winters and the arrival of the first ship in spring was a real occasion for celebration. The feeling still lingers and when the long ore boats appear again on the horizon — especially when the first one arrives at night with its array of lights winking the darkness — I hold a personal, quiet ceremony. The desire to go down to the sea in ships is still deeply imbedded in many hearts.

I drove down close to the tall ore dock, switched off the engine and rolled down the window. I could hear the muted night sounds of the harbor and smell the rich pungent odors emanating from the boats rocking impatiently in their fog-shrouded berths. The fog horn guarding the harbor at the end of the breakwater issued its sonorous warning again and again. Now the ore boat responded: three long and two short blasts, the salute. No longer tired, I watched in awe as the giant freighter, at least 700 feet long, glided slowly through the fog to its berth beside the ore dock.

The pioneer iron ore shippers who built the first dock in Marquette harbor would scarcely believe the present immense structure. The men labored mightily with simple hand tools to erect a crude platform of logs piled in the water and covered over with gravel. The very night it was finished a Lake Superior gale blew the primitive dock away — weeks of backbreaking work washed away overnight by the giant waves. The modern pocket ore dock is 80 feet high and built of reinforced concrete; it is so huge and so sturdy that trainloads of iron ore pellets can be pulled along atop the structure. The pellets are then dumped into waiting bins; these huge metal bins or pockets can then be lowered directly into the cavernous holds of the long ore boats.

It was not always so easy. In the early days, the raw iron ore was brought in horse drawn carts down to Marquette from the mines in Negaunee and piled on the primitive docks. The heavy red ore was then carried on board and placed on the open decks of windjammers and steamers; sometimes it was shoveled laboriously into barrels for the transit. Not long after the Civil War, a startling new development in marine architecture appeared which revolutionized the transport of ore to the blast furnaces.

A wooden bulk freighter was designed with engines aft and navigational quarters in the bow; a long, low compartment for carrying large loads lay between. Commissioned in 1869, the *R. J. Hackett* was 211 feet long and could carry a cargo of 1200 tons. Ship builders then turned to metal construction and the boats lengthened. The *Onaka*, the first iron freighter, was built in 1882 and at 282 feet was almost the length of a football field. The first of the modern steel ships, the *Spokane*, was commissioned in 1886; she was an incredible 310 feet long with a capacity of 3000 tons of the red metal.

Over a century has passed since the historic launching of the *Hackett* and today more than 250 bulk ore carriers ply the waters of the Great Lakes. They have grown to immense proportions. Freighters in the 600 foot class are common; there are fifty ore boats as long as 750 feet and a few scale almost 860 feet — the *Roger Blough*, for example, is 858 feet. There is even a 1000 foot behemoth, the *S.S. Cort*, which can carry a mind-boggling load of 60,000 tons! Most modern long ships, however, carry between 20,000 and 30,000 tons; unlike early ore carriers, they can be loaded and unloaded swiftly. When water transportation is used, speed is essential and it takes only 6 1/2 - 7 days to make the transit from the Peninsula down to the midwestern steel mills and return. All summer the ore boats glide silently past, long sleek profiles on the horizons of Lake Superior, linking the mines of northern Michigan and Minnesota to the mills in the heartland of the country, As they have for centuries, the waters of the north country continue to serve as highways for men and their craft.

Probably the first boats to float upon Lake Superior were simple dugout canoes — hollowed and burned-out logs built by Native Americans. Then an unknown time later, the magnificent light birch bark canoe was invented. The craft varied in length from 13 foot river canoes to 30 foot war canoes for use on the big lake. Although fragile looking, the birch bark canoe was ideal for water travel: very light and easily portable, it gives against the thrust of the water but will not break; it was easily repairable with spruce or balsam pitch and could carry enormous loads. The Chippewas had great respect for the winds and waves of Lake Superior and no doubt kept the canoes close to shore when shifting their camping spots at different seasons, when trading goods with other tribes or waging war.

The first white travelers to enter the region were Frenchmen in search of adventure, new lands for France and a passageway to the Orient. Often they were accompanied by Catholic priests who sought the salvation of unbaptized souls. The impetuous young explorer, Etienne Brule, and his companion Grenoble undoubtedly used a native birch canoe to explore the shores of Lake Superior about 1622. Brule brought back the first description of the huge lake and an ingot of copper which he had bartered or stolen from the Indians. Claude Allouez, a Jesuit priest, circumnavigated the Lake in 1665 and described the immense wealth of the region in forests and furs. In the next century men would make fortunes and alter the north country and its native residents forever in their search for beaver pelts.

The French fur traders invaded the region in force — Groseilliers, Radisson, Joliet, Sieur Duluth, the names roll melodically off the tongue. The clergy was never far behind. Fathers Rene Menard, Claude Dablon and Jacques Marquette suffered sickness, torture and privation to bring the message of Christ to the indians. The traders and soul-seekers expanded and improved travel on the lake. Two-man canoes were succeeded by 25 foot North canoes which could haul a ton of cargo and a crew of eight; the North canoes were followed by the 35 foot freight or Montreal canoe which held two tons of furs and 12 men. The urge for larger, more stable craft led to the bateau, a flat-bottomed boat made of cedar planks and pointed at both ends; it could carry huge loads and sails were improvised for wind power. The Mackinac boat, a barge built of oak, was also sailed. Soon tall white sails were seen on the horizon.

As early as 1771, Alexander Henry, celebrated fur trader and explorer, sailed a sloop on Lake Superior. Johnathon Carver crossed the lake and described the north shore in 1766. Between 1815 and 1822, a British officer, Lt. Bayfield, did an extensive survey of the lake and devised a chart of the more prominent features. But it was the lumber boom which dramatically expanded the wind borne fleet: at the peak of the lumbering period in 1870, 1500 sailboats coursed back and forth between ports in the Upper Peninsula and southern markets hungry for wood. Very few lighthouses existed on Lake Superior, lake charts were very limited and many of the early schooners were lost on the rocky shoals and in the gales which blew across the expanses of water. With the advent of efficient steamships, the windjammer fleet declined.

The first steam craft on Lake Superior was the side-wheeler *Independence;* the 260 ton capacity ship was piloted in 1845 by Captain A.J. Averill. Many more followed. The early steamers burned wood and had to stop along the shore to pick up fresh fuel during the long journey along the south shore of Lake Superior.

In 1891, a radical new concept in ship design was invented by Captain Alex McDougall. The whaleback was shaped like a giant metal whale; it featured a flat bottom and rounded decks and hull. More than 40 whalebacks were built and for years they hauled grain and oil on the great lakes. The *Christopher Columbus* saw service as a passenger vessel during the heyday of water travel. In less than four decades, the historic Soo locks had made not only passenger travel aboard whalebacks and other vessels feasible, it literally revolutionized the iron and copper mining industries.

The entire history of the Lake Superior region swings on a single hinge — the Sault Ste. Marie. Where the waters of Lake Superior descend 21 feet to Lake Huron was a series of rapids forming a formidable barrier to early travel. Although the St. Mary's River is only 63 miles long, it is ranked eighth in size in the United States because of the volume of flow. This unique spot at the head of the turbulent river was the focal point of early travel, military expeditions and commerce for more than a century before the American Revolution. It is today the greatest shipway in the world; more tonnage traverses through the Soo Locks each year than through the Suez and Panama Canals combined.

As early as 1615, a French missionary, Joseph LeCarron, later followed by Friar Gabriel Sagard, introduced the doctrines of the Catholic Church to the Indians residing on the islands of the St. Mary's River. In 1641, two Jesuit priests, Isaac Jogues and Charles Raymbault, preached to the Indians engaged in catching whitefish at the outlet of Lake Superior. The two missionaries dedicated the place in honor of the Blessed Virgin by naming it Sault de Saint Marie, literally the leap of St. Mary. In 1668 Father Jacques Marquette established a mission for the Chippewas here. In an elaborate ceremony, St. Lusson claimed all the land by the Sault on June 14, 1678, and the French flag flew over the small settlement until the British took over in 1762.

The British influence in the area was still strong when Lewis Cass, territorial governor of Michigan, came north through the St. Mary's River on his 1820 expedition. In a show of defiance, the Indians encamped at the Sault raised the Union Jack. Cass, in an amazing display of courage against over-whelming odds, marched over to the Chippewa stronghold, tore down the British flag and raised the Star and Stripes. Accompanying Governor Cass on his official inspection tour of the Peninsula was Henry Rowe Schoolcraft, geologist, writer, ethnologist — a man for all seasons. Schoolcraft was later assigned to the Soo as Indian agent and it was here he conducted his Algic Researches, a compilation of Indian legends and customs. A New England poet named Longfellow based his epic, *Hiawatha*, on Schoolcraft's descriptions of the Chippewas. Now explorers and adventurers flocked to the new northern frontier.

The early fur traders simply portaged around the mile-long rapids — their old route now forms Portage Avenue in the Soo. A tramway was constructed so that furs, goods and later copper and iron ore could be drawn across the portage in carts by draft animals. As commerce grew between the Lake Superior region and the population centers in the south, however, the rapids at the Soo posed a significant barrier. If only there were a way to get ships around the dangerous white water. The Northwest Fur Company did build a small lock in 1797 but it was destroyed by American soldiers during the war of 1812; the Americans built a base, Fort Brady, near the spot.

The next attempt to conquer the rapids was undertaken in 1838 by the young state of Michigan. But before the workmen could even commence digging, troopers led by Captain Jackson marched out of Ft. Brady with fixed bayonets and claimed the site as the property of the United States Government. There is some speculation that the contractor had simply overestimated the job and arranged the debacle with the Captain so that he would not have to forfeit his bond on the projected canal around the rapids.

After the discovery of iron and copper in the Peninsula, the demand for an easier, faster way to get around the rapids became urgent. It was simply too expensive and time-consuming to pull heavy ships around the rapids on greased skids or to carry the barrels of ore in carts and laboriously reload the cargo onto ships waiting below the falls. A few large ships attempted to negotiate the rapids with disastrous results —the *Discovery* and the *Otter* were severely damaged in such attempts. Politicians heard the clamor for a new waterway and promised 750,000 acres of federal land in compensation to anyone successful in constructing a lock or canal around the St. Mary's sharp drop.

In 1853, a young salesman for Fairbanks Scales Company happened to be recovering from an illness in the Soo and became entranced with the idea of constructing a water lock to lower and raise ships between Lake Superior and the less turbulent waters of the St. Mary's River. Although only 23 years old and inexperienced in heavy construction, Charles T. Harvey began efforts to secure a federal grant to begin work on the lock. Despite the fact that both Daniel Webster and Henry Clay condemned the project in the U.S. Senate as a flagrant waste of money in a "worthless wilderness," the grant was finally awarded to Harvey. On June 7, 1853, the young salesman pushed the first wheelbarrow of dirt out of the cut. Despite the frigid cold, an epidemic of cholera, dysentery, inadequate machinery — Harvey invented a steam hammer on the spot — and the difficulty of cutting through Cambrian rock, 1600 men completed the project on schedule. The first lock was 350 feet long and 70 feet wide. The canal opened on June 18, 1855. The first ship to go through the locks was the northbound *Illinois,* a side-wheel steamer under the guidance of Captain Jack Wilson. The *Columbia,* laden with iron ore, was the first southbound vessel.

The locks have expanded over the past century. In 1876, the Weitzel lock was built — 515 feet long, 80 feet wide and 17 feet deep. In succeeding years, the Poe, the David and the McArthur Locks have been increased to 1000 feet. Now the Corps of Engineers is studying the feasibility of a new "Superlock," to handle ships up to 1500 feet long, 150 feet wide and up to 36 foot draft.

I admire the profile of a large ore freighter on the Lake Superior waters, yet another jump in size poses potential problems. Larger ships will mean more extensive dredging of harbor bottoms at lake ports, and a possible increase in pollution of the already fragile lake ecosystems. To dredge six feet would produce millions of cubic yards of spoil materials laden, in some ports, with a variety of toxic substances . . . and there is simply no safe place to put this material. The long ships also could create water pollution in pristine Lake Superior when they dump ballast water collected in lower Lake Michigan and Lake Erie into the clear northern lake.

There is an additional concern. The demand for a superlock comes from shipping interests planning to build even larger lake freighters. The present size carriers are causing serious erosion problems along some narrower portions of the waterways; larger ships with more intensified wake effect would magnify the problem.

Ocean-going vessels also pass through the narrow water valve at the Soo and many foreign ships make the circuit during the eight-month and now lengthening shipping season. Opening of the waterways to the sea for commerce, notable the Welland Canal around Niagara Falls in 1929, also opened a pathway for the sea lamprey to enter the Great Lakes. The ocean eel found conditions favorable and by 1942 the parasite had destroyed the lake trout fishery in Lake Huron. Sometime in 1955, it found its way into Lake Superior. The aquatic vertebrate is voracious; it will kill a 15 inch lake trout in only 14 hours. Over the 18 months of its life, scientists compute that a single lamprey can destroy 20-40 pounds of fish. The efforts to control the parasitic eel, using metal weirs, electric weirs and specific chemicals, has met with some success and the fish populations have been expanded. The lamprey saga is an example of the long range, and at times unexpected, problems that can occur when large changes in lake conditions and balances are undertaken.

The old balances which the Chippewas and French voyageurs knew were changed dramatically when the giant steel ships began moving up and down the inland seas hauling the materials of the region. The long ore boats are unique to the Great Lakes; the ore freighter has no counterpart elsewhere in the world. If we learn to husband our resources carefully and if we can live wisely and not just very well, then the parade of the long ships on the horizon will continue for the next century — and, it is hoped, many more.

—◄◼►—

T H E R A P Y   V A L U E S   I N   N A T U R E

The calmest, most genuine and healthy existence for humans is a life close to the natural world. There is an abundant source of nurture in nature. Long before reading Thoreau, I discovered that the solitude and wonder of a forest path, a lonely shore, a mountain meadow soothed me with their slow rhythm. As a youngster I stuttered quite severely and the affliction troubled me deeply; unable to share my thoughts, subject to penalties and endless frustrations, I found in woodland rambles the surcease which I needed. I drank deeply of the tonic of wildness and by the time I reached adulthood and more fluent speech, the habit had indelibly marked my life. Nature is a skillful therapist.

It was only natural, then, when I started my career as a university teacher, to feel an urge to share my affection for the woods and waters with my students. Whenever possible, we abandoned the lecture halls and speech clinic for hikes and cookouts in remote spots. My colleagues raised their eyebrows — and my guilt level — when they made sly remarks about the Pied Piper professor and his entourage tramping in the forests. A few bluntly asked, in rhetorical fashion and with a distinct ruffling of their academic feathers, what a sojourn to a spring waterfall had to do with a college education. Perhaps, I worried, I was simply indulging my own need to relate to others in the context of the out-of-doors.

But the students responded to the outings, even to the extent of arising before dawn — no small sacrifice for a collegian — to watch a sunrise before we cooked breakfast. We called these excursions "hegiras" and a list for the semester was posted on my office door; the adventures became so popular that we had to limit the number of participants in order to retain the quality of each experience.

It was not difficult to notice changes in the students on these hikes: they seemed more spontaneous, free and open. At first I thought they were simply less guarded outside the formal classroom setting, relating better to the professor as a person without textbooks, tests and other trappings of academe. I am sure that was part of it. But there was more. The students — even tense, anxious Master's candidates — seemed to relax and visibly grow calm as they sat and watched an open fire or picked their way on snow-shoes through a winter forest. Why not see, I thought, if the wilds would weave the same magic with some of our clients in the speech clinic?

We picked five adolescent stutterers for an experimental four week summer therapy program. Each of the young clients had previous unsuccessful treatment and now felt little hope. Two were rebellious failures at school and at home. All five were surly and uncommunicative. I was astounded by what happened during those four weeks. After an initial period of resistance the youths plunged into a tough, intensive program to alter the way they talked. Again the catalyst was nature. We practically lived in the woods — camping, hiking, exploring. As they shed their defenses and settled down to work together, they laughed more and took pleasure in little things; the woods offered solace and set them back into the slow cycles of nature. The talk around the campfire and on the trail was *real* talk, not artificial conversation contrived in a sterile treatment room with acoustic tile, tape recorders and two-way mirrors. Removed from the stress of everyday life, they had time to look carefully at themselves, form their own ideas and act upon them. By the end of the summer they were talking very well indeed.

A move, research for a doctoral degree, and the press of daily teaching duties delayed me from following up on our nature therapy revelations. As Edward R. Murrow discovered, the urgent takes precedence over the important. The ideas remained dormant until two events propelled me to explore more fully the path we had found.

Quite by accident a brochure describing the Outward Bound program crossed my desk. According to the literature, when participants undertake physical challenges and learn survival techniques in the context of the outdoors, they benefit in terms of self-reliance and self-confidence. I learned that a local psychologist was investigating the impact of wilderness experiences on young boys using an Outward Bound approach. Camping in a remote forest, the youths learn to use map and compass, to find survival foods and make shelters; they are taught to rappel a steep cliff and spend a day and night alone in the woods. Such experiences served to expand the participants' self-esteem and feeling of adequacy and, it was felt, increased their ability to cope with exigencies of day-to-day living. Researchers in the mountains of Utah were finding similar benefits with adults; their studies suggest that prolonged experiences in wilderness areas may be useful adjuncts to preventive and remedial mental hygiene programs. The most interesting article I encountered described a unique freshman orientation program in an Arizona college: instead of large assemblies in square rooms, the students are divided into small groups for a camping experience in the desert canyons. The student groups erect a tent with all members blindfolded except one . . . and the sighted member cannot touch the tent. They divide responsibilities for finding firewood, cooking, getting water; each participant also has a solo experience. Group rapport and cohesiveness are built swiftly as each student tests his skills and endurance and comes to know his capabilities.

The second event which refocused my attention on therapy values in nature was more direct and personal. During a sabbatical year, our family took an extensive camping trip throughout the western part of the United States. As we roamed the ancient cliff dwellings of Mesa Verde or hiked along the rim of the Grand Canyon, my then-second grade children soaked up history, geology, anthropology and biology through their pores. The learning was real, a product of ongoing experience. Then, because the school system insisted, we had to drag out workbooks and "cover" so many pages each day. The instant that formal school began, my children changed dramatically; posture and demeanor were altered. School and formal learning were not supposed to be joyful and spontaneous as was the learning they had absorbed while climbing among the rocks. Finally, in the deep verdant coolness of the Solduc Valley in the Olympic rain forest, we finished the last of the dreaded workbooks and went back to learning directly from nature. Now I was very intrigued. There is powerful medicine in those hills. I returned to the university eager to explore the therapy values in nature with a small class of sensitive students.

Alas, before we could offer a new course our innovation would have to pass through the university committee hierarchy, a system which moves creakily and incredibly slowly. It has been said many times in rueful jest that the camel was the product of a committee which set out to design a horse. It so nearly could be true that it is not really funny. After more than three decades of laboring in the vineyards of academe, I have come to understand that committee meetings are gatherings where minutes are kept and hours are wasted.

One would surely think that academicians would welcome innovation and look with favor upon novelty. However, professional boundaries are carefully guarded and each department patrols its territory (and student enrollment) with considerable jealousy. There was collective alarm when members of a key faculty committee scrutinized our course proposal:

> *A tutorial investigation of therapeutic values derived from experiences in natural settings. Students and instructor-guide will systematically explore the unique impact of "wilderness" encounters upon personal growth and adjustment. Activities will include:*

scrutiny of classic writings (Thoreau, Muir, Sigurd Olson, W.O. Douglas and others); personal interviews with individuals living in primitive settings; practicum experiences in natural settings both group and individual.

The professor of English was doubtful that we could really understand classic literature without his expertise. The clinical psychologist suggested none too gently that therapy was his own special bailiwick. The biologist wanted to be included so he could name and classify everything we viewed with appropriate Latin terminology. I winced at that point for his suggestion was the last thing we wanted. Although we recognized that knowing the names of birds and plants enhances a personal relationship with nature — like knowing a friend's name — we remembered Colin Fletcher's warning: If you don't miss some rare specimen, then you may well miss the wonders of nature's pure display. We were not going to try to identify everything for we were not taxonomists, merely a small group of persons deeply intent on increasing our awareness of the natural world. To lose ourselves in the music of a thrush was more important, we felt, than knowing its genus.

Interestingly, the most strenuous objection to our proposed course came from teachers of humanities and social sciences; they simply could not see what exploring therapy values in nature had to do with a university education. I linger over this issue — the notion that man and his works are of sole importance to a liberal arts education — because it is, in my judgement, part of the reason we are currently in an environmental crisis.

It is commonly asserted that students should acquaint themselves with their vast cultural heritage; we have no argument with that admonition. All too often, however, the keepers of social status and academic programs interpret it to mean exposure exclusively to the works of man — literature, music, dance, art. The person who knows and loves nature, who may have mud from a marsh on his boots and bird songs filling his ears, is somehow unusual and probably not very "cultured." Yet, why should it be more cultured to recognize ballet steps than the habits of thrushes? Why is it more cultured to recognize a series of sounds as Bach than to thrill to the wild call of a loon on a remote northern lake? The sounds of nature are primary; they flow naturally from real life experiences. The actor feigns his moods and the play after all is just a play. But it is a real living drama when a small wren, sputtering and protesting, fills a nesting box entrance with sticks to prevent its use by other birds.

I told the committee that I was not denying the greatness of man and his achievements but that there is an even larger circle which includes all of us; when we say that no man is an island we mean that he is joined not only with other humans but with all creation. A person is whole when he is in tune with the winds, forests and waves as well as with his neighbors. I saved my most convincing argument for last: many students come to this small northern university because they know or sense that its surroundings have as much to offer them in their growth as does the classroom. They migrate from the noisy warrens in the lower part of the state in search of the solitude, beauty and challenges available in the unique setting of the Upper Peninsula. Why, I concluded, not use our locale to teach about the meliorative effects of nature and do it in a systematic manner. Finally, our course was approved and we set out joyously to explore a new frontier.

In order to create an intimate climate for the initial exploration of therapy values in nature, we limited enrollment to only five persons: John, an expert professional counselor; Mary, a warm, quiet explorer; Lucy, an unusually sensitive undergraduate student; my wife, Lynn, the most perceptive woodswoman I know; and myself as guide and coordinator. We met one evening over dinner and eagerly planned our program of psychoenvironmental immersion.

The program we evolved had three facets. First, we visited persons living simply in primitive settings and interviewed them extensively: why had they chosen that life style? What values did they see in living close to nature? Secondly, we read and discussed the works of John Muir, Sigurd Olson, Aldo Leopold, William O. Douglas, Edward Abbey, Annie Dillard, Curtis Stadtfeld and many, many others. They all suggested that humans need to relate to nature for rest, for recharging, to refill the main-spring of life. Thoreau was the most explicit with his prescription: "You must converse with the field and woods, if you would imbibe such health into your mind and spirit as you covet for your body." Following his advice, the third facet of our course was devoted to spending much of our time in the fields and woods.

Most of our sojourns were taken jointly — we prepared for the excursion, immersed ourselves in the experience and then analyzed the results together. Some hikes were taken in complete silence to deepen our personal reflections; each class member also took solo rambles and kept a diary of their observations. We practiced building fires in a rain-dampened forest, found our way across country by map and compass, and studied survival techniques. At the end of spring semester I asked each member to summarize — in any chosen fashion — what impact the class had made upon their thinking or their lives.

What had we learned? Rather than discovering that something had been added to our lives, we found that old longings for a deeper relationship with the out-of-doors had been re-awakened and layers of civilization had been peeled off during the sixteen weeks. What of our main purpose — to identify possible therapy values in nature? We knew we had been touched, even changed profoundly in some ways . . . but how could we describe what had occurred so that others might recognize the directional signs and follow a similar path? Early efforts were difficult and the dimensions of our findings eluded the group. Perhaps the difficulty in translating our experiences into verbalistic forms stemmed from the fact that much of what we had undergone was simply not amenable to sequential, cognitive analysis. Rather, our understanding of humans and nature was on the level of feelings, intuitions and a grasp of relationships among the many things we had experienced. We persisted and gradually a list of values emerged, values which not only are of merit for therapy with troubled persons but also can be recommended to all human beings.

- Nature offers eternal truths. Unlike the unease of the swiftly changing world of men and machines, we found in the forests, beside the streams and on granite overlooks comforting constants to which we could return again and again. Changes do occur but in a slow natural progression that is in keeping with the cycles of the seasons and the balance of nature, not the latest social whim. As Sigurd Olson observed, civilization has abandoned the intuitive wisdom developed over time, we have substituted mores (what people are doing) for morals. The natural realm offers a timeless counterpoint to fleeting social customs and popularities.

- Nature offers simplicity. Let us recognize it: nature offers the lowest common denominator of life, the baseline for all existence. Despite the bewildering array of life in a single square foot of forest soil, there is order and a sense of basic purpose. When we lose ourselves in a personal relationship with woods and waters, we are forced to abandon the many pretenses which clutter our existence and confuse our minds. Nature is unaffected, direct and unadorned.

- Nature offers perspective. The easy rhythms of nature unlock the corridors of our mind, free us from the mundane matters of day-to-day existence. A good long hike in the forest tumbles our demons about until they are reduced in stature and obedient to our desires. Nature truly can refresh us with its vigor; it permits us the leisure to sort out what is really important in life.

- Nature offers humility. In addition to perspective, but related to it, the natural world teaches us that we are but a small part of a community, that it is vain and arrogant to believe that our problems and our needs are center stage in the universe or that we have the right to alter the natural world to suit our purposes.

- Nature offers an expanded awareness. We discovered that an immersion in the natural world brought an expansion of our physical and mental awareness, an increase in our sensitivities, not only toward rocks and trees, but toward each other. Lynn chose a Japanese poem form, a *tanka*, to convey her impressions:

Expansion

World above, around
Makes me stretch to feel, to grow
To become as one.
Elemental as aspens
Responding to touch.

- Nature offers authenticity. There is little time or purpose in social posturing or other forms of calculated *presentation of oneself* on the trail. Persons sharing life in the woods and hills become real, drop their defensive social armor and experience honest, genuine relationships. Let me make it even more pointed: experiences in nature foster a true *expression of oneself.*

We found, in summary, that nature has much to do with human emotions and attitudes, that experiences in remote places offer an antidote to the mental price we pay for life in modern times. Even Sigmund Freud realized it when he wrote that "It is easy for a barbarian to be healthy; for a civilized man the task is a hard one." In my judgement, the tonic of wildness is an untapped source of medicine for troubled souls. It is, to be sure, addictive, but without the dangerous side effects of drugs or liquor — and far less cumbersome to learn and enjoy than meditation or other pop psychology formulas. The key is a personal relationship with nature: the medium. The wind, the water, the forests are the message. My wife's tanka says it better:

Mystery

I wonder why, how
Each wilderness adventure
Takes on afterglow.
Miles, aches, cold and being lost
Fade; the quiet joy remains.

THE PICTURED ROCKS

At first glance it seemed that the elderly man was permanently bent by spinal arthritis. He shuffled slowly down the rock-strewn beach near the water's edge; in one hand he carried a well-worn stick with which he appeared to paw casually through the wet stones. Occasionally he stopped and retrieved a particular stone, studied it briefly and deposited it in a brown bag which hung from his thin shoulders on a leather thong.

I scrutinized his agate-searching behavior surreptitiously for several moments, trying to pick up stones of the same sort he was placing in the brown bag. Finally I could stand it no longer. I didn't care if I did reveal myself as a neophyte rock hound, I had to know how to identify agates as swiftly as he seemed to be doing.

"What do you think of this one?" I asked in a diffident manner.

He looked at the wet stone carefully, turning it over several times in his calloused old hands. Only then did he straighten up — to a height almost as tall as myself — and reply.

"That's a leaverite, young man," he said, a faint smile playing at the corners of his mouth.

"Really?" I yodeled. "What is a 'leaverite' . . . are they rare?"

There was a long pause and, thinking the old man had not heard me, I was about to repeat my query when finally he spoke.

"It means 'leave 'er right' where you found it," he responded and shuffled on down the Grand Marais beach. It did not help my ego much when my wife returned from her private rock hounding a short time later with a stone clutched in her palm.

"I think this is an agate," she said, wetting a cream-colored stone at the water's edge. A series of parallel rings separated by narrow opaque bands shone through a clear surface; the thumb-sized rock was silky smooth from years of tumbling in the waves of Lake Superior. It was indeed an agate, a small bit of crytocrystalline quartz which had probably broken off an ancient pre-Cambrian shelf in the depths of the lake. During spring or fall storms, scores of such agates sporting various colored rings are washed ashore.

"That's no leaverite," I replied sagely.

Lynn looked at me questioningly.

"It's a long story," I shrugged and joined my daughters in building an elaborate sand castle.

We were camped near Grand Marais (which means 'Great Marsh') a small village with a beautiful natural harbor on the eastern boundary of the then new Pictured Rocks National Lakeshore. Just the previous autumn the United States Congress had passed Public Law 89-668 which established a new national park " . . . to preserve for the benefit, inspiration, education, recreational use and enjoyment of the public a significant portion of the diminishing shoreline of the United States and its related geographical and scientific features."

During the time since the enacting of the legislation and our first camping trip to Grand Marais, we have come to know and enjoy the National Lakeshore in all seasons; we have tramped its tall shifting sand dunes, swam in the crystalline waters, combed its fine beaches and admired its colorful sculptured cliffs. Our favorite season for exploring its many fascinating charms is spring when wildflowers bloom in profusion along the shoreline footpath which winds the entire 40 mile length of the park.

Although it takes its name from the dramatic sandstone cliffs, the Pictured Rocks National Lakeshore is actually comprised of three rather distinct features: the Grand Sable Banks and Dunes in the east, a lengthy center stretch of sand and pebble beach and, at the western extreme, the fifteen mile section of multi-colored cliffs.

The Native Americans who dwelt on the south shore of Lake Superior called the huge sand formations *Gitche Nagow*, "Big Sand," and, according to legend, believed that the dunes were born at Hiawatha's wedding when the dancing feet of Paupakkeewis tossed sand aloft until it lay in great heaps upon the shore. The French explorers adopted the same name — Grand Sable — for the tall banks of sand just west of Grand Marais. Modern geologists, however, have a less romantic but probably more accurate version of their origin. The Grand Sable Banks and Dunes are the result of ancient glacial, wind and wave activity.

The Grand Sable Banks is the exposed part of an old bay-mouth sandbar extending for five miles along the Lake Superior shore; the huge formation rises to 275 feet above the lake level at about a 35 degree angle. The banks are composed of sand and gravel which filled an enormous formation in the rapidly retreating glacier. Perched on top of the banks are the Grand Sable Dunes covering an area of five square miles and rising 80 feet taller than the banks. The sand was blown into the great dunes at the edge of ancient Lake Nipissing — which preceded Lake Superior. Winds off the lake are slowly moving the dunes inland where they become partially stabilized by vegetation.

One spring I spent a long solitary day hiking and exploring the Grand Sable Dunes. Moving across its surface was like walking, as Charles Penny suggested in his 1840 journal, on " . . . a vast, undulating plain of moving sand, looking perhaps much like a desert." As a matter of fact, I glanced northward to Lake Superior often to remind myself that I was not hiking on the Sahara or Mojave. Very little vegetation grows atop the dunes — some isolated stands of jack pine in flat areas, a few stunted sand cherry trees, some indomitable white cedars looking a bit like gnarled Joshua pines, and scattered patches of beach grass.

Near the western end of the dunes I found the famous Devil's Slide where years ago hundreds of white pine logs were sent cascading down the steep embankment to the waters of Lake Superior. The timber was then pulled together in huge rafts and floated to the waiting sawmills at Grand Marais. Sitting near the edge, I inspected the old slide; the deep marks of the log chute could still be seen on the sand banks. Moving even closer I reflected on what it must have been like to make the swift descent to the water almost 350 feet below. Impulsively, I leaped over the edge and plunged down the steep sandy incline; in huge bounds covering more that 20 feet I soared out and down, sliding, tumbling, barely skimming the surface of the soft sand. What a sense of reckless freedom and abandonment was mine as, shouting loudly, I cascaded down the precipice and slid to a halt in a shower of yellow sand beside the lake. The frenzied descent took less than 30 seconds but in those few seconds I felt as one with the giant white pine logs that raced down the Devil's Slide more that a half-century before. The climb back up on the crumbling, shifting sand of the steep bank, however, took more than 30 minutes.

The dunes are at their scenic best in early morning or late afternoon when shadows soften the harsh landscape; then, a surrealistic glow of gold, beige and brown coats the sand in point and counterpoint of light and dark. My most memorable view of the dunes, though, occurred one night when the great sand formation was bathed in the pale silver rays of a full moon; spellbound, I could only think of the lines Charles Penny had written in his journal under similar circumstances more than a century earlier: "The scene is magnificent beyond my powers of description. In fact, I do not think a description or drawing could convey any just idea of it, though executed by the hand of a master." My companion, who had not uttered a word during the moonlight walk on the Grand Sable, summed up his impressions with a simple but apt phrase: "What incredibly beautiful desolation."

The center section of the park, although just as scenic as a great sand formation, is less austere, more sedate and comfortable. Here the shoreline along a 12-mile stretch is a broad, sand-and-pebble beach. It is in this section of the National Lakeshore that our family has spent the most time — exploring the old lighthouse near Au Sable Point, fishing in the Hurricane River and Sullivan Creek and camping beside the shining waters of Lake Superior.

We pitched our small backpacking tents well up from the high water mark on the beach near Seven Mile Creek one evening in late May. The beach at this point is broad, perhaps 40 feet across; the sand is very fine grained and light yellow in color. Near the water's edge are windrows of rocks ranging in size from large, round boulders to tiny specks. Driftwood is scattered about in casual but artistic fashion. We spent a lazy weekend searching for agates — Lynn was again successful, finding this time a large stone with pale blue and brown striations — picking up small pieces of driftwood with which to make napkin rings, exploring inland up the small rushing creek, building sand villages and watching for migrating shore birds. I indulged in my favorite idle-time occupation: watching the moods of Lake Superior. The big lake was calm, almost quiescent, and steely-gray in the overcast sky.

A 30 foot sand bluff rises above the beach for most of its length; it is densely covered with a forest of pine, hemlock, and mixed northern hardwoods. Under the trees we found blueberries and bearberries in bloom, their tiny bell-shaped white blossoms contrasting with the dark green leaves. A rich carpet of reindeer moss grows on the forest floor where the pines dominate. Hiking back toward Twelve mile Beach Campground, we came upon a stand of beautiful white birches; some time ago this area had burned and now only clumps of paper birch grow in close ranks which seem to cover every hillside. That evening, as we sat by a small campfire, the clouds lifted and we could make out, far to the west, the high promontories marking the beginning of the famed sandstone cliffs of the Pictured Rocks escarpment. We remembered these lines from Longfellow's *Hiawatha*,

On the shores of Gitche-Gumee,
Westward by the Big-Sea-Water,
Came unto the rocky headlands,
To the Pictured Rocks of sandstone.

The fifteen mile section of high bluffs at the extreme western section is the most spectacular and awesome portion of the National Lakeshore, and the one most travelers come to see. The rocky formations rise abruptly from the lake as high as 200 feet in some places; the erosive action of waves, ice and wind has carved the red sandstone bluffs into dramatic arches, columns and promontories while mineral-bearing water seeping between the sandstone strata continues to paint vividly colored murals upon the perpendicular walls. A tasteful sign near Miners Castle, one of the many well-known sculptures, tells of transformations still occurring:

Dominated by Lake Superior, the Pictured Rocks tells of the strife
between land and water. Waves assault the cliffs; they tunnel and
probe and climb the steep walls, crashing in a crescendo of exploding
spray. The cliffs must resist but pay a ransom in sand and rock to
appease the fury of the tireless sculptors.

The rocky cliffs were fashioned on the bed of a warm Cambrian Sea. About a half-billion years ago, large deposits of sand, lime and coral formed on the bottom of the sea; layers of the material were pressed down by enormous weight. Then, when the seas subsided, the deposits were exposed and hardened into rocky strata. Subsequently, the glaciers polished and scraped the marine sandstone bluffs; when the heavy ice sheets retreated, the earth's crust rebounded, lifting the ancient layers of hardened sand into spectacular cliffs.

Like the Grand Canyon, Niagara Falls, the Canadian Rockies, or any great scenic wonder, no one can really believe the beauty and splendor of the Pictured Rocks until they see the escarpment. Photographs do not really convey the impact of the majestic formations, the display of intense colors, the compelling blend of water and rock. Most of the formations are visible only from the water. Along with several dozen other admirers, we boarded a sightseeing boat in Munising one late afternoon for our first view of the red sandstone bluffs. As the sleek white ship cruised slowly along the length of the escarpment, we passed tall columns of rock, worn and fluted into fantastic shapes — castles, arches, overhanging walls, caverns. All along the shore were gigantic piles of rubble which had fallen from the cliffs over the years.

Miners Castle was the first major formation we passed that afternoon. With its tall tower topped by an overhanging battlement turret, broad walls, loopholes and, at the waterline, a large arched doorway, it does resemble a real Norman castle. The rock is worn and pitted as if the fortress has withstood showers of arrows and other missiles in countless battles. A fellow passenger told me that, according to local folklore, Father Jacques Marquette used a shallow depression atop the Castle as a holy water font when he baptized a small band of Chippewa Indians in the autumn of 1670.

Beyond Miners Castle, the bluffs are stained with a variety of exciting colors. Rainbow Cave was my favorite display. The cave is shallow but high, extending to within 30 feet of the rim. The topmost layer is composed of dark brown sandstone mixed with coarse gravel; its width is stained by vertical bands of black, brown and russet. Spread across the lower level of light buff sandstone are vertical overlapping bands of black, white, green, yellow, bright red — even a vivid orange. The colors seemed to shimmer and pulsate in the afternoon sun. The exotic mural is exquisitely complemented by the clear green waters of Lake Superior. Later I found a comment in David Bates Douglass' journal of the Cass expedition in 1820 which succinctly summarizes my impressions of viewing the painted bluffs:

"The effect produced on the mind as we approached these rocks cannot be described — picturesque in the distance they become sublime, awfully sublime, when we drew near."

The passengers amused themselves by looking for meaningful shapes among the forms and colors on the cliffs. The multi-colored walls are like a natural Rorschach plate; each person sees in the ambiguous chromatic array a fragment of his own mind. Some tourists made out a herd of wild horses while others identified a band of Indians painted for battle.

But there is no mistaking the Grand Portal — the Great Door. Early explorers, Brule, Radisson, even the laconic Schoolcraft, were awed by the immensity of the aperture in the bluff. Although the roof of the original arch collapsed in 1906, there still remains a deep interconnected cavern which tunnels through the steep rocky headland at the waterline; small boats and canoes can pass through the portal. The captain switched off the engines on the cruise ship and we could hear the waves rumble and moan in the dark recesses. The Chippewas believed that this spot was the dwelling place of the Manitou of thunder and lightning. On the very top of the Grand Portal formation is a large rookery and the air was alive with gulls.

The tour boat turned for the homeward voyage near Chapel Rock, a sculptured formation which resembles the ruins of a small Byzantine temple. Several sandstone columns, worn and shaped by waves and weather to a replica of baroque architecture, form the outside of the chapel and support a high vaulted roof. The roof projects several feet beyond the columns into an ornate cornice. On top of the roof a large pine tree grows eighty feet above the lake; it seems to form a lofty spire for the sandstone temple. Since the tree first began to grow many years ago, the rock formation has separated from the mainland; the roots now extend back over several feet of open air to the nourishing soil on the cliff.

As the boat swung around and picked up speed on a heading for Munising, I caught a fleeting glimpse of a human figure standing within the Chapel. Looking again quickly with binoculars I could see a bearded hiker with a pack on his back waving toward the boat. At that moment I resolved I must get to know the Pictured Rocks more intimately. From a distance the cliffs are austere and seem to hide behind an ancient reserve; it would take time and much personal contact to understand the land fully. As Joseph Wood Krutch pointed out, there is a great deal of difference between looking at something and living with it: a person never really sees an aspect of nature for the first time until he has seen it for the fiftieth, until it becomes a world of which the viewer is a part.

Vision alone is such a fleeting sense — I must store up other images: the feel of the coarse sandstone, the cries of the gulls at close hand, the sounds of wind and waves slowly slowly eroding the rocky formations. What began as a rather simple goal — to walk astride the sandstone cliffs — has since become an obsession. Let me confess it: I am hopelessly addicted to the Pictured Rocks National Lakeshore. One step onto the trail and the environment seems to envelop the hiker; he becomes immersed in beauty, in the space, silence and solitude which sets this very special place apart. It is here, to paraphrase Thoreau, that a person can cultivate the tree which bears fruit in his soul.

As I prepared to write this account of the Pictured Rocks, we returned once again to hike the trail which traverses the top of the sandstone cliffs. It was spring and the wildflowers carpeted the narrow path from Sand Point to Miners Castle. At several places along the trail, small vernal streams cascaded over the edge of the bluff and tumbled down the steep escarpment 200 feet to Lake Superior. The birches and maples were budding and in the morning sun each tree wore a halo of Nile green. At Miners Castle we rescued an elderly couple who had attempted to take a short cut up the steep east side of the formation. As we led them down a makeshift path, somewhat shaky and embarrassed but in no serious distress, I was reminded that there are still places such as this where a person has the freedom to put himself in danger, where he must rely on his own agility and intelligence to cope with potential disaster. I like that. Consider what would be lost in human character and experience if there were no more hazards, if, for example, the trail along the length of the Pictured Rocks escarpment were groomed and guard-railed for its entire 40 mile length. How can an individual experience peak moments where all risk has been removed? As a former teacher and wise mentor once remarked, "It is better to break a bone than a spirit."

Our spirits soared as we pushed along the trail past Miners River, across the sparkling beach and on through the beech and maple forest to where the escarpment descends to the Mosquito River. We rested under a hemlock and admired the long slabs of red sandstone which extend out into the lake. Inexorably, the trail pulled us onward: up again on the rim of the high cliffs, past Lover's Leap, through the sand above the gull rookery atop the Portal, around the deep fjords at Battleship Row and finally down to the long crescent of white sand beach near Chapel River. It was fitting that our spring journey along the Pictured Rocks should end at this beautiful stream where the water rushes over an apron of rock and creates a filmy white veil of spray and mist.

It is fitting, also, that the entire Lake Superior shoreline from Munising to Grand Marais is now set aside for all time. On the high sand dunes, the broad beaches and the myriad rock ledges and escarpments, the sensitive seeker will find a wealth of beauty, silence and space to expand his awareness of the natural world and of himself. The experience will, I hope, send him away renewed, refreshed — and humble.

WHITE-THROATED
SPARROWS

The May dawn glow filtered dimly through the tent rousing me gently from a light sleep. Shifting in my warm down bag, I listened for the melodies of early morning, my favorite time of day. The sounds were familiar — the caroling of a robin, the harsh alarm call of a blue jay, the high voices of spring peepers celebrating in the marsh beside the creek. Then close beside the campsite, I heard it: the clear pensive song of a white-throated sparrow. "Old Sam Peabody, Peabody, Peabody," he seemed to chant with a rising, slightly quavering whistle; residents of Canada maintain his call really translates to "Oh, sweet Canada, Canada, Canada." It really doesn't matter as long as he returns each May and sings of springtime, of woodland glades and sparkling morning dew.

Then further away, perhaps across Harlow Creek from our campsite, came the song of another bird; obviously it was a white-throat — no mistaking the clear almost querulous whistle — but this singer had a different melody. Instead of a rising inflection, the songster came down the scale on his trilled "Peabodys." But now other birds began to sing — a flicker, a brown thrasher, and then a veery each heralded the daylight with its own particular musical score — and I forgot about the unusual song of the distant white-throated sparrow.

Randy stirred on the other side of the tent, and raised up on one elbow.

"If we're at Harlow Creek, it must be Saturday morning," he yawned.

"And we have miles to go before we reach camp number two on the Yellow Dog River," I replied, crawling out of my bag. Mike, the third member of our hiking clan, was already awake and out of his tarp tent checking the set line he had left in the big pool under the old railroad bridge. A cry of anguish came from near the creek.

"There goes our breakfast trout," Mike groaned. "I missed a nice brookie in the same spot where I caught the one last night."

The three of us were hiking to Bay Cliff Health Camp, a residential treatment center for handicapped children, as a demonstration to call attention to the camp's important work. We would follow the old Lake Superior and Ishpeming Railroad tracks northwestwardly twenty-five miles to Big Bay, a small village distinguished primarily as the site of a famous homicide retold in John Voelker's novel *The Anatomy of a Murder*. Randy and Mike were new residents of the region and I was eager to share with them the verdant May hills the way they should be seen: on foot, slowly.

Carrying heavy packs but with light hearts we began our weekend trek early one Friday morning from an abandoned railroad station near the city's island park. We passed through a railway graveyard of retired steam engines and ancient passenger cars; shrouded in the morning fog they looked like phantom trains restlessly waiting, ever waiting for a load of passengers. As I lingered beside the rusting locomotives while my companions inspected the old Pullman cars, I reflected on how extensively the automobile has shaped and dominated our culture. How basically senseless and wasteful it is for thousands of individuals to shepherd their personal vehicles in and out of crowded cities and towns each day. When passenger trains disappeared across the Upper Peninsula, we lost one of our connections to an earlier, simpler time. Walking the old railroad tracks, I mused nostalgically about powerful engines huffing asthmatically as they pick up speed, the click of steel wheels on steel rails, the urgent moan of a train whistle on a spring morning.

Where the old railroad tracks cross Compeau Creek we surprised a man carrying a sizeable string of fish; from a distance they appeared to be brook trout but it was impossible to be certain. Shocked momentarily to see persons walking down the abandoned tracks, the successful fisherman recovered quickly and slipped off into the bushes beside the creek before we could admire his catch. Spring (and summer) is trout fishing time in the north country and each angler guards his favorite pools with military secrecy; it is considered very poor manners to ask, or even look questioningly about where someone seeks for speckled trout. Randy and Mike would angle for trout near our campsite so we continued our hike along the old grade.

A few miles down the tracks we removed our packs and rested on a pile of discarded railway ties beside Wetmore Pond, a spot of blue surrounded by cattails, tamaracks and white spruce. The pond is gradually filling in with vegetation and now all around its perimeter is a quaking bog. A great blue heron stalked in the shallows; it, too, was fishing

— for frogs, small fish — in a territory staked out and defended against intruders of its own kind.

It was late morning and the sun had burned off the fog permitting us to admire Sugar Loaf Mountain, a granite knob which rises to 1,077 feet close beside Lake Superior. Both Henry Schoolcraft and Charles Penny mention this spectacular high summit in journals of their expeditions along the south shore of Lake Superior in the early 19th century; at that time the mountain was called *"Tatosh"* which means "woman's breast" in the Chippewa language. *Tatosh* is certainly more fitting than Sugar Loaf and the native name is more in keeping with the personification of, and reverence for the land. After seeing the "Tall One" in Alaska one summer, I vehemently agree with those who propose a change from "Mount McKinley" back to the original native name, *Denali.* How arrogant it was for European immigrants — "discovering" North America several thousand years after the original Americans were here — to set about renaming prominent geographical locations!

At lunchtime we climbed a granite bluff where we could see Hogback Mountain ("Cradle-Top" is the original name), a slightly higher twin-peaked mountain to the west. Now, as we sat quietly eating a simple trail lunch, we began to notice many birds; it was the third week in May and the spring migration was at its peak. American redstarts displayed in the pines overhead, stopping occasionally to dart after small insects; a yellow warbler sang again and again from a clump of red osier near the tracks; an ovenbird called insistently for a "teacher." But one ethereal voice seemed to come from everywhere: our luck was good and the hike would coincide with the spring serenade of white-throated sparrows.

The white-throats were still singing on the dewy Saturday morning as Randy, Mike and I assembled and packed our gear for the long trek to the Yellow Dog River. Birds, and especially bird songs, have been an abiding interest for a long time, ever since I inadvertently killed a cedar waxwing in my parent's cherry orchard during my tenth summer. That summer my brother and I had been armed with new air rifles and ordered to protect the ripening fruit crop against the voracious foraging of flocks of starlings; we were sternly admonished not to shoot robins, the only bird other than a crow I could identify. We had just settled beneath the trees when a flock of birds lighted on the branches and began to pull off cherries; they were backlighted but I knew that robins feed alone or in pairs, rarely in flocks. I fired at the nearest silhouette and a new and strange bird fluttered down almost at my feet. It was a sleek olive-green with a yellow band on its tail, a black mark and a rakish crest. As I turned the bird over in my hands and noted the small red waxlike beads near the ends of its wing feathers, I was appalled at what I had done.

Yet my interest was piqued. What was the name of this beautiful creature? Were there other birds which I had simply lumped into broad categories of sparrows, thrushes and so forth? At that moment began a life-long interest in ornithology.

My most memorable outdoor experiences are associated with birds. Once I was taken into custody briefly by campus security police while scrutinizing — with binoculars at 5:30 a.m. — a rare Wilson's warbler in a mountain ash tree outside the girls' dormitory. When I maintained I was merely looking for birds and showed my identification as an Audubon Society member, one of the officers affected a British accent and admonished me to watch my "birds" in the college woodlots thereafter.

At Itasca State Park, birthplace of the Mississippi River, my wife and I hiked one May to a small lake near the west boundary of the park. A heavy wet snow was falling. Suddenly out over the water appeared scores of tree swallows circling and darting through the large snow flakes close to the surface of the lake. Their dark blue wings and backs contrasted vividly in the field of pure white. Another time, in Prince Rupert, British Columbia, we ate a late dinner of salmon steaks and, awestruck, watched a dozen bald eagles fishing and riding the air currents above a mirror-smooth bay.

But now as we hiked along in the dew of the May morning, my special avian friend, the white-throated sparrow, seemed to be singing from every balsam and spruce beside the old tracks. Spring in the north country would not be the same without his special sweet melody. His song is so pure and clear, like a cold draught of water from a deep well or a fresh breeze from Lake Superior. When I hear it again each May after the birds' long winter sabbatical, it fills up my senses and floods my mind with woodland memories.

We paused to admire one particular songster: the striped black and white crown (some are closer to tan than white), white throat patch and yellow spot beside its bill and eye could be seen clearly in the morning sun. Some beginners confuse the white-crowned sparrow with the white-throated but the two are quite different. The white-crowned sparrow lacks a white bib, is more fastidious and clean-looking and seems to carry his crown higher, puffier; he rarely stays around the Upper Peninsula to nest and his song is different from that of the white-throat.

As we hiked through the continual spring serenade it was difficult to believe that all bird songs are simply utilitarian melodies designed to establish a territory and attract a mate. They seem so joyous about their tasks! To be sure, feathered singers are by and large exhibitionistic: "Here I am," they announce, "I am a white-throated sparrow and this is my turf, so stay out all you other white-throats." Ornithologists have discovered by careful scientific analysis of recorded songs that within some species, each singer has a personalized melody: "I am a *particular* white-throated sparrow."

Then, carried on a soft breeze I heard again the strange white-throat song I had heard at dawn. Later I was to discover that professional ornithologists have cataloged 15 distinct song patterns of white-throated sparrows! The four most common patterns vary demographically: the most common song in the east, the only one I had learned as a student, rises in inflection; however, the most usual melody among mid-western white-throats was the "strange" whistled notes with downward inflection that I had heard. Not all white-throats sound alike but to qualify as a member of the species, the song must be a clear whistle (pure tone, no harmonics) and feature at least one pitch change.

While I pondered on the vagaries of bird songs, Randy and Mike had spotted several rainbow trout in Wilson Creek which meanders through the forest near Saux Head Lake. Here beside this small woodland lake years ago, a Chippewa hunting party surprised and killed every member of a Sioux raiding party which had previously massacred an entire encampment of their women and children. The Chippewa cut off the heads of the unfortunate warriors and hung them in trees around the lake as a grisly warning to other Sioux invaders. Tales of the incident later accounted for the name of the lake.

Fashioning crude poles from alder limbs, my companions quickly dug a supply of worms from under the wet leaves beside the stream; admonishing me to be quiet and not even cast a shadow on the water, they stalked carefully along the banks in search of deep pools. Trout fishermen — even when lowering themselves by using bait instead of small bits of fluff and feathers — tend to magnify the importance of their task and even invest it with a degree of unctuous mysticism. It seems to come with the territory. I have often wished I was addicted to fishing because my presence in the forests would then have a ready sanction: a fishing pole in hand. Nonetheless I can still enjoy the cool shadows beside wilderness streams, I can admire the soft green moss on rocky shelves along the bank and, most of all, I can listen to the sound of water making its magic music upon the rocks.

But rather than risk offending the serious anglers as they went about their religious fishing ceremony, I wandered out to the road to inspect the former townsite of Birch. The lumbering town grew up around the timber cutting operations of the Northern Lumbering Company which commenced about 1908. At the height of the logging activity the town had 45 homes, two schools, a large shingle-covered hotel and daily train service. All that remains is a large open grassy area, an ancient lilac bush and a graveyard upon a knoll covered with a thick stand of maple and white birch. Here, too, the white-throated sparrows were singing their timeless melodies in the thickets and among the fallen grave markers.

We pitched our tents that night beside the singing waters of the Yellow Dog River. The original French name, *Riviere Chien Jaune,* apparently sounded like St. John to English speaking explorers; on some early maps the river is labeled St. Johns. One branch of the Yellow Dog flows out of Bull Dog Lake in the highlands of the McCormick Experimental Forest forty miles to the west; it winds its way through sandy jack pine plains, leaps over Pinnacle Falls and rushes over granite slabs, finally emptying into Lake Independence near the village of Big Bay.

I sat on the bank watching and listening to the water as my hiking companions once again attempted to outwit a trout. Another angler in search of fish, a belted kingfisher, flew back and forth emitting his dry rattle. He seemed less self-conscious about his attempts at gathering fish; he was also more successful.

Later that evening we sat quietly beside a small campfire admiring its orange flames and listening to its soft guttering. It takes a while for each hiker to get into a woodland experience, to drop the layers of civilization and social facade, to shed the uneasy feeling that each moment should be occupied with some activity or filled with idle chatter. Unlike the usual social gathering, the silence around our fire was comfortable for we were sharing on a far deeper level than words. Conversation was redundant. As dusk closed in around the circle of flickering yellow warmth, the most compelling feathered songster of all, a hermit thrush, favored us with a solo; his flute-like melody echoed and re-echoed hauntingly from the dark shadows.

I lay awake a long time in a pleasant fugue-like state that night. When the fire had burned down to only a few glowing coals, a whip-poor-will, accenting the first and last syllables, called his name over and over again. A full moon appeared from behind a cloud and briefly flooded the forest beside the river with its pale silver brilliance; than a white-throated sparrow roused himself and whistled a single sleepy note.

The next morning we hiked the last leg of our weekend demonstration walk in a soft spring rain. We found ourselves moving more swiftly now; although not wanting our adventure to end, as we came closer to our goal we were drawn inexorably to complete what we had begun. Marching around the shore of Lake Independence, we passed through the village of Big Bay and soon saw the white buildings of Bay Cliff Health Camp looming out of the morning mist. Although the camp was quiet now, almost two hundred children would soon be in residence for the summer. Here, at this unique treatment center, they would receive many kinds of assistance — speech therapy, physical and occupational therapy, dental care — in a healthy outdoor environment. A curl of smoke issued from a chimney of the Big House, the large central dining facility, and we headed over for a cup of coffee and a chat with John Vargo, then director of Bay Cliff, who had sponsored and encouraged our weekend hegira. The original structures at Bay Cliff, including the Big House, were erected by Charles and Edna Korsan; they started a large dairy operation which, using both their first names, they called "Chedna Farms." The floors in the large farm house were made of select birdseye maple and painted wallpaper was imported from France to decorate the many halls and rooms. It is fitting somehow that such opulence is now given over to the important job of helping handicapped children find a place in the world.

As we retraced our route by car to our homes in Marquette, Randy, Mike and I felt that we, too, understood our place in the world a bit better.

The following Monday as I sat in my office at the university pondering a particularly perplexing academic problem, a white-throated sparrow outside my window perched atop a forsythia bush and sang just once but so sweetly it sent chills up my spine. Instantly I was transported to the old railway grade: I could smell the pungent resins of miles and miles of balsams and hemlocks warming in the sun; I could see the grasses sparkling in the morning dew; I could hear the gentle gurgle of small creeks finding their way past ancient moss-covered stones. The song lingered in my synapses all day and I smiled inwardly at my good fortune to have hiked through the spring serenade of the white-throated sparrows.

T H E   P A T R I A R C H S

No one except the venerable white-haired patriarch had protested removal of the huge, gnarled pine which had stood at the edge of the village square longer than anyone could remember. He had stood up feebly at the council meeting and, in a voice trembling with emotion and age, he recalled the grandeur of the lumbering era until he became lost in personal reminiscence and, embarrassed and confused, sat down.

> *If only the old lumber kings, Ike Stephenson, Alger Smith or George Orr had been there, maybe they could have told the city council how the white pines grew so thick they blotted out the sunlight. Beneath that dense canopy of needles no underbrush grew and the hiker walked in a perpetual purple twilight among the gigantic boles. Good lumber trees they were, straight and tall — some rose to 120, even 170 feet — and 70 feet to the first limb; many, like the old village pine, measured as much as five feet in diameter at the butt. If they only knew they would let this one last giant remain. But I failed . . .*

Now the old man sat in the sun watching the three young city employees in orange hard hats prepare to cut down the ancient white pine. A faded gray double-breasted suit, its hue almost matching the thick bark of the old pine, swallowed his shrunken frame; the wrinkled tie knotted carefully under his grizzled chin was spotted with gravy and his socks did not match. A battered wooden crutch leaned against the dark green bench beside him. His hands trembled slightly as he tamped a few shreds of dry tobacco into the bowl of a well-worn black briar pipe. But his eyes were as bright and restless as the sparkling azure waves of Lake Michigan that endlessly lapped the edges of the village harbor.

The big timber was gone . . . but we thought the days would never end. The white pine made magnificent lumber — creamy-white, even grained and so easy to work with. No doubt about it, it built the homes and shops, the schools and churches of the midwest. What were the figures? Oh, yes, over 150 billion board feet — enough to build 10 million six room homes — flowed out of the forests and shores of the Upper Peninsula. The sawmills at Escanaba, Manistique and all those other towns screamed around the clock; huge piles of fresh lumber crowded the busy docks. Scores of lumber barges — we called them 'hookers' in those days — steamed across the lakes with cargoes for Chicago and Detroit. It seemed just like yesterday . . . where had the years gone?

The tree had to go. True, it was the village Christmas tree, had been for years. If you looked closely you might even see a piece of straw from the creche beneath the clusters of soft green needles. And it was true too, that the old tree symbolized the lumbering origins of the small northwoods town. But the white pine was a thing of the past. So were the men who had cut them. The sawmill was silent, boarded up against vandals. The lumber barons who made their fortune from the seemingly endless forests were gone, too, except for one old man nodding and remembering in the warm May sun.

Land had been cheap in the old days, not much more than $1.25 an acre for cutting rights. That's why the timber cruiser or landlooker was so crucial to a lumber company's success or failure. We had a good one. He disappeared into the woods for two or three weeks at a time with an axe, compass and a few supplies to look for the tallest, straightest tracts of timber close enough to the Manistique River or connecting streams to make the spring drive to the company mill at Manistique. The landlooker was even responsible for picking a likely spot for the logging camp. Like Camp number 60 on Cusino Lake, one of our finest and last.

The old man remembered. It seemed but a few days ago — was it really over seventy years — he had arrived in the forest village, a lad of sixteen seeking his fortune in the giant white pine covering every hillside. That bright Sunday morning he had felt suddenly very lonely standing on the dock while the steamship churned out of the harbor. The village was quiet and he wandered slowly inland until he came to Indian Lake. The sight overwhelmed and exhilarated him: The lake, nearly three miles across, was clogged with huge pine logs! He had grown like the pine. Starting as a clerk, he worked and fought his way up to a partnership in the oldest and one of the largest timber producing companies in eastern Upper Michigan. He hungered again now for the masculine bustle of the logging camp filled with husky French-Canadians, Swedes and Finns; he longed to see the timber piled high again on the rollways waiting for the spring thaw, and feel the excitement of one last big river drive. But the big timber was logged off and the sawmills and shanty boys had moved westward. If only he could do it all over again.

The Chicago Lumber Company built a large logging camp beside the placid waters of Cusino Lake in 1897. What, so many asked today, was life like in an old time logging camp? Well, it was no place for weaklings! The day began abruptly an hour before dawn when the foreman opened the bunkhouse door and shouted, "It's daylight in the swamps!" With no central heating — just an iron stove or a large barrel in the middle of the bunk house — no one lingered over dressing or his morning toilet. The shanty boys (as they called themselves) pulled on thick trousers, held up by galluses, a heavy wool shirt or two, socks and slipped into rubber-bottomed boots. Grabbing mitts, a hat and a plaid Mackinaw coat, they headed for the cook shanty. Morning chuck was usually pancakes covered with molasses, some fried ham or venison if the men were lucky and gallons of steaming coffee — all consumed in absolute silence to speed the eating and prevent arguments among the rough and ready men at the table.

After breakfast the men headed through the deep snow to the cutting area. By the first rays of dawn, the sawyers working in teams of two men, were selecting trees to fell. First a notch was made with their axes to determine the direction they wanted the tree to fall; then the men went into action with a sharp seven foot long cross-cut saw. Back and forth they pulled with smooth, powerful strokes until the huge pine quivered and tumbled to the forest floor. When the tree was down, other workers, 'choppers,' lopped off the branches and the sawyers then cut the trunk into 16 foot lengths. Urging on their teams of horses and oxen, teamsters then skidded the logs to an area where 'loaders' placed them in huge piles for the spring river drive. Younger workers, or sometimes older men who could no longer keep up the pace required in the cuttings, spent their day making icy skid roads and keeping them free of horse droppings. Those attending the latter task were known as 'chickadees' in logging camp jargon.

All the logs were marked with the individual timber brand of the company so they could be sorted in the sawmill during spring drives; the impression was stamped into the end of the logs with a special hammer by the scaler who kept careful records as the timber cutting proceeded.

Lunch, generally beans, 'red horse' (corned or pickled beef), bread or biscuits, coffee — was brought out to the men on the job in a crude portable kitchen — the 'swingle-dingle' — by several 'cookees' (young boys who served as the cook's helpers). The shanty boys sat around on stumps and relished a plate of hot food (they called it 'flaggins') and the brief rest. At dusk the men filed wearily back to camp, washed in crude basins and headed again for the cook shanty and supper. Venison, pork, hash, the ubiquitous baked beans, homemade bread, perhaps a pie or cake all were washed down by the ever-present mug of black coffee.

After the evening meal the men visited the 'van', a small company store where they could buy tobacco, new socks and other sundries and then retired to the bunkhouses. These crude shelters were made of logs and usually measured 30 by 60 feet. Tiers of narrow low bunks — called 'muzzleloaders' because you could only crawl in at one end — lined the walls; they were not constructed for comfort. Slats were made from small poles; cedar or hemlock boughs or a generous supply of straw served as a mattress. What remained of the evening was devoted to smoking, playing checkers or swapping stories as they sat on the Deacon's bench, a crude board seat which ran the entire length of the bunks. The oil lanterns were blown out not long after nine o'clock and the men settled down to try to sleep in the smoky, poorly ventilated quarters with smells of drying clothes hanging from the rafters and sounds of snoring echoing in several keys.

The men were paid about 25 dollars a month for six days a week, twelve hours a day of hard labor in the woods. Strangely, there was little complaining about the work, just about the food. The shanty boys, for the most part, prided themselves in what they could do by their own efforts and sawyer teams often raced each other to cut the most trees in a day. They did what they could, did what they must and tried to have fun doing it.

Sunday was a free day. No liquor or women were permitted in camp so the men wrote letters, played cards, tramped about in the woods or simply rested. Among men who lived close and worked hard, tempers often flared and the rough and tumble fights, at least in the retelling, were legion. The legends of Silver Jack Driscoll and other great fighters undoubtedly grew better and better as they passed from camp to camp.

In the spring, the best, most agile men were selected to shepherd the logs down the swollen rivers. These 'river pigs' received extra pay for the dangerous job of riding the logs in the swift current to free the inevitable log jams. Now the kitchen, called a 'wanigan', followed the men downstream.

The old tree had to come down. Didn't the village council vote unanimously to have it removed so that a new highway bypass could shuttle the honking hordes of tourists through the town? A hazard it was, too, struck by lightning several years ago and leaning badly toward the road. It would be replaced by a blue spruce, trimmed and tame, from a nursery in the lower part of the state.

Nothing replaced the big pine we cut so many years ago, not for a long time. The twilight years of the lumbering era are not so pleasant to remember. When the trees were gone, the shanty boys followed the cutting westward and the bright lights of Seney, Hurley, Watersmeet and many others winked out and the towns slowly died. Then the fires came. Again and again the flames roared through the dry slashing left from logging; the air was filled with smoke and soot for days. The humus which had been built up over centuries was destroyed. Maybe this land was meant just to grow pine because once we stripped it so clean, many areas simply didn't come back. There are miles and miles of fire-blackened stumps on the Kingston Plains . . . and little else of any size.

The yellow chain saw spit into life. One husky young man hefted it up to the old pine and it bit deeply into the soft white wood. The old man leaned forward slightly and peered more closely. Weren't they wearing stag pants? Didn't they have a long, sharp cross-cut saw? Couldn't he hear the cry of 'timber' in the distance?

The old ways were better: the men I knew had to work to beat the tree. You had to survive the weather, the long hours of labor, the primitive living conditions. Modern logging is all machines. One large yellow giant rumbles up to a tree, cuts it off, delimbs it, cuts it into eight foot lengths and then stacks it. No teamsters driving horses; now the loggers drive huge trucks that can load and unload themselves. Seems as if we've traded human minds and spirit for mechanics and efficiency.

Down came the giant white pine — the roaring tumble of branches its own funeral dirge. The wizened old man sank back on the green park bench and sighed deeply; his eyes filled with tears of regret and longing. As the workmen began to cut off the limbs and buzz the tree into sections, he slowly, painfully made his way to the crown of the old pine. Bending down, the old lumberman plucked a single cluster of five soft green needles; leaning heavily on his crutch, he pressed the cluster to his face and drew in the familiar resinous odor.

Later that evening when the orderly was making rounds in the nursing home, he found the old man slumped in a chair. The cluster of white pine needles was still clutched in his withered hand. When they gathered his belongings, they discovered in the night-table beside his bed an unfinished manuscript entitled in longhand, *"My Name is Legion: the Story of the White Pine in Upper Michigan."* Although his scrawl was difficult to decipher, the last entry was clear enough to read easily:

> *Like the village tree, men also can live too long, can become anachronisms, living relics of a different era. Today I attended the funeral of the last giant white pine in the town limits. Like Thoreau so many years ago in Concord, I was the chief, if not the only mourner. When that old pine went down today, my spirit went with it . . .*

—◆—

T H E   L O N G   H I K E

The idea arose out of an excess of affection — the notion to cover on foot and in a single day the narrow waist of the Upper Peninsula from Rapid River, on Lake Michigan to the south, all the way to Au Train on Lake Superior, a distance of fifty miles. Lovers' enthusiasms typically run to excess and I felt the need to fill up my senses with as much of this region as I possibly could in the span of one daylight period.

The idea lay dormant for several years. One spring as Lynn and I roamed the far reaches of the Hiawatha National Forest, we chanced upon signs proclaiming "Bay de Noc Grand Island Trail." We followed the blue blazes down through the aspen covered hill-sides, through a dense plantation of young Norway pines and admired for a long time the clear ripples and flower-covered banks of Davies Creek. There is something about a foot-path extending through a forest which beckons the hiker on and the notion of following it to its end began to germinate.

Sometime later, when I had almost forgotten my resolve, I discovered in the historical archives that Au Train — the north end of the trail — means "place of the dog sleds" or *"traineaus"* (French for sleigh or sled used by the early fur trappers). The article suggested that Au Train was the starting place for the trips that were made during the winter and spring through the Au Train River valley down to Bay de Noc on Lake Michigan.

My interest was piqued. Still, physical challenge hiking — making miles simply to make miles — is not my style. I like to savor the country through which I walk. Some macho hikers and backpackers derive satisfaction from speed. Eric Ryback, for example, apparently storms along the most scenic stretches of North America — the Appalachian Trial, the Pacific Crest Trail, the Continental Divide — at 25, 35 or even more miles a day. I don't mind, particularly, that some choose to walk this way (though I sometimes wonder what is chasing them) until the hurrying hikers attempt to define *my* pace in terms of their accomplishments. Hiking is not, in my view, a competitive sport, let each march to his own favorite drummer.

So I pondered and weighed my decision to march from Lake Michigan to Lake Superior in a single day. The reactions of persons with whom I shared my vacillation were interesting, but not very helpful. Most simply could not understand why I would want to walk fifty miles in one day. A few suggested, not too gently, that it was impossible for a middle-aged professor to travel that far that fast. The latter remark hardened my resolve to make the attempt.

In early spring two other things occurred which helped to make up my mind. First, I remembered the rash of interest in long range hiking which emerged during the early days of the Kennedy administration; John Kennedy revived the Marine Corps endurance test of a fifty-mile, one day march. Then I chanced to re-read an article by Bob Marshall, one of the elders of the tribe devoted to self-propelled exploration of the wilderness. Marshall wrote that "A man must work for his wilderness enjoyment. Only when he is tired can he really know what it means." Now I was just about ready to make the long hike, but the doubts lingered.

Then one evening I was shocked to find an article in the local newspaper proposing a canal across the narrow waist of the Superior Peninsula. The headline leaped out at me: *U.P. Canal Talk Revived by Shippers.* The article read: Shippers are reviving a nearly century old idea for a canal through Michigan's Upper Peninsula.

> *Paul Trimble, president of the Great Lakes Carriers Association, said a canal through the central U.P. may be more feasible than renovating existing locks at Sault Ste. Marie. The U.S. Army Corps of Engineers presently is studying the possibility of building a new lock at the Soo or combining two smaller locks into one giant lock.*
>
> *Only one of the five locks at Sault Ste. Marie is capable of handling the thousand-foot freighters which are beginning to ply the lakes.*
>
> *Trimble said the move toward larger vessels points up a need for renovations at the locks. He said the big ships also need wider navigation channels on the St. Mary's River. He said his group isn't demanding the canal, but added:*
>
> *"We think it is an alternative to renovation of the Soo locks that should be explored." The proposed canal would be only 38 miles long, running from Au Train Bay on Lake Superior. Then, ships would pass*

through an existing waterway consisting of the Au Train River, Au Train Lake, Mud Lake, the Cleveland Cliffs Iron Co. water storage basin, the Whitefish River and then into Little Bay de Noc on Lake Michigan. The canal would trim 300 miles off the trip from Lake Superior iron mines to the Lake Michigan steel plants. It also would circumvent the St. Mary's River, where ice breaking in the winter causes problems for island residents.

No costs have been estimated for either a new canal or renovations on the Soo locks. The idea for a central U.P. canal first surfaced in the 1820s and also was considered as a federal works project in the mid-1930s.

During World War II, the War Department considered it as an alternative if the locks were destroyed.

The U.S. Geological Service and the corps of engineers studied the possibility in the mid 1950s and decided such a project wasn't economically feasible.

But Trimble said new factories on Lake Superior and increasing demand for coal make conditions more favorable.

That did it. Now I must go if only as a lonely protest at the outrageous notion of another possible intrusion on this precious land. I set about some serious planning.

My intent was to travel light — a small dayhiker pack containing high calorie food, a canteen of water, halazone tablets to purify additional water from the many little streams along the way, an emergency kit and extra socks. Lynn designated several spots as checkpoints where the trail came close to or crossed a forest road; in the event of an emergency, I would wait at one of these points and she would retrace my steps by car late in the day. Finally, on a frosty clear morning in the second week of May, I waved good-bye to my family and started on the trail. Here are the entries I made in the diary of the journey.

7:30 a.m.

Got lost first thing on the maze of old logging roads where the trail commences. Now, after a detour, I am at Milepost One. According to the Forest Service folder, each mile is duly recorded on cedar posts beside the trail. It says here on the brochure that the Hiawatha National Forest was dedicated in 1931 by Herbert Hoover. Thanks, Mr. Hoover.

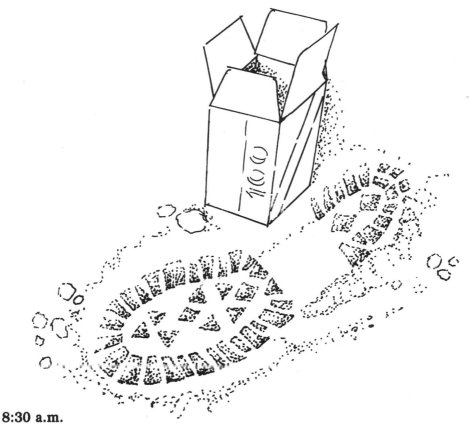

8:30 a.m.

Milepost Three. Spent some time listening to a couple of barred owls having a hooting match. Wonder what they were discussing? The trail passes through mostly cut-over land here — aspen, some jack pine barrens, even an open grassy area. Next to a sign which read, "Take only pictures, leave only footprints" there was a discarded film box and a clear Vibram-soled boot print. Litter is an American cancer — bottles, cans, cigarette butts. Mostly beer cans. But only at places where the trail crosses a woods road.

Several years ago we formulated a litter law: *the amount of litter and trash found in any given area is inversely proportional to the amount of physical effort that must be expended to reach a given area.* Let us admit it: the litterbug campaigns, all the pious attempts to educate people, are not working. Our national roads, forests, and streams are still garbage pits for cans and bottles and other artifacts of our affluent society. And likely to remain so because — and this is a corollary of the litter law — *litter breeds more litter.* Piles of trash encourage the next passerby to discard a can or bottle. But here in Michigan the bottle deposit law has had a dramatic impact; not only do most containers get picked up for the ten cent deposit, the overall amount of litter has decreased.

Sure wish I knew the cause or how to cure the litter disease. Picking up — or the unctuous slogans of the manufacturers' front, *Keep America Beautiful*, is like putting a bandaid on an advanced case of skin cancer. Anyway, I'd like to catch the guy who hiked the trail before me who chews a lot of gum. Mr. Spearmint, I presume.

9:30 a.m.

It takes a while to "get into" a long hike, to find your pace and rhythm. Now, lulled by what Colin Fletcher calls the comforting constants — the slight creak of my small pack, the dull thud of my boots hitting the damp trail, the smooth surface of the walking stick in my hand — my mind is springing free, following flights of fancy, spinning large plans on the morning air. Crossed several small streams. They are clear and surging with water from the melting snows. One in particular, Bill's Creek, was cool and shady with moss-covered banks.

10:30 a.m.

All the Forest Service signs banning motorized vehicles on the trail have been torn down. In one case, a post blocking entrance by motor vehicles had been neatly sawed off! The tracks of a three-wheeling toy — an ORV or Off-Road Vehicle — lead off down the trail. This system of letting motorized travelers go anywhere *except* on closed hiking trails simply does not work. It is too easy to remove the signs and then claim one didn't know trail bikes were banned. It would be far better to designate where the ORV user *can* roar their machines and then put the rest of the forest off-limits. Hence, if they are found anywhere except in their area, they are in violation. Whither comes this mystique of the motor? It appears that some persons believe it is their inalienable American right, guaranteed by the constitution, to take their vehicle wherever they want. Let's see, life, liberty and the pursuit of speed and noise - doesn't sound just right!

11:30 a.m.

I have been dawdling along. Only at Milepost Nine. I saw a flash of red and blue down through the aspens and was surprised and delighted to meet Lynn and the girls; they were checking to make sure I was on the trail and to offer me some encouragement.

Onward! Each stride is a celebration: How fortunate I am to be able to live in this marvelous country. I feel like today on this hike I am embracing the Superior Peninsula about its small waist.

12:30 p.m.

Stopped for lunch near Milepost 13. I really picked up the pace this past hour. This part of the trail, from Haymeadow Creek to where the path next crosses the forest service road is quite scenic: aspen and white birch knolls, tall red and white pines, deep valleys with spring beauty and Dutchman's breeches blooming, vistas of the Whitefish River Valley off to the west. Saw some morels under the aspens but they were well beyond prime picking condition. (There are many different kinds of mushrooms up here but morels are the favorite — they are recognizable by their caps and tops which are pitted with little hollows as if holes had been punched part-way through.)

I am tired but there is a joy in extending myself physically; it makes me feel more alive. Ideas for articles and future books are tumbling around in my head as I walk.

2:00 p.m.

Well down the road, or trail, I should say. Passed through an extensive cut-over area and was reminded of the so-called multiple-use policy. Often seems that multiple-use is a euphemism for selling the national forests, which belong to all of us, to the highest bidder among commercial interests; logging, mining, sheep and cattle grazing in the west. They seem to come to think of national forests as their land then, even to the point of shooing away the non-commodity users — the hikers, fishermen, backpackers, bird watchers. Is it possible to use a natural area for hiking *after* it has been logged in a clear-cutting program? I suppose so, but it's just not the same experience. The persons who manage the national lands are decent, honest men and women but their training and interests lie closer to the lumber merchant than to the lover of wild lands. Foresters like to see planted forests, all the same size, all the same species, in nice even rows all ready for easy harvesting. A tree plantation does not a forest make.

3:30 p.m.

Milepost 22. What an exquisite pleasure it is to remove my boots, peel off my sweaty socks and cool my feet in a cold stream! Saw three deer, all does — still in their grey winter garb. They watched me curiously from beside the trail and as long as I kept up my pace, eyes forward, they did not move. The moment I stopped, up went their white tails — what else could they be called but white-tail deer — and they bounded away. Maybe there is a lesson there.

How much do we miss by marching along with eyes forward and with an unchanging pace? Thoreau knew. Also saw a redtail hawk perched on a large dead white pine near Pole Creek, and heard a loon where the trail comes close to Saul Lake.

4:30 p.m.

I am going much more slowly now and stopping much more often for a drink of water or a rest in the dry leaves beside the trail. But I am beginning to really understand that without weariness there can be no appreciation of rest, without hunger no enjoyment of food.

6:00 p.m.

I am sitting at the end of the formal Bay de Noc-Grand Island trail. I had planned to follow the edge of the Au Train Basin up to Lake Superior but that is an additional 19 miles and my legs and blisters will not permit it. It is good to test oneself and it is also good to realize when you have reached your limit. I marched over 30 miles and although I am tired, my senses are clear and my mind is still very active. I will wait here at the checkpoint for Lynn and the twins. Map miles are sure different from actual trail miles. Or feet miles!

Several friends asked me after the long hike what my impressions were, what I had learned. For several weeks I declined to answer and then, one day, it fell into place and I penned this addendum to my hiking diary:

Physical challenge hiking is not my kind of hiking. I don't think I will try another endurance day. I have done it, although I didn't go the total distance, and I am glad that I did. I learned that I am not a superman, nor do I have to be; in fact, it is not a bad old body.

I learned too, if I had forgotten, that man without his machines has limits. That's nice. It is humbling but it is comforting to know.

I learned that there are values in pitting yourself against some odds, that Don Quixote lives on in each of us.

I had seen another part of the countryside intimately, had made it "mine" without disturbing it or changing it for the next person to pass that way. I had walked where the Indian traveler and French trapper-voyageur walked and knew again with all frustrations, disappointments and discouraging changes it is a beautiful world! Far from dimming, my affection has grown.

PORTAGE BAY

Rounding a sharp bend in the narrow woods road, we emerged slowly from a dense cedar forest to catch sight of the morning sun sparkling on the waters of Lake Michigan. Suddenly, out of the corner of my eye I saw a flash of yellow at the edge of the cedars, then another, and many more. With a shout of delight, I braked the camper truck sharply, threw open the door and rushed to the edge of a small clearing. There they were in full bloom: yellow lady's slipper plants. I knelt beside one plant and examined the delicate, bright yellow slippers; one, two . . . five hung on slender stems from one plant. Lynn, now recovering from my precipitous exit from the truck, joined me and quickly discovered more of the beautiful northern orchids growing nearby. Our daughters emerged from the back of the camper where they had been reading and coloring to see what had attracted their parents to the clearing beside the road.

Further back among the trees, almost hidden in the grass, we discovered another wild flower, a crested dwarf iris; its three petaled purple flower with distinctive yellow crest was shining everywhere and we hesitated to take a step lest we crush one of the small plants. Lured on through the woods we came upon another larger clearing. The blaze of red-orange which leaped out at us almost took our breath away — a whole field of Indian paintbrush in bloom. The clearing looked as if it were in flames. On the way back to the truck we found columbine, hawkweed, fringed milkwort and several other late spring wildflowers in bloom. Quite by accident we had discovered a colorful wild garden.

We had followed the winding road through the forest to find the Portage Bay state forest campground on the east side of the Garden Peninsula in the south-central portion of the Upper Peninsula. Just to the east of the cities of Escanaba and Gladstone, two peninsulas — Stonington and Garden — jut down into Lake Michigan like a giant thumb and forefinger. Featuring a somewhat milder climate than areas inland from the lake, both peninsulas are heavily farmed, less so than in the past but still to a greater extent than most other parts of Upper Michigan. The explorer will find old orchards, rolling green hills, rocky cliffs and sleepy fishing villages. Although it is difficult to make such choices, our favorite is the Garden Peninsula because it is the site of a ghost town, Fayette, which has been brought back to life by Michigan's Department of Natural Resources.

Lynn and I knew little of the history of Fayette when we visited the ghost town before its restoration. We admired the high limestone bluff, swam in the beautiful harbor and poked around in the old ruins of blast furnaces and charcoal kilns in complete solitude. We inspected the well preserved company store and opera house and spent long hours sitting on the bluff watching the nuances of color on Lake Michigan. When the pioneer iron smelting town was restored during the early 1960s, we learned about its origins, the extensive operations during its heyday and its eventual demise.

About the time the Civil War ended, Fayette Brown of the Jackson Iron Company explored for a location to smelt pig iron in large quantities for shipping by lake vessel to the mills in the industrial centers of Chicago, Cleveland and Gary. His search ended at Snail Shell Harbor, a deep well-protected cove on the west side of the Garden Peninsula. The harbor provided excellent anchorage for large ore boats and plenty of space for docks and loading facilities. An abundance of hardwood trees for making charcoal to feed the blast furnaces grew within easy hauling distance. The cliff on the north side of the harbor provided a ready source of limestone, a material that was essential for smelting pig iron. Brown was delighted with his discovery and rapidly made plans for a town built exclusively for the business of processing iron ore.

Construction commenced and by 1867 two stone blast furnaces and several charcoal kilns had been erected; a stock barn, carpenter shop, boarding house and other support buildings mushroomed around the edge of the harbor. Now the smelting began in earnest.

Raw iron was shipped from Negaunee by rail to Escanaba and then brought on Lake Michigan barges to Fayette. In two short years production was booming: over 5000 tons of pig iron were shipped to the industrial centers, making Fayette the single largest producer in the United States. By 1875, production had increased to an astounding 14,000 tons and the population of the town grew to 500 people.

Then the bubble began to disintegrate. One of the two blast furnaces was destroyed by fire. The supply of hardwood was running out and making pig iron required enormous amounts of charcoal; it is estimated that it took 125 bushels of charcoal to produce one ton of iron. The manufacturers at Gary and Pittsburgh found that coke was superior for making iron and it proved easier to ship raw ore in the huge bulk vessels and do the smelting at the large factories. In 1892 the last load was shipped from Fayette, the remaining furnace was extinguished and the people began to drift away looking for other work.

The boom and bust cycle — rapid expansion, peak production and then exhaustion of the natural resources — has been typical of the economic history of the Upper Peninsula. In most cases it is the land and the people which have suffered the consequences; the owners, generally from outside the region, took their losses or their profits (often huge) back to Boston or Cleveland and left the residents with empty dreams and ugly scars on the land. Fortunately in the case of Fayette, there was minimal impact on the land and the town, now restored as a historical state park, offers a provocative insight into life in an earlier era. The trees have come back — large white birch even grow from within the old charcoal kilns — and Snail Shell Harbor still offers a lovely port of refuge, now for modern sailors on pleasure crafts.

Five miles south of Fayette near Fairport, there is evidence of much earlier inhabitants of the Garden Peninsula. At Burnt Bluff are the only known Native American paintings in Michigan; estimates place the pictographs at over 1500 years old.

Since our discovery of Portage Bay Campground, we like to believe that the peninsula is called "Garden" because of the profusion of wildflowers which grow here. Since that initial fortunate discovery several years ago, we return each spring to supervise the blooming of the last spring flowers.

Our favorites are the woodlands orchids, or lady's slippers. We are especially partial to the yellow lady's slipper because it does not grow in the Lake Superior region where we live, though the pink variety can be found in profusion — and rarity makes the affection more intense. The bright yellow blossoms, backed and accented by two brown, purple-veined and twisted lateral petals, sit daintily atop slender stems; shaped like tiny slippers or moccasins (moccasin flower is another name for the yellow slipper), the blossoms are very faintly veined and have a shiny almost wax-like appearance. A fairy princess never wore a slipper more lovely.

The pink lady's slipper doesn't look at all like a slipper or even a moccasin; the blossom resembles a deeply cleft pouch or a small heavily-veined two-chambered heart. Not too far from the hand pump in the campground we were delighted to discover a small, more rare lady slipper. The blossom of the ram's head is a conical pink pouch which is veined with crimson and lined with silky white hairs.

The orchids blooming at Portage Bay are so lovely and so dramatic that it is easy to overlook the many other species of wildflowers which grow here: star flowers, yellow clintonia, swamp butter cup, St. John's wort, and between the campsites and the beach an abundance of fringed milk wort in magnificent lavender blossom.

There is another reason why we return to Portage Bay each year in early June. The campground offers a measure of quiet and solitude; its isolation at the end of a five mile poor dirt road tends to discourage most casual visitors. Camping is popular now, a big business operation in many states. During the summer months the parks in northern Michigan, especially those which feature full "services" — electrical hookups, flush toilets, showers, paved parking lots, laundries, grocery stores, rangers with harried looks — resemble small cities. The activity and noise levels are numbing: kids on minibikes, barking dogs, portable radios, adults on motorcycles letting the good times roll, portable record players, ad nauseum.

We avoid the crowded parks in favor of unmarked spots in state or national forests or small, out-of-the-way campgrounds like Portage Bay. The area supports an interesting variety of wildlife. Deer frequently cross the campground on their way to drink from Lake Michigan; we see their tracks in the moist sand on the beach most every morning. Chipmunks dash about the picnic tables searching for scraps of food and red squirrels scold from the jack pines which shade the campsites. On their way to get water, the twins found a large box turtle, the only species which can withdraw and close itself up completely in its hinged shell. They spent several hours trying to make friends with the gentle terrapin.

One evening just about dark as we returned from a stroll, a large porcupine emerged from a thicket beside the road and ambled slowly toward us. We stopped and watched as it came closer and closer. I clapped my hands loudly and the prickly creature stopped, barely four feet away, raised up and peered at us in the gloom. After a long moment he shuffled to a nearby tree and climbed out of sight in the foliage. Late that night we were awakened by a strange sound under our camper; when I investigated there was our porcupine, or a close relative, gnawing on the frame of the truck, apparently for the salt which had splashed up during the winter driving.

Winter is far from our minds as we sit on the long clean beach and swim in the warm waters of Lake Michigan. Lake Michigan, although we are very fond of it, has a totally different character than our beloved Lake Superior. It is more sedate, tamer. The shoreline is predominantly sand beach unlike the formidable rocky shores of Superior. There are storms on Lake Michigan, of course, and many ships have gone down in its waters. In fact the first major shipwreck on the Upper Great Lakes was thought by some to have taken place in the depths off the Garden Peninsula, perhaps even near Portage Bay. As I walked along the beach toward the north arm of the bay, I tried to remember the saga of the *Griffin,* the first major sized commercial vessel to ply the waters off the Upper Peninsula.

Robert Cavelier, Sieur de La Salle, known simply as La Salle in most historical accounts, came to the New World in 1666 with the mission to garner the fur trade on Lake Michigan and explore the upper Great Lakes. To accomplish his mission, he built a brig on the Niagara River near the mouth of Lake Erie. The ship was 65 feet long and weighed 45 tons; it had two large square sails and a high poop deck. It was christened the *Griffin**, an allusion to Count Frontenac's coat-of-arms. Some historians feel that the name was a non-too-subtle slap at the ubiquitous black-robed Jesuit priests who sought souls while the explorers searched for fame and fortune; the griffin, a mythical beast with the head and wings of an eagle and the body of a lion, could fly above and beyond the dusky raven.

The vessel set sail on Lake Erie in early August, 1679, with La Salle in command and Henri Tonti as first lieutenant. La Salle chose Tonti for the expedition because he was completely loyal and a fearless soldier; he had cut off his own hand in battle and now wore a crude iron claw. A third notable, Father Louis Hennepin, a Recollect friar accompanied the mission. Hennepin was more adventurer than priest and he kept a meticulous record of the events of this most eventful journey; his enthusiasm exceeded his accuracy, however, for he reported that Niagara Falls was 600 feet high and that its roar could be heard for 90 miles!

The small brig sailed uneventfully through Lake Erie, past what is now Detroit and across Lake St. Clair into Lake Huron. They encountered a severe storm near Saginaw Bay, so severe that a frightened and disheartened La Salle commended his mission to God and all hands, except the ship's pilot, prayed for deliverance. The storm passed and the *Griffin* sailed through the straits of Mackinac, skirted the Garden Peninsula and put in at Green Bay, Wisconsin, where a load of furs awaited.

The furs were loaded — their value was estimated at between 50 and 60 thousand *livres* (perhaps $60,000) — and La Salle dispatched the vessel back to Niagara with orders to return as soon as possible. The ship's pilot, a giant Dane named Lucas, objected, pointing out that he had only five seamen for the return voyage. La Salle was adamant. The *Griffin* set out on September 18, 1679, and sailed into history; she was never seen again. What happened to the ship? I wondered as I walked along the beach at Portage Bay.

*sometimes spelled *Griffon* or *Gryphon*

Did the crew scuttle the vessel and make off with the valuable cargo of furs? Did the helmsman lose his way in a thick fog, miss the turn southward into Lake Huron at the straits and run aground on some rocky isle? There is some credence to this latter theory. On Manitoulin Island in northern Lake Huron a lighthouse keeper recently found four skeletons in a cave; two more were discovered nearby. With the remains were 17th century coins, part of an ancient ship hull and a bolt very similar to those used in boat construction at the time of the *Griffin*. Ship timbers and bolts matching the description of the *Griffin* in every detail were found near Tobermory in northern Georgian Bay in the 1950s*. Or did the vessel and crew perish in a storm in the northern part of Lake Michigan as Father Hennepin believed? Hennepin reported that a band of Indians had observed the ill-fated ship tossing about in heavy seas.

A piece of smooth board protruding from the sand at the water's edge attracted my attention. Quickly I dug around it and exposed a portion of a thick oak plank; digging further I discovered modern bolts and abandoned my search. Perhaps the plank came from an ore barge which foundered en route to Fayette but it clearly did not belong to the *Griffin*. Maybe, I thought, there is a fourth possibility: perhaps the wraith-like *Griffin* still sails the waters of Lake Michigan, a phantom ship forever moving before the wind. Reaching the end of the bay, I paused to rest near a point on a large piece of driftwood. A flash of blue caught my eye near the edge of a large backwater a few yards behind the point. Investigating, I found three blue flags just beginning to bloom; their three-part blossom resembled closely the *fleur de lis* which graced the flag of the courageous French adventurers who explored this country centuries before. For a long time I sat and gazed out over the water.

That night a spectacular electrical storm flashed and pulsated far out on Lake Michigan. I lay for almost an hour watching the bolts of lightning knife out of the sky toward the dark waters. During one particularly large flash, the lake was partially illuminated and — just for an instant — I thought I saw a ship with an eerie silhouetted griffin springing from its bow making her way through the heavy seas. The flag of French royalty, golden lilies on a field of blue, billowed in the wind from the brig's high transom. I blinked and it was gone. Perhaps it was merely a dream.

Portage Bay is often in our thoughts and dreams as we go about our daily activities. As I write these lines I can see in my mind the spectacular yellow lady's slippers, the tastefully restored ghost town of Fayette and, yes, I can even make out faintly through the lightning the good ship *Griffin* in full sail.

*See *The Fate of the Griffin,* by H.J. MacLean

S U M M E R

Seasons in the Upper Peninsula of Michigan

"An old woods road"

"Old Reliable"

PHOTOS BY LON EMERICK

"The twins played beside the water"

—————

S U M M E R

The sun edged over the rim of Lake Superior spreading a glow of pale gold upon the water. Far below me, Middle Island and Partridge Island, dark and brooding, seemed to sail on the smooth glistening surface. I was stationed atop Sugar Loaf Mountain, a tall granite knob north of town, observing an annual June ritual: greeting the summer solstice, the day of the longest light. As I watched the lake slowly turn to its usual deep blue and felt the subtle warmth of the sun's early morning rays, a line from one of Emily Dickinson's poems ran through my mind: "Oh, sacrament of summer days!"

The days of summer are sacred indeed to those who dwell in the north. Many, like myself, cannot bear to miss a single dawn nor be absent when the sun exits in a splash of orange and pink. We savor the sunlight; there is, in fact, almost a regional obsession with absorbing as many of its rays as possible, to lay up treasures of light and warmth to last through the long dark winter. The summer season is very special in the Upper Peninsula.

After sampling many parts of the nation, I can say — with obvious bias — that no place has a summer to rival ours. No residents who can prevent it spend the summer season out of the Peninsula — who needs a vacation anywhere else when you *live* in a vacation land? The first summer I moved back here, many years ago, I began to notice a few tourists filtering into the area in late June; by July summer vacationers could be seen everywhere on the highways and at the beaches. Suddenly it occurred to me: I am privileged to reside in a region which tourists plan and scheme all year to visit for a week or two!

It's not the climate that makes our summers so special. We have weather. I agree with John Steinbeck: a climate is boring. I once spent a week visiting friends in southern California. Each day we awoke to yet another cloudless, windless, warm — another bland

and beautiful day. It almost made me ill — for, let me confess it, I like weather. I admire thunderheads gathering out over the lake, I love the stiff winds when they send the water into a towering frenzy, I even yearn for rainstorms which soften my footfalls in the forest and leave the pines drenched and sparkling. Although summer is our most predictable, most stable season in the north, the weather can still be chimerical. Several times I have seen the temperature plummet from over 80 degrees to near 40 degrees in less than two hours.

Even so, summer is still a season for long hikes, canoeing wild rivers and lakes, exploring old woods roads and gathering the wild fruits which grow abundantly in forests and fields. It is also a time of serenity, a time to reflect and ponder.

I have two very special places where I go to think the long thoughts of summer, two spots close to home which provide a supply of warm images to last all through the cold days that will follow. The first is a grassy knoll in an old pasture of a former dairy farm. I go there and lie on my back in a sweet-smelling bed of red clover, daisies and wild grasses. I watch clouds, feel the sun on my body and listen to the wind flutter the leaves in the small apple tree near the crest of the hill. It feels open and expansive and free; so also do I while I'm a part of the farmer's old field.

My other special place is a woodlot, in late afternoon or early evening when the slanting rays of the sun send soft shafts of yellow and gold filtering through the leaves. The forest is quite dense with red and striped maple, aspen and birches well started. I have an insatiable hunger for the delicate play of light and shadows through the trees; a single leaf may be turned to bright burnished copper against a backdrop of deep green, or a single shaft of light will touch the forest floor illuminating the ripening purple berries of a solitary clintonia. Its dimness shelters me and the softness of the shadows gentles me.

The environment and the feeling of the woodlot and of the field are unlike in every way — yet each forms a portion of summer. Along with the granite hilltops, the sparkling waves of Lake Superior, the streams and inland lakes, the curving sand and jumbled rock beaches, my special woodlot and field hold the beauty of summer in the Upper Peninsula.

R E T U R N   T O   T H E   P O R K I E S

The trail spiraled down from the rocky cliff. It was cool and dim where it wound under virgin white pines and hemlock and the path was soft and pungent with needles — nature's wall-to-wall carpeting. We located one last trail marker, a small orange tag imbedded in a tree, and then came out on a rocky crag overlooking Lake Superior.

The water sparkled in the sunlight; a herring gull wheeled slowly catching the warm updrafts beside the steep cliff. We dropped our packs by a nearby log and looked at each other with a sense of accomplishment. We had returned to the Porkies.

A little more than a decade earlier my wife and I, then newly married, spent a delightful week hiking through this midwestern wilderness. Near the end of our stay, along the rocky trail which twists upward from the cabin at Buckshot Landing on Lake Superior, we made a promise to each other beside a solitary birch tree. Someday we would return to hike again through the Porcupine Mountains in the western part of the Upper Peninsula.

Now, ten years later, I searched for the same birch while Lynn and our twin daughters rested against their packs. I found the tree — its present girth exceeding my own — where the trail makes a steep descent to Buckshot cabin. After a long moment of reflection and a cold drink from our canteens, we shouldered our packs and hiked on toward the cabin.

We were returning to the Porkies to introduce our children to this very special wilderness park and to our favorite mode of exploration — walking. We wanted also to see if Michigan's Department of Natural Resources had been able to preserve the wilderness character of the park's interior despite determined onslaughts by road-building, lumbering and mining interests.

The Porcupine Mountains, a prominent landmark of rugged terrain rising from Lake Superior, are widely acclaimed for their scenic beauty and virgin forests. Made up of a series of broken ranges roughly parallel to Lake Superior's shoreline, they rise to an elevation of 1,958 feet above sea level — one of the highest land masses in the midwest. From the lake the park looks like a huge shadowy porcupine crouched down by the shore for a drink. The Chippewas called the rocky redoubt the *Kakewishing* Mountains and propitiated the spirits they believed dwelt among the high granite cliffs. Early in the 17th century, Brule and Grenoble, the first white men to explore the south shore of Lake Superior, paddled past the Porkies; Radisson, John Johnston, Henry Schoolcraft and many other adventurers admired the flinty hills and dark forests. This kind of wilderness park, still barely touched by axe or road, isolated from cars and other impacts of modern life, is rare, and becoming even more rare.

There had been no park, just a vast heavily timbered area, when my grandfather fished and explored in the Porcupine Mountains in 1917. Now in his nineties, he still remembers vividly the clear rushing streams, the wild lakes and, best of all, the expanse of virgin timber, largely white pine, hemlock and yellow birch. At that time most, if not all, of the forests of the Upper Peninsula had been converted to lumber; the Porkies escaped this relentless juggernaut because its rugged terrain made logging nearly impossible by the methods of that time. Only a narrow strip of timber along Lake Superior was cut, but later lumbermen began making plans to harvest all the primeval forest: in 1937, 170,000 acres of virgin timber remained; by 1941 it was down to 140,000. Alarmed at the swift disappearance of this irreplaceable portion of our natural heritage, several men of great vision had a dream.

The dream began beside a campfire one May night at the mouth of the Carp River in the heart of the Porkies. Ben East, Ed Johnson and Raymond Dick set in motion that night the Save the Porcupine Mountains Association which caught the imagination and support of thousands. P.J. Hoffmaster, then Director of Conservation, and Governor Harry Kelly pushed through the legislature a bill calling for a million dollars to purchase the land and, in 1944, the Porcupine Mountain State Park was dedicated as a forest museum. The area was saved. Or so they thought.

In 1958 the price of copper zoomed upward and a mining company sought state permission, under the archaic mineral rights law, to enter the Park and extract the metal. The famous nonesuch shale — rich in copper deposits — underlies most of the 60,000 acres which comprise the Porcupine Mountains. The controversy raged. Thousands of letters, telegrams, and phone calls from persons protesting potential intrusion flooded the state capitol. Many of those protesting had never seen the park but were somehow comforted to know that a small portion of our natural heritage remained intact. Permission for mining was denied. Again the area was saved. Or so it seemed.

Enter the road builders. A concerted effort was mounted to construct a north-south macadam highway through the heart of the park along the very spine of the mountain chain. Conservation groups raised a mighty protest. A highway would mean destruction of the virgin forest, degradation of the pristine streams — let alone the complete loss of the wilderness character of the area. There was already a fine paved highway to the lookout above Lake of the Clouds. Nonetheless, a bill funding the road construction plan passed both the House of Representatives and the Senate and was sent to the governor for his signature. Governor George Romney made a wise, though unprecedented move: Instead of making a decision in his Lansing office, he came to the Porkies, looked at the land and walked the trails. Visibly moved by what he had seen, he vetoed the bill. Again, the advocates of wilderness relaxed. But they were cautious.

Wilderness lovers remembered Thoreau's comment: "Most men, it seems to me, do not care for nature and would sell their share in all her beauty for a given sum." For many years lumbering interests have coveted the large timber in the Porcupines; seen through the eyes of a commercial forester, the trees are "rapidly deteriorating, declining in vigor and soon will be gone with the wind." To be sure, blowdowns do occur in the Park, just as they occurred for centuries before lumbermen existed to mourn the loss of merchantable board feet. Far from deteriorating, the woodlands in the Porkies are healthy mixed communities of trees unlike the highly disease-susceptible even-aged monocultures that are cultivated for highest yield.

Yes, the price of preserving a wilderness is eternal vigilance. There are some individuals who would even replace the music of waterfalls with the tinkle of cash registers. One of the most inane plans to convert the park's natural beauty to dollars was promulgated by a local legislator who wanted to install fish ladders around the several falls on the Presque Isle River and promote a salmon fishing industry. Not within the mountains themselves, but along the western foothills and forming the western boundary of the park, the Presque Isle River flows in a torrent of foaming, swirling water. The largest and most beautiful river in the region, it rushes from the upper tableland through narrow precipitous gorges, over a series of waterfalls, to blend with the waters of Lake Superior. In order to build the elaborate sequence of fish ladders, it would have been necessary to blast away portions of the falls and replace them with ugly concrete steps. Once again the protest was overwhelming and the ill-conceived project was abandoned.

Finally it was decided to prepare a master plan which would, once and for all, preserve the interior of the park as the wilderness while permitting some development around the perimeter to handle the large numbers of summer visitors. The plan called for four zones: a wilderness zone comprised of 35,000 acres of the most undisturbed forest with no motorized travel or disposable items in hiker's packsacks. A second zone, consisting of 5,000 acres was designated for wilderness study; here scientists can investigate ecological parameters in an untrammeled setting. For camping, picnicking and other similar uses, 19,000 acres was set aside for development and a buffer zone outside of the wilderness boundary. Lastly, 2,000 acres which contain particularly attractive and scenic areas — the Escarpment Overlook, Presque Isle River, Summit Peak and Union Spring — were designated as scenic sites. According to House Bill 4881, the area is identified as Porcupine Mountains Wilderness State Park. Will it now be safe? We shall see. If the increasing army of wilderness enthusiasts and backpackers will continue to monitor for potential commercial assaults, many future generations can enjoy the Porkies as they are today.

The Park is a backpacker's delight; more than 70 miles of excellent trails criss-cross the interior. The paths are well-marked with orange metal tags; distance and directional signs are placed at trail heads and major junctions. Nine log or board cabins are placed unobtrusively in natural settings beside the lakes and streams. They are fully equipped except for sleeping bags and personal items and may be rented for a nominal fee. Tent camping is also permitted in the interior under a permit system and with certain restrictions regarding location of campsites.

We chose the two mile hike from the main park road to Buckshot cabin for this initial backpacking adventure with our twin girls. It was rugged and long enough to discourage casual day hikers but short enough for the four-year-olds to accomplish. We took the trail slowly, making frequent stops to rest, eat trail snacks and enjoy the scenery. Soon we came around a bend in the trail and there stood Buckshot cabin in a small clearing by the rocky shore of Lake Superior. We dropped our now-heavy packs and silently soaked in the panorama of sparkling waves, rocky slabs and thick forest. It was exactly as we had remembered it.

For the next few days we lived simply and quietly in this wild beautiful place. We adults felt the layers of civilization dropping away. Almost all our meals were prepared and eaten on the rocky beach. We explored the many coves and wooded bays along the shore, collected driftwood, hunted for agates and relaxed all over. Our girls enjoyed themselves even more than we imagined they could. Their major activity was spending hours pretending that a huge slab of granite by the shore was a ship and they were sailing down to the sea with their dolls.

Beside the campfires, we shared with the girls a few delights of our first hiking adventure in the park — ten years before. Lynn and I had, with other tourists, seen Lake of the Clouds from the rocky escarpment, a short walk from the end of the main road. This clear, almost transparent, lake set in a valley of surrounding dark hills is probably the best known scenic site in the Porcupine Mountains. The dark green forest seems impenetrable from the escarpment; the only evidence of man is a small log bridge crossing the outlet of the Lake of the Clouds far below. We had crossed that same bridge ten years before and headed over the ridges through the heart of the park for our campsite beside Mirror Lake, the only other sizable body of water in the region. Mirror Lake could not properly be named anything else. The surface seemed almost breakable; the reflections of the giant white pine were as sharp and clear as the reality which towered more than a hundred feet above us. We remembered, too, the Big and Little Carp Rivers. These two pristine streams, with water so clear and cold we could see trout lying in ambush in deep pools, originate and terminate within the park boundaries; in their journey to Lake Superior they twist and turn through dense groves of pine and hemlock. Someday, we promised, the children would see it all with their own eyes.

Our last evening at Buckshot was a bittersweet occasion. Each girl, with some carving help, had fashioned her own Paddle-to-the-Sea* and we christened each one solemnly before the tiny craft were slipped into the restless currents of Lake Superior. We collected a pile of driftwood, built a fire and savored the twilight. Three silhouetted forms, pied-billed grebes, swam across the path of gold reflected on the water. Silently we watched as the sun made its descent and the sky changed from orange to delicate pink and finally deepened into mauve. We were quietly together, closer perhaps at that moment than we had ever been as a family, each of us wishing, we found out later, the same thing: to return again.

As the woods turned dark behind us, a sudden far-off storm lit up the big lake. White fingers of lightning stabbed down from the dark sky and into water. As we watched, we talked quietly of the things we had enjoyed — the porcupine, as startled as we were, which waddled up and sat beside us outside the cabin; the young boy, camping alone who hiked past one evening. How contented he seemed compared with teenagers of loud rock music, fast cars and street corners. The big-eared deer mice which chewed on our soap each night; the smell of damp hemlock and pine in the morning; the sound of the water and the wind as we fell asleep each night.

*Holling C. Holling, *Paddle-to-the-Sea*

The hike out the next morning was accomplished with dispatch thanks to a rain-threatening sky. As we climbed out on the overlook to Lake Superior, we could see, far below, the small clearing where blue waters touched the shore at Buckshot cabin. We were agreed that we all wanted to come back again to hike in the Porkies; even more importantly we were convinced that for children growing up in an increasingly more crowded, confusing world, there must always be such places.

THE COPPER COUNTRY

*A*lthough couched in conservative language and containing explicit cautions to the naive, the little doctor's geological report still precipitated the first large land rush and mineral boom in the young United States of America. The guarded excitement in this sentence of Douglass Houghton's scholarly treatise caught the imagination of the fortune seekers: "Upon the whole (while I would carefully avoid exciting any unfounded expectations among our citizens, and caution them to avoid engaging in wild schemes with a view to gain sudden wealth), the examinations and surveys which have been made would serve fully to justify the conclusion that this region of the country will prove a continued source of wealth to our State." That did it. In 1841, thousands of speculators, prospectors and adventure seekers (but, curiously, few if any experienced hard-rock miners) headed straight for the remote and wild Keweenaw Peninsula. It is fitting that an historic city of the Copper Country, now home of Michigan Technological University, which started as a college of mining engineering, is named for Dr. Houghton.

Born in Troy, New York, the diminutive Douglass Houghton was a five foot, four inch man for all seasons: chemist, physician, geologist, educator, politician, wilderness explorer, accomplished flute player. Endowed with a keen inquiring mind and boundless energy, he joined Schoolcraft in discovering the source of the Mississippi River at Itasca, Minnesota, served as mayor of Detroit and helped to organize the University of Michigan — all before his untimely death at the age of 34! But it is for his geological surveys of the Upper Peninsula that he is best known. Commissioned the first State geologist in 1840, Houghton was allotted the sum of $3000 and charged with conducting an analysis of the possible mineral wealth in the vast reaches of the Peninsula recently acquired by the State as a consolation prize in the mini-war with Ohio over the Toledo Strip. Accompanied by three assistants, Dr. Houghton systematically explored the region for mineral wealth five months each season; from May to October, the small party traveled and camped on remote beaches and river banks.

In the Keweenaw Peninsula (Chippewa for "place of crossing"), a rocky finger of land which curves out into Lake Superior, Houghton found traces of copper almost everywhere he looked. Most of the metal he found was float copper, chunks of native copper which had been discarded capriciously by the glaciers which scoured the region thousands of years before. Douglass Houghton did not live to see later discoveries of the bonanza lodes of copper found in ancient laval flows (amygdaloid) and sedimentary beds of sand and gravel (conglomerate) which brought fleeting wealth and glory to the area. On the evening of October 13, 1845, the young geologist was steering a Mackinaw boat on a course toward Eagle River when a wet snow storm erupted on Lake Superior. A sudden gust capsized the boat, throwing the men in the icy waves. Only two men, Peter McFarland and Baptiste Bodrie, managed to reach shore and relate the tragic death of the little doctor who played such a big part in the development of the Copper Country.

Centuries before Douglass Houghton searched for mineral wealth, even long before the Chippewa tribes camped along the shores of the Keweenaw, a mysterious race of miners looking for copper hacked shallow pits, ten to twenty feet deep, into the flinty hills. Throughout the area, early prospectors found these ancient pits; most of the later prosperous copper mines were located on the sites. The Chippewas did not know of the people who had mined in the region and did not use the metal themselves, although they revered it as a manifestation of the Great Spirit. Who were these prehistoric miners — Vikings, Phonecians, Central American Indians? They left no remnants of dwellings, pottery, burial sites or personal artifacts, just hundreds of crude stone hammers, abandoned in the pits as if they were ready to begin mining again tomorrow. Whoever they were, these early miners were prodigious workers: It is estimated that it would have required at least a thousand men working for a thousand years to remove the quantity of copper they extracted by the primitive methods employed! Their mining techniques, albeit crude, were effective. Fires built against the copper bearing rock and cold water poured over the hot rock caused the boulders to spall; the miners then simply hammered the copper free from chunks of the boulder. Carbon dating of the charcoal remains from their fires indicates that the mining commenced as early as 5000 years ago — and then suddenly ceased about 1400 A.D. Archeologist have traced weapons and other artifacts of Michigan copper all the way down to the Yucatan Peninsula in Mexico, and in Central America.

In the mid-17th century, Jesuit missionaries learned of the rich copper deposits during their travels along the south shore of Lake Superior. The Chippewas escorted

Father Dablon up the Ontonagon River to show him an immense boulder of pure native copper lying free in the riverbed. Alexander Henry, sole English survivor of the massacre at Fort Michilimackinac in 1763, also visited the boulder; he made an abortive attempt at mining in the area in 1771. Schoolcraft and other explorers inspected the now famous boulder, chipped off specimens of the copper and described it in their journals. But it took an enterprising American, James Eldred, to devise a scheme for making money from the slab of copper (unlike granite, the Ontonagon boulder is a slab, four feet six inches long, four feet wide and only 17 inches thick). He skidded the boulder out of the river and exhibited it in Detroit in the fall of 1843 at an admission fee of 25 cents a person. Although copper was obviously not a precious metal, and there were then very few uses for it (it was not used for making brass for bullets until the Civil War and electrical wiring was of course still unheard of) a flood of treasure seekers arrived the next summer at the very tip of the Keweenaw Peninsula.

It is difficult to imagine today's picturesque small village of Copper Harbor as a boom town in 1844. So many prospectors poured into the area poking, chipping and exploring that the State government feared for their safety; although the Chippewa had ceded all the land from Marquette to Duluth in the Treaty of LaPointe, a band on Isle Royale rumbled threats to take it back. The Federal government erected a garrison, Fort Wilkins, but no trouble developed and the troops were summoned to fight in the Mexican War. There is an interesting footnote about Fort Wilkins which reflects how the modern visitor feels when it is necessary to leave the Copper Country. One noncommissioned officer, Sergeant William Wright, was assigned to watch over the Fort when the rest of the troops were withdrawn. When the Army finally decided to transfer him to a different part of the nation ten years later, Wright found he could not leave the enchanting natural beauty of the Keweenaw, mustered out of the service and opened a hotel at Eagle River. Today Fort Wilkins has been tastefully and authentically restored by the Department of Natural Resources; it stands beside Lake Fanny Hooe, a clear mountain lake named after the young sister of the commandant who, one version relates, wandered away while picking berries in the summer of 1845 and was never seen again.

Very little copper was found at Copper Harbor — only enough to keep the grandiose dreams of wealth alive, but not in sufficient quantities to pay for the expense of sinking shafts in the hard rock. The early prospectors did not know that the major deposits of copper lay in a narrow band, three to five miles wide and more than a hundred miles long, on an elevated greenstone ridge which cuts down the center of the Keweenaw Peninsula and as far south as Ontonagon and the Porcupine Mountains. The search shifted southward.

The first really large copper lode was discovered at Cliff, 25 miles south of Copper Harbor. According to legend, the rich deposits were found when a prospector slid down a cliff and barked his derriere on a piece of projecting copper. When shafts were sunk deep into the greenstone, the miners, most of them experienced Cornishmen, found massive deposits of amygdaloid copper within lava flows; in this case the ore is found in cohesive masses, some as small as raisins, others in great chunks weighing tons. The Cliff mine produced over 40 million pounds of the red metal. Shortly after the discovery of the lode at Cliff, large deposits of amygdaloid copper were found near the twin cities of Hancock and Houghton. Here the Quincy mine was sunk into a hill overlooking the waters of Portage Entry, a waterway which now provides a shortcut through the Keweenaw Peninsula. Dubbed Old Reliable because it continued to produce copper ore for over 70 years, the shafts went down 9,400 feet into the very bowels of the earth. Shaft house number two still stands today, a much photographed sentinel overlooking the cities.

The glory years of the Copper Country really began with the discovery of the *great* Calumet and Hecla conglomerate deposits near the present communities of Calumet and Laurium. It earned the adjective great in every way — at one time the C and H employed 66,000 people, and between 1869 and 1946 paid over 200 million dollars in dividends for the investors. The word *Calumet* is French for "pipe of peace," while *Hecla* was the name of a volcano in Iceland.

The rich deposit was found, according to a local anecdote, by Billy Royall who was looking for his lost pigs. He heard squealing from between the roots of a tree and when he pulled out one of his pigs, a chunk of copper came along with the creature. More probably it was Edwin J. Hulbert, civil engineer and nephew of Henry Rowe Schoolcraft, who found outcroppings of ore while surveying for a road between Hancock and Eagle River. Later, after a dispute over management, Alexander Agassiz, son of the Swiss naturalist, Louis Agassiz, took over the direction of the C and H Company. The Calumet and Hecla flourished in the late 1800s and the population of the area reached 100,000 persons (now down to 30,000). It was a veritable melting pot of nationalities including Cornish miners, Finns, French Canadians, Italians, Irishmen and many others. During those glory years C and H was the major producer of copper in the United States and the residents could apparently afford their desires for culture in the isolated north country. There was much local pride when a large ornate opera house was erected in Calumet; it was the only theater owned by a municipality at that time in the United States. Lillian Russell, John Philip Sousa and Jane Addams appeared on the stage.

By 1910, the mines were wearing out and the copper boom days were almost over; the shafts by now descended far into the earth and it was becoming very expensive to bring the ore to the surface. A prolonged labor dispute in 1913 was the beginning of the end. Encouraged by gains made by unions in the western part of the nation, 13,000 copper country miners went out on strike on July 23, 1913; they demanded eight hour shifts, a minimum wage and better safety and working conditions. The Company refused to negotiate with the union and imported laborers to keep the mines going on a token basis. Violence flared and the Michigan National Guard patrolled the streets and guarded the mines. Advocates of workers' rights, including John L. Lewis and Clarence Darrow, came to speak at union rallies. The tension was extreme and finally exploded into tragedy during the holiday season. On Christmas eve day, 1913, more than 400 miners' children were attending a party in the upper floor of the Italian Hall when someone yelled, "Fire!" In a frenzy, the crowd rushed down the long stairs, failed to pass through the inward-opening door and piled in a heap in the stairwell. Sixty-two children and eleven adults died of suffocation in the resultant crush. *There had been no fire.* My mother remembers watching the long sad funeral cortege winding its way through the center of the village; with the horse-drawn hearses holding large coffins, and small ones carried by grieving miners, the procession moved slowly toward Lakeview Cemetery. Although the strike ended in April, 1914, the community in some ways never recovered from the strife and tragedy.

Many other mines were opened in the region during the boom copper era: Minesota, Mohawk, Ahmeek Seneca, Kearsarge, and many others. On reflection, the activity in the Copper Country during the last half of the 19th century was fantastic. Consider the statistics: 11,000 miles of tunnel dug, 10 billion pounds of copper removed; over 400 million dollars in dividends were paid. And yet despite all this effort, there is today little visible evidence of the mining activities which dominated land and life in the Copper Country. An abandoned shaft house, piles of waste rock, remains of old stamping mills, remnants of villages — they merely enhance the mystery, romance and incredible beauty of the region.

I find myself drawn to the Copper Country not only because my roots are there but also because of the surcease I feel when I contemplate its rugged charm. When scenery was handed out, the Keweenaw Peninsula must have been at the head of the line. Its shoreline, particularly the stretch between Eagle River and Copper Harbor, is incomparable; between Eagle Harbor and Copper Harbor are the starkly beautiful Brockway Mountains; rivers — the Montreal, Gratiot, Silver — surge down narrow gorges, tumbling and foaming toward Lake Superior. Located at the very tip of the Peninsula is the Estivant Pines, a tract of huge virgin white pines, with one leaning giant measuring seven feet in diameter. Dotting the region are tranquil granite-ringed inland lakes — Medora, Lac la

Belle, Gratiot, and others; dominating the landscape are trees, maples, oaks, birches, row upon row of pines. In autumn, leaf-lookers are drawn to the Copper Country from great distances to partake of the color display.

The copper industry slumbers now — only an underground mine at White Pine near the foothills of the Porcupine Mountains continued until recently to produce the red metal — but the people wait and continue to hope that a new discovery will someday bring back the glory days of the Copper Country.

A GRAND ISLAND TREK

*T*he tree branches embraced above the ancient dirt road creating a leafy tunnel as we trudged toward the circle of blue ahead. Spiraling down from the steep North Light escarpment, we emerged suddenly upon a magnificent sweep of sand beach; Lake Superior danced and sparkled in the late summer sun. We all felt that exhilaration described so well by John Burroughs: When they approach a beach, all humans beings seem to emerge into a larger, more primitive space; it is like standing in the open door of a continent.

The immaculate white sand extended for nearly a mile; a small clear stream, the North Light Creek, divides it almost exactly into two equal segments. Gnarled silvered driftwood dotted the beach artistically. Sheer sandstone cliffs rising like surrealistic pink and buff towers from the lake, guarded each end of the sandy oasis. To the west, we could see the very tip of the North Lighthouse through the dense forest atop the cliffs. By the time Randy and I had completed a survey and selected sites for the two small tents, Lynn and Jane were busy picking high bush blueberries under the hemlocks where the woods bordered the beach. Spirits were high — under our own power and carrying our home on our backs, we had reached this beautiful timeless spot.

Grand Island sits like a large emerald on Lake Superior. Separated from the mainland and the city of Munising (*Kitchi-minissing,* place of the Great Island in Chippewa) by a narrow strait, it buffers the roll of Lake Superior and creates a deep well-protected harbor. Unlike Mackinac Island, the historic resort in Upper Lake Huron, and Michigan's famous wilderness national park, Isle Royale, few people are acquainted with this largest island on the south shore of Lake Superior. It is truly a *grand* island. Shaped like an open hand — with the thumb extended toward the east — Grand Island is approximately eight miles long from north to south, and three miles across at the widest point. Its 13,500 acres are heavily forested with hemlock and mixed northern hardwoods; some of the most

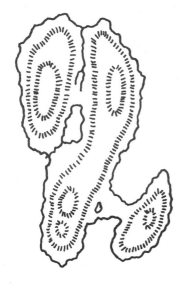

extensive stands of beech in the Upper Peninsula are located here. In addition to small streams and ponds, there are two quiet lakes on the island. The larger, Echo Lake, is situated in the center of the "hand." A mile long and half a mile wide, the lake was created by a giant beaver dam. Duck Lake is located near where the "thumb" joins the main mass of the island.

High cliffs of sandstone rim most of Grand Island; sculptured by waves and weather for eons, they are of the same geological formation as the fabled Pictured Rocks a few miles to the east. On the island's highest point, three hundred feet above Lake Superior, the federal government established a lighthouse in 1856; at 750 feet above sea level, it is the highest lighthouse in the United States. Another lighthouse was built on the East Channel in 1869 to provide easy navigation into the harbor. The area around Grand Island has been a hazard for ships; a total of 29 vessels were lost here from 1829 to 1973.

As we sat around a crackling driftwood fire on the remote north beach, we wondered aloud if others had shared this lovely campsite long before us. The Native Americans had permanent dwellings on the island years before the French adventurers and priests explored the south shore of Lake Superior. The Chippewa call Grand Island *kitchi-miniss* which means Great Island and expressed great reverence for their home. According to Chippewa legend, the island was created by the Great Spirit, *Kitchi-Manito.* The Great Spirit fashioned several large creatures to amuse Himself but then, fearing they might be more powerful than Himself if he gave them life, He placed them around the harbor, forming the hills which surround the present city of Munising. *Kitchi-Manito* cast one of the huge creatures into the lake where it became Grand Island, a sleeping giant; nearby Wood and Williams Islands are its hands rising above the water of the lake.

The Native Americans lived in harmony with the land, fishing, hunting and gathering wild foods.* They understood intuitively that nature's resources were renewable because they considered themselves as one with all wild creatures; the native hunters were careful to always leave enough animals and plants to replace what they had taken. A way of life honed by centuries of adaptation changed forever when the French and English explorers discovered that the north country contained fabulous wealth in furs.

*See Loren R. Graham, *A Face In The Rock*

The French came first — Radisson, Allouez, Marquette, Joliet and many other adventurers and priests camped on the shores of Grand Island long before the American Revolution. Early maps of the region clearly depict the island and show that the French adopted the Chippewa name, calling it "Les Grandes Isles." The island was a vital link in the burgeoning fur trade from the 1600s well into the 19th century. The French, the English and finally the United States established posts here or on the mainland close by.

Unable to sleep that night, I crept from the tent, stoked the fire and sat quietly thinking about the flamboyant romantic era of the fur trade. Between May 2, 1670, when the Hudson's Bay Company was formed, and the mid-1800s when fur bearing animals were nearly extinct, an enormous quantity of pelts flowed out of the midwest and northwest. Ernest Seton estimated the total number of fur pelts at 60 million! In the two decades between 1853 and 1877, almost at the end of the fur trading era, three million pelts were harvested.

I tried to picture the small tireless men who transported the bales of fur across the endless reaches of the north country. What a romantic figure is the *voyageur!* The voyageurs were hired canoemen, mostly of French-Canadian extraction, who thrived on the adversity and adventure of the wilderness waterways. Mile after mile, for as many as 15 hours a day, they traversed the lakes and streams, eyes narrowed from scanning the sun-drenched horizon, red paddles flashing in the light, singing gaily. They lived on soups, dried corn and pork, carried enormous loads — at a trot — over portages and slept on the ground under their canoes. Why did they sign on to the crews again and again? Certainly not for fame and fortune. It must have been the adventure and the lifting sense of freedom which comes when one immerses himself in a wild and primitive environment with none of civilization's rules to follow and only himself to depend upon. The voyageurs lived their hard life with gusto.

But the Indian lost his unique way of life as well as his independence during the fur trading epoch. Encouraged by white men eager for fast profit, the Native American ignored his own values and trapped *every* beaver from a colony. Gradually, insidiously, he became ever more dependent upon the materials of the trader — food stuffs, clothing, implements, guns. The last trading post at Grand Island was built by a pioneer whose name and personal industry left a permanent imprint on the island.

As we scanned the map for the second day's hike, we noted frequent references to the name Williams — Williams Island, William's Landing, William's Hotel. Abraham Warren Williams, the first permanent white resident of the island, was born in 1792 in Burlington County, Vermont. He first came to the Lake Superior country in 1818 when he fished for lake trout and whitefish off Whitefish Point. Later he drifted down to Illinois where he farmed for several years. He must have been drawn back to the Upper Peninsula, however, for in 1840 he sold the farm and brought his family to Sault Ste. Marie. The Sault was a rough frontier town at that time, no place to raise children, so when *Omonomonee*, chief of the Grand Island Indians invited him to establish a trading post and live on the island, Williams accepted swiftly. On July 30, 1840, the Williams family arrived at Grand Island aboard the schooner, *Mary Elizabeth*.

Williams set to work immediately. A man of prodigious energy and ingenuity, he built a warehouse, log cabins for travelers, a stockade and a large home for himself. He ran a trading post, farmed and raised 12 children. The values of hard work, diligence and self-reliance were shared by other pioneers — miners, loggers, fishermen — immigrating to the Upper Peninsula, and to a remarkable degree, are still extant in contemporary residents. Mr. Williams was also a fiercely proud and independent man. On one occasion two of his sons were sent to Marquette (two days to the west by rowboat) for supplies. Thankful for the business, the merchant included a gift pair of shoes for his customer. Williams thought he was being patronized and sent his weary sons rowing right back to Marquette with the shoes and a note that he neither accepted nor gave gifts.

Williams died on April 21, 1873, and lies buried beside his wife in the Williams-Powell family cemetery on the island. A simple weathered stone shaped like a gothic church window and inscribed with his name, the dates of his birth and death, and the Masonic insignia marks his grave. Ferns and bunchberry grow in the small cemetery and, on the afternoon we stopped to pay our respects to the old pioneer, a gentle wind was rustling the pine needles overhead.

While we waited by the shore for the chartered boat to take us back to the mainland, we watched the barge *Timber Queen* come into the pier at Williams Landing. The barge and almost all of the island were owned by the Cleveland-Cliffs Iron Company (C.C.I.). At the turn of the present century, C.C.I. purchased Grand Island from descendants of the Williams family for $93,000. The president of the company, William Mather, a direct descendant of the famous colonial preacher, Cotton Mather, constructed a game preserve and imported elk, moose, caribou, antelope and other species of wildlife. The old Williams home was restored and converted to a small hotel; a few years later the hotel was expanded to accommodate 150 guests. The Inn continued operation as a fashionable summer resort until 1958.

Until the late 1980s, Cleveland-Cliffs owned almost all of Grand Island (portions were leased to several families who maintain summer homes). The Company had been a good steward of the land and much of the island remains as it was for centuries. The exotic game species died off or fled across the ice to the mainland but the island supports bear, deer, many kinds of small mammals, fish and birds.

Since we took that first backpacking trek on Grand Island with Jane and Randy almost 25 years ago, we have returned often to hike, bike and look for birds. Happily, *the island now belongs to all of us.* In 1990, Congress authorized the purchase of the island and directed the U.S. Forest Service to prepare a management plan which would ensure the "preservation and protection of Grand Island while allowing for a range of recreation and economic opportunities."

At times it seemed almost an impossible task to create a plan for the new Grand Island National Recreation Area that would please everyone. Finally, the decision was made to combine elements from several alternatives. Under the compromise plan, there will be limited development — confined for the most part to the southern part of the island — and protection for many of the natural features unique to Grand Island. With the exception of an extant road leading to the north beach, motorized travel, including public transportation, will be limited to the southern tier of the island. Campgrounds, a small lodge (20 rooms) and restaurant (serving 30 persons) will also be located in the southern portion.

Grand Island National Recreation Area: A remarkable, beautiful island gem on the south shore of Lake Superior. A visit here promises adventures in a natural setting, providing a link through time with earlier island travelers and settlers whose lives no longer will seem so remote, so alien to our own.

—•—

A   S Y L V A N I A   D I A R Y

*I*n 1966, the Ottawa National Forest acquired a large tract of land in the western Upper Peninsula. Close to the border with northern Wisconsin, the area is dotted with lakes and the Forest Service intended to create a canoe camping wilderness. As long time aficionados of canoe travel, we could hardly contain our eagerness to explore Sylvania. Our first sojourn to Sylvania in 1973 is captured in my diary of the trip:

May 23

The long awaited letter from the Forest Service finally arrived! Although our excursion was a couple of months away, we were anxious to learn more about Sylvania, the newly acquired national recreation wilderness canoe area. Eagerly we tore open the envelope and scanned the short message:

Thank you for your inquiry regarding the Sylvania Recreation Area. As you may know, Sylvania is part of the Ottawa National Forest and is a unique region of many undeveloped lakes. Camping is primitive (and by permit only) and travel within most of the area is limited to canoe or other non-motorized means.

Regarding rentals, please be advised that there are a few outfitters in the local area. You may write to the Chamber of Commerce in Watersmeet to obtain listings; supplies are available at nearby towns such as Watersmeet and Land O' Lakes.

A brochure describing Sylvania and a map of the area are enclosed. If we can be of further service in this regard, please do not hesitate to write.

June 9.

After studying the Sylvania brochure and a map of the Ottawa National Forest, I wrote again to the district ranger inquiring about the history, size and vegetation of the area. His detailed reply came swiftly:

The size of the area is 18,325 acres and the United States Forest Service purchased it in July, 1966, for $5,740,000.

Originally the land was owned by timber and mining companies, plus a few homesteaders. In the early 1900s the land was bought by officials of the United States Steel Corporation for an exclusive hunting and fishing club they called Sylvania. Their shares were later acquired by heirs of the estate of William Ellis Corey, U.S. Steel President from 1903-1911, and William Boyce Thompson, a copper magnate whose son-in-law, Anthony Drexel Biddle, Jr., was Ambassador to Poland.

There are 36 named lakes in the area and when the Forest Service acquired the tract there were twenty-six buildings consisting of lodges, boathouses and guard quarters. All of them except the Thompson Lodge at the south end of Clark Lake have been removed.

The timber is northern hardwood forest consisting of sugar maple, yellow birch and hemlock. Some pine logging took place in 1880 between Whitefish and Loon Lakes where the stands were heavy. In the fall of 1949 considerable damage was caused by high winds; some of the down timber was removed but this, to our knowledge, was the only logging done since 1901.

August 9.

All the gear is stowed in the car ready for an early morning departure. Just checked the road map again; the best entry to Sylvania is from U.S. Highway #2; four miles west of Watersmeet we'll turn south on the Thousand Island Lake Road. We feel the familiar urge to jump in the car and take off right away now that all the planning and preparation are complete. My psychologist colleagues put it more formally — the closer an individual is to his goal, the faster he tends to move!

August 10.

We stopped at the Visitor Information Center located near Clark Lake to obtain a camping permit. After some study of their giant wooden map, we chose Loon campsite on Loon Lake.

Within minutes we're paddling down Clark Lake in our wood and canvas canoe. The water is so smooth, vividly reflecting the heavily wooded shores, that we hesitate to plunge our paddles into its surface. A gentle stroke sends cascades of sparkling drops skittering along the still water like diamonds on a black velvet tray. The canoe seems to glide effortlessly, leaving cares far behind.

The children are trailing their dolls (now somewhat soggy) in the water and I have just paused for the traditional voyageur's pipe rest after nearly an hour of paddling. What a sweep of blue water with no cottages, power boats and water skiers in view! Any type of self-propelled craft is permitted (motors are allowed only on Crooked, Big Bateau and Long Lakes) and we have seen rowboats, small sailing craft, and even one raft that looked a bit like the Kon Tiki.

Over the portage from Clark into Loon Lake. What a breeze — only 30 rods. This had been a short carry but we knew that the longer portages have welcome places to rest with a bar to balance the canoe. The French voyageurs who transported furs throughout the north country called these places *poses* or "places of deposit," where they dumped their two or more 90 pound packs upon the hard-packed trails and rested. A neophyte canoe camper also traveling the trail lamented that he despised portaging, yet I like the freedom of portability. I'm no masochist. Carrying a canoe on my shoulders is not necessarily high on my list of fun things to do, but the essence of traveling this primitive, historic way is the fact that you can tote your transportation over to the next pond and thus leave the crowd behind.

We found our campsite with no trouble and spent the rest of the afternoon setting up camp and gathering downed deadwood for an evening fire. The Forest Service has done an excellent job of locating the campgrounds near, but not on, the shore of the lakes; this tends to preserve the wilderness character of the area. From the lakes, the only sign of human habitation are canoes drawn up on shore and small brown campsite signs at water's edge. Each campground has three sites spaced sufficiently far apart to ensure privacy. Shortly after we finished a magnificent meal of freeze-dried chili, fruit and pan biscuits, another family paddled in. I think they are just as disappointed as we are not to be camping alone, but we seem to have negotiated a mutual, though unspoken, agreement not to impinge upon one another.

Just about dark now, the fire glows cheerfully, and our twin daughters swap stories. All our food is in a large stuff bag dangling from a sturdy limb of a red pine tree far from our tents. Black bears are plentiful in Sylvania and the camper should be scrupulously clean in meal preparation and dispose of all residue by burning whatever possible and carrying out the rest.

August 11.

A beautiful quiet summer morning. Hey, those are fish jumping out in the lake. Gulping our breakfast, we headed out to troll and cast (only artificial bait is permitted) around the coves. Due to the previous inaccessibility of these lakes for fishing, an extraordinary fish population developed. Most fish, though relatively large, are quite old. Fish populations are similar to what might have been found in the western Upper Peninsula by the first white man; the lakes contains bass, trout, northern pike, perch and sunfish. We checked the regulations carefully because on some lakes fishing is for trophy-sized fish only and on other lakes, just for fun — no keeping the catch, not even the big ones. We had several strikes, but caught no fish.

The quiet is shattered. Late this morning, Ralph and Frank, two mongrel dogs, exploded into the campground with their "parents." Ralph is black and white and surly; Frank is brown and aggressively friendly. Their owners, a young couple, are loud and uncouth. When we finally asked that the dogs be leashed as the rules plainly require in Sylvania, the owners were dumfounded that we did not enjoy the playful antics of their pets. Ralph and Frank were just then howling after a chipmunk my children had befriended, stopping in their wild chase only to adorn bushes, trees and picnic tables with liquid mementos. Assuring us that their dogs were "like members of the family," the rude pair proceeded to prove it by peeling a birch tree to kindle their fire. Incredulous, we retreated.

There has been in the past few years a veritable explosion of dogs on the forest trails; apparently more and more couples, particularly young ones, are hiking with "me and you and a dog named Boo," instead of having children. I like dogs, too, but not when they limit my enjoyment of seeing wildlife; I dislike hearing pets bark and whine when I want to listen to natural sounds; I cannot abide being challenged by a formidable St. Bernard or German Shepard on a wilderness trail; it bothers me to worry about where my children can walk and play without being fouled with canine excrement. I think the answer is common courtesy: people should keep their pets under control. The alternative will be to limit the entry of dogs into wilderness areas and on hiking trails.

Later, we were further outraged to witness the boorish couple troop to the lake and use its clear waters for a personal bathtub — complete with soap and shampoo! As calmly as I could, I pointed out that it is better to take water from the lake, bathe and then dump the waste water on land where it can be filtered and cleansed back through the earth. The couple responded laconically that it was a big lake. When I asked what would happen to the water quality if every visitor to Sylvania used the lake like that, they shrugged arrogantly and went back to their ablutions. What better illustration of the "tragedy of the commons," the notion that *my* little bit of litter or abuse of the environment does not matter.

The lakes in Sylvania do have exceptional water quality; the chemical character of many of the lakes is similar to that of rain water. We found that it is sometimes possible to see the bottom — particularly of High and Mountain Lakes — in as much as 30 feet of water. These conditions occur primarily because portions of these lakes sit on the Mississippi-Lake Superior divide with no inlets to supply nutrient matter. Recognizing the possibility of serious damage to a unique ecosystem, the Forest Service makes the plea in the Sylvania brochure:

It is important that those who use Sylvania today treat it with utmost care. If they do not they may destroy its fragile character and deny its beauties to others who will follow them.

To save our psyches further damage, we took the canoe and paddled back to Clark Lake for a refreshing swim. Late that evening, revenge was ours, for Ralph (or was it Frank?) neglected to leave the tent for his nightly needs. This caused much distress for the dog owners and much amusement for us.

August 12.

Got up early and stole quietly down to the rocky shore in time to watch the mists rising from the waters. A loon laughed querulously from the far shore and the call echoed and re-echoed across the lake; no other sound is so in keeping with wilderness waterways.

The neighbors, with Ralph and Frank, and one soggy tent left at midmorning. Sylvania is once more soothingly still.

We are settling in. It generally takes two days or so to drop the cares and preoccupations of our workaday world — "to sit," as Colin Fletcher says, "and think that it is nice to sit and think about nothing at all." In preparation for our trip we read about the Ely canoe country. Sigurd Olson, who has lived on the edge of the Boundary Waters Canoe Area in northeastern Minnesota for many years and guided throughout the area, has written several books which make the north country come alive. From the pages of *Listening Point*, *Runes of the North*, *The Lonely Land* and especially *The Singing Wilderness*, the woods and waters, the wildlife and the portages seem like familiar places, already enjoyed.

We also explored a bit. Portaged 42 rods into Deer Island Lake — our favorite so far — and fished along its bays and lovely pine-covered points with no luck. We were reminded of the remark made by Mrs. Lyndon B. Johnson at the dedication of Sylvania: "What a magnificent part of the world this is!"

August 13.

Our last day. Reluctantly, we loaded our canoe and paddled up Loon Lake, then found the portage once again into Clark Lake. Leaving our canoe safely beached, we hiked over to inspect the famous Thompson Lodge, the only one of the original structures still standing. (Note: several years later, before it could be moved, it burned to the ground). It is immense! I quote from the Forest Service folder:

This magnificent lodge was built as a summer home by William Boyce Thompson, a copper magnate from Colorado, and one of the original owners of Sylvania. Construction of the lodge, of Swiss Chalet design, started during the early months of 1930. However, in the spring of 1930, Mr. Thompson died. Work continued on the building and it was completed in August of 1930. Elaborate furnishings were moved into the building at that time but the Lodge was never occupied as a living quarters. The lodge is 212 feet long and contains 25 rooms, including 16 bedrooms and a large indoor tennis court. Western red cedar logs, all carefully selected, were used to construct the exterior; these logs, all hand hewn, were set in place by expert craftsmen from Minnesota.

We walked around the impressive structure and peered in the windows. It is grand, opulent and certainly reflects the era of the super rich: While many suffered during the Great Depression, here was conspicuous consumption at its zenith. We could only wonder as we gazed at the huge log structure how many Colorado hills and mountains, how many clear streams and lakes were permanently damaged by the copper mining that enabled one man to indulge his wealthy whims.

As we paddled slowly up the long sweep of Clark Lake, I reflected on our canoeing adventure. After several excursions to northeastern Minnesota, I had been a bit skeptical of what Sylvania might have to offer; there was, in my mind, only one canoe country, the Quetico-Superior or Boundary Waters Canoe Area. Even so I had been impressed with what I had seen. All those, like ourselves, who find enjoyment and recreation in gliding silently down a tree-rimmed lake and scanning a shoreline with no cottages, docks, power lines or cleared lots are fortunate indeed that this unique place has been dedicated to wilderness adventures.

Postscript. In 1987, Sylvania was accorded wilderness status under the Michigan Wilderness Act. In a very recent ruling, only small electric motors will be allowed on Crooked and Big Bateau Lakes, two lakes which border the Sylvania Wilderness. The lovely lakes and the remnants of old growth forest still abide.

T H E   S U M M E R ' S   B O U N T Y

y hike this evening through an old pasture near my home brought an exciting and unusual discovery. During my short ramble, I was surprised and delighted to find three different wild fruits already ripened: a few juicy wild strawberries lingering on the shaded north slopes; a handful of red raspberries along the edges of an ancient farm lane; and, close beside a pile of stones at the far south side of the abandoned pasture, seven low bush blueberries. It's only July 1 but the annual bounty of wild fruit is already beginning.

July was the Moon of the Sweet Berries for the Indian tribes of the Superior Peninsula and many modern residents abandon all other pursuits and pleasures of summer to gather the delicious wild fruits. In fruitful succession, strawberries, raspberries, thimbleberries and blueberries appear, almost miraculously all over the region. Then, in late August, large succulent blackberries begin to ripen, wild apples assume a reddish hue and rose hips swell. It is like a sweet summer symphony — form, progression, beauty, all the proper ingredients are present.

Gathering berries from the wild food chain creates a living link between ourselves and our forebears, it reminds us of our roots in a real and vivid way. For eons humans lived on nature's bounty and when we pick edible food in the wilds it fulfills an urge to forage which lies buried beneath a shallow veneer of modern sophistication. Picking wild berries and concocting pies and jams from them creates a sense of personal accomplishment that plucking items off the shelves in a climate-controlled, neon-lit supermarket can never match.

The gathering season begins in June when we search the fields for the tiny red fruit of *Fragaria virginiana*, the wild strawberry. Although the plants may grow in most any open area, we find them often in poor or sandy soil. During our hikes in May, we look for the three-leaved plants with the pretty white blossoms and mark their location carefully. I am not very good at *picking* strawberries; I cannot resist sampling too many of the sweet, juicy morsels while they are warm from the early summer sun. Often I find myself simply sitting among the plants smelling the delicious aroma of ripe berries and enjoying the hum of life in the lush green meadows. June is the month of vibrant, unlimited growth and life is proceeding on all sides at full tilt. Hawkweed, daisies and clover bloom extravagantly. Bobolinks, vesper sparrows and meadowlarks sing continuously. It is a fitting time to celebrate life.

The Native Americans of this region did, in fact, hold a strawberry thanksgiving ceremony, a festival to fete the first fruit of the year. Although our own ceremony is more modest, we too herald the ripening of the wild strawberries. Returning home with our sweet treasures, we prepare small turnovers; after the pastries have cooled we climb a nearby high granite peak and savor the dessert as we watch the setting sun. Then we begin thinking of the next wild berry that will ripen.

Soon after our family strawberry festival, we sally forth to find our favorite wild fruit, red raspberries. This delightful species of *Rubus* grows on prickly canes in thick stands along old woods roads, under powerlines and around the edges of clearings or old pastures. One winter I searched through several weighty tomes in an effort to learn more about this tasteful fruit. Astonishingly, botanical authorities were not even sure where the name "raspberry" came from; one scholar traced the origin of the word all the way back to 1290 A.D. when the delicious fruit was apparently called "raspeium." No matter, a handful of ripe red raspberries on a warm July afternoon would taste as sweet by any name. Interestingly, experts maintain that raspberries are not really true berries. They are, rather, aggregate clusters of droplets, each with its own seed surrounded by succulent pulp. Amen for the succulent.

Although we are secretive about the location of all our favorite berry patches, we are especially security conscious when it comes to our raspberry picking sites. We approach them slowly, carefully, making certain that no one has spotted us turn off the highway onto the old dirt road or fire lanes. If anyone dares to ask where we pick berries, a gross impropriety among berry-picking enthusiasts, we provide only vague directions. "South of town" is a favorite explanation.

Raspberries are a bit more difficult to pick than other wild fruits. In order to retrieve the really good berries, the picker has to actually immerse himself in the prickly canes — and then he has no difficulty at all understanding why they are called *rasp*berries.

The best, the ripest, the largest berries are always hidden beneath the canopy of leaves. I find that picking raspberries evokes the glutton in me; I cannot resist the urge to try to get *all* the berries, to keep on picking just one more berry. And another. There is also frustration. Only those who have searched among the tall canes for ripe raspberries know the agony of having a large berry drop off just as your fingers are about to close around it.

Birds, chipmunks and squirrels often are gathering berries in the same patch; on one memorable occasion, a large black bear and I were picking almost from the same cane. A few seconds before seeing the bruin I detected his distinctive fetid odor, and then his shaggy black head and small pig eyes appeared over the bushes. We both beat a hasty retreat . . . and I am proud to relate that I didn't drop a single berry from my pail. A more frequent hazard when picking raspberries is stepping upon the nests of yellow jackets and bumblebees which have been built beneath the thick tangles.

But the delicious rewards are more than worth the possible hazards: pies, short-cakes, tarts and jam delight our taste as well as our souls. A goodly supply of the red fruit goes into the freezer; then on a cold day in January, we savor a dish of red raspberries or warm raspberry pie and remember the long summer days when we gathered them.

Another member of the *Rubus* genus, the thimbleberry *(Rubus parviflorus)* is unique to the north country, growing only in the Upper Great Lakes region (a related species is found in the Rocky Mountains, British Columbia and Alaska where it is known as the salmonberry). Like other members of the large raspberry clan, thimbleberries grow in new clearings, along woods roads, old railroad grades and under power lines. The plants are tall — 4 to 6 feet — and rather handsome; they grow in veritable tangles or thickets but are not as prickly as raspberry canes. The foliage resembles large maple leaves with smooth tops and furry bottoms and may measure as much as eight inches across. They turn a distinctive pale yellow hue in autumn.

The thimbleberry plant flowers in June and may continue into July; it features a large white flower, generally in groups of two or more. As the name suggests, the fruit resembles a small red thimble. Although it looks like a raspberry, its taste is quite unusual — my daughters say they taste like moist, furry raspberries. I think they taste like, well, only like thimbleberries. As thimbleberries are pulled from the plant they tend to squish at the touch. The local saying is that no one ever picks a full pail of thimbleberries, they just keep sinking in the container. Many oldtime thimbleberry pickers use flat, shallow pie pans to collect their favorite fruit.

But, oh, the jam they make! All one does is combine equal quantities of berries (but don't wash them for all that will be left is red, watery mush) and sugar; bring to a boil for a moment or two, pour into jars and seal with paraffin. The morning toast in February will take on special delight when spread liberally with thimbleberry jam.

The most prolific and most sought after berry, though, and the one symbolic of the north, is the blueberry. The Peninsula is blueberry country and the plant is found in great abundance. In fact it is so common here that, until a few decades ago, the local railroads offered special day trains to and from the best blueberry picking areas. The blueberry is a hardy plant — experts distinguish 35 separate species — and grows in well-drained, acid soil. The plants are found in almost any area of the north but grow abundantly in logged areas, recently burned forests and almost everywhere in the sandy jack pine barrens. We have two main varieties, the low bush which ripens early and the high bush which continues to bear fruit into late August. The darker huckleberries grow among the blueberries and are an added bonus for the picker.

The small fruit with the powder blue bloom is my twin daughters' favorite berry to pick. Sitting in a patch when they were younger, they pretended to be Indian maidens and as they filled their buckets they sang songs and chanted back and forth to each other. It is one of summer's simple pleasures to hear the berries drum into a metal container and to watch the blue mound grow. To me, blueberries are the very essence of a northern summer: the small sweet morsels remind me of accumulated sunshine, nature's little blue beads of delicious warmth. Anyone who has enjoyed wild blueberry pancakes, muffins, pies or tarts knows what I mean.

Near the shank end of summer, when the birches are already showing tints of their autumnal brilliance and platoons of goldenrod wave triumphantly along the edge of every meadow, the oblong juicy blackberries ripen (it is the only berry that is red when it is "green"). The blackberry picker is presented with a formidable tangle of tall spiny canes; *Rubus alleheinsis* grows in thick, near-impenetrable thickets. I have a secret patch quite close to my home which I have savored for over a decade. From it I have picked many quarts of blackberries for pies, jams, breakfast fruit and other late summer delights. Last season someone else found "my" patch and, as if discovery were not enough, they committed an outrageous violation: they drove a car through the patch, knocked down the canes and left three discarded beer cans. Obviously no true appreciation of blackberries.

From the blackberries we gather, we also make two Cornish beverages: a non-alcoholic shrub and a tasty wine. For blackberry shrub, take the juice from a quart of berries, add pale gingerale, sweeten to taste. For an added touch, freeze a single blackberry in each ice cube and serve one cube in each glass.

The wine recipe was vouchsafed to me by my grandfather. Take three quarts of blackberries, three quarts of water and four pounds of sugar; add 1 1/2 tablespoons of yeast. Let the mixture "work" for about a week and then bottle and age the brew for at least six months. Stand back when opening.

There is, of course, much more on the natural smorgasbord of summer. We gather choke and black cherries for jelly; mint and goldenrod are selected and dried to make delicate teas; a supply of rose hips, a rich source of Vitamin C, is gathered for combining with apples and grapes to make jelly. Acorns, when crushed and leached of their bitter substance, make a very tasty and healthful bread.

One year we prepared several jars of wild fruit jam and jelly to give to relatives and friends as Christmas presents. The reactions we received were, to put it mildly, very interesting. Some persons were bemused ("Wild cherry and rose hip jelly?"), a few were obviously insulted to be given a present which was "homemade." The latter seemed to believe that a item purchased in a store, a gift processed and perhaps even wrapped by machines, was somehow superior, as though the expenditure of money reflected greater consideration. Older persons could still remember when all their Christmas presents were homemade and they were clearly touched and warmed by our gifts from the summer's bounty. Some of my students and other young people who are searching for more natural life styles were also pleased by our gifts and sought the recipes so that they might prolong the experience. They sensed that presents made by hand bear the signature of the human spirit; they knew that the jams had the mark of life whereas mass-produced merchandise, while attractive in a gaudy way, is interchangeable and gives little of the personal touch.

Gathering wild foods helps us to feel closer to the natural world, it increases our rapport with what is real. Picking one's own food is like chopping one's own wood — it fuels our bodies and more importantly, nourishes our spirits. It reminds us also that food comes always from the earth, not from the supermarket. Summer's bounty here in the Superior Peninsula provides a many splendored feast.

G H O S T   T O W N S

*L*onely, silent, crumbling, they bear only a shadowy resemblance to their former existence. Deserted logging camps, abandoned farms, weed-choked old railways, ghostly mining towns — there are no places in the Superior Peninsula quite so nostalgic. Walking quietly among the weathered remnants, memories of oldtime residents crowd in and cast a lingering spell, an eerie feeling that phantoms of former dwellers still inhabit the ruins. All about are poignant reminders of the hopes and dreams of the departed pioneers. When I pause on the silent streets of a deserted town, or rest against a piece of rusting machinery on an abandoned farm, I often wonder if the people who lived there shared my affection for the region. Like John Donne, "I long to talk to some old lover's ghost."

Several cycles of boom and bust swept across the Peninsula; scores of dwellings and diggings were abandoned throughout the area. The deserted spots range in size from a small log cabin in an old clearing to rather large copper mining communities. In almost any part of the vast forest which carpets the north country, an observant hiker can find the site of an old logging camp; the signs are a clearing, remnants of log homes, discarded tools and huge weathered stumps. Also hidden among the pines and granite knobs of my home county of Marquette are abandoned gold mines which offer the additional lure of imagined wealth still secreted in some unexplored rocky redoubt.

The Holyoke, Ropes and Kreig claims were, around the turn of the present century, active gold and silver mines. Julius Ropes began searching for wealth north of Ishpeming in 1881 and, in one month of digging, recovered $700 in gold and $900 in silver. Only six years later his annual yield of the precious metals totaled over forty thousand dollars. However, the fabulous mother lode of which he dreamed was not found and in 1897 the mine was closed. A winding sand road through the forest leads the modern explorer to the water-filled mine shaft and the ruins of several structures. The Kreig family failed to unearth enough gold to continue their mining operations in the hills north of Marquette. All that remains of their labors is a horizontal shaft sunk 120 feet into a hillside of solid rock, another shallow hole filled with dark water and decaying vegetation, and a few pieces of rusty broken machinery.

Very little remains of a 35 mile railroad from the village of Champion to the mouth of the Huron River on Lake Superior. Built at great expense and requiring an enormous amount of human labor — it went through perhaps the wildest portion of the Peninsula and created a seven mile rock cut through sixty foot high granite cliffs — it never carried the ore and slate dreamed of by its developer. Milo Davis created the Iron Range and Huron Mountain Railroad in 1890; he raised two million dollars for the ill-fated project and built a huge wooden dock on Lake Superior in anticipation of shipping iron ore and other products. When, after several delays and spiraling expenses the railway was finally ready, they fired up the steam locomotive and commenced the maiden ride. The railroad bed gave way after only a short distance and the new engine tumbled ignominiously into a deep ditch. Fortunately, much more remains of the communities which flourished around the fabulous Keweenaw copper mines.

The majority of the Superior Peninsula's ghost towns are located in the Copper Country and most owe their origins to the mining of the plentiful red metal. Bete Grise, Delaware, Mandan, Wyoming, Phoenix, Gay — the names reflect the great expectations which the early mining companies had in every discovery of native copper. In each instance a community sprung up, homes, schools and churches were built, a company store erected and stocked with the belief that the rich ore would last forever and a day. I return often to one particular Copper Country ghost town, Central Mine, for it was there that my maternal ancestors chiseled a livelihood and a heritage from the ancient copper-bearing rock.

Central Mine is located in Keweenaw County, the northern-most tip of the copper-laden peninsula which juts far out into the waters of Lake Superior. Keweenaw County lies closer to the North Pole than does Quebec, Canada, and has an average annual snowfall of 265 inches. Although it is the least populous county in the State of Michigan and has the smallest county seat, Eagle River, it has the longest, most beautiful shoreline — eighty-four miles of high cliffs, pebbled beaches and tall sand dunes. The ghost town drowses on the southeastern slope of the greenstone ridge which extends the full length of the Keweenaw Peninsula; the site commands a magnificent view of Mt. Bohemia and Mt. Houghton almost twelve miles away near the shore of Lake Superior. Almost directly south of Central an Air Force radar base used to crouch ominously atop Mt. Horace

Greeley, an anachronistic reminder of the uncertainties of this more modern world.

No one knows for sure why the mining community was called Central, although it may have been because it was located between two older mines, the Winthrop and the Northwestern. A small impoundment and a rushing stream also bear the name Central. A wooden sign along U.S. Highway 41 tersely describes the origins of the village:

> In 1854 heavy masses of native copper were discovered in the bottom of an ancient pit dug by prehistoric miners. In November of that year the Central Mining Company was organized. A rich ore body was soon opened which had produced a total of $9,770,528 by July, 1898, when the property was finally abandoned. Until the Kearsarge Lode was discovered in the 1890s, the Central Mine was the biggest and most profitable producer in the Keweenaw District. At one time the population reached a total of approximately 1,250 people and reunions of former residents are held here annually.

It was difficult to imagine a busy mining town on the gloomy late summer day when I first visited Central. Dark clouds hung low over the hills and a fine mist coated the tall grass and made the leaves slick and shiny. The empty streets, the unpainted houses, the crumbled ruins of the old pump house, the huge pile of gray waste rock all created a somber mood. Pausing by one of the old houses. I inspected it carefully. At the height of the mining operation, around 1876, there were over 200 homes; most are gone now and only the stone foundations mark where they stood. Of those that remain, the majority are owned or rented by summer tenants. Despite its 100 years, this one looks to be in remarkable condition. Built of fine white pine lumber by the mining company it is a tall, two-story rectangular structure; in addition to a front porch, there is a large kitchen attached to the rear of the home. The foundation is sturdily built of native stone. There are two yellow brick chimneys, one in the main portion of the house and one in the rear kitchen. Clumps of lilacs now crowd close, almost protectively, near the porch and along one side of the old home. Several ancient apple trees, one still bearing fruit, grow behind the house.

I walked up a steep hill to the vast pile of waste rock and searched for an overlooked fragment of copper or a small piece of greenstone to keep as a memento. Finding none, I put my pack on a large rock for a dry seat and reflected on the old townsite before me. There were four shafts sunk at Central but only #2 and #4 were productive. What enormous human labor was required for mining in those early days! Black powder was used for blasting tunnels, of course, but the ore was extracted by men chiseling and shoveling in cold wet surroundings with only the feeble light of candles to illuminate the rocky caverns. How, I pondered, did one workman hold a slender chisel in his unprotected hands, twisting it after each blow, while two others alternated striking the head of the tool with heavy sledge hammers? With elan and daring, an old Cornish miner told me recently. It was inevitable that hundreds of Cornishmen flocked to the new copper mines in the Keweenaw Peninsula; for centuries the sturdy, independent residents of Cornwall, England, had worked deep underground in search of tin and copper in their native country. The men from Cornwall were consummate hard rock miners, they knew the dangers and drudgery and accepted each new challenge with typical Celtic enthusiasm. Their indomitable spirits must have been tested severely in the wild and rugged terrain of the Upper Peninsula.

Central must have been an awesome challenge to the early miners and their families. Consider the conditions that confronted them: the isolation of being many miles by stage coach from a town of any size; sickness, particularly childhood diseases such as diphtheria which swept through communities claiming the lives of scores of children; accidents in the mine which maimed and killed many, including my great-grandfather; crowded living conditions in the dormitories and boarding houses where beds were used around the clock by three miners working on different shifts and the long cold winters. Scratched on a windowpane in the home of the mining company clerk, now tastefully and authentically restored by the Stetter family, is the terse inscription: Feb. 8, '88, 34 below.

Yet life on the copper range was not totally devoid of culture and amenities. According to Charles Stetter, retired high school principal and historian-laureate of Central, the community was actually rather sophisticated. The town supported a band and, weather permitting, a concert was held every Saturday afternoon on the village green. The top floor of the spacious school was designed as a hall for the performing arts. In addition to the many church activities and social clubs, several fraternal lodges (Sons of St. George, Knights of Pythias) had chapters in the small community. There was a well-stocked company store, a post office and a number of small shops, including a candy store and a millinery supply. The small stores were generally run by miners' widows trying to keep food on the table and their large families together. Despite the isolation, the community seems to have eaten well. Inspecting the yellowed records of the old company store, I noted that on October 7, 1876, my great-great grandfather, Samuel Satterley, purchased a barrel of flour ($8.75), five pound of codfish (50¢), saffron, a few coconuts, damask material and a gallon of syrup. What really pulled these people through the hard times, though, was pride in meeting adversity and, more important, a strong sense of belonging to a common community,

"Hit was like coming back 'ome," said an old Cousin Jack describing his first impression of Central after the long journey from England. Here he found the familiar goods, customs, faces and names — Uren, Trevarrow, Trevarton, Trezona, Polglase, Rosemergy — the list of surnames might just as well have come from St. Austell, Penzance or Redruth in Cornwall.

I climbed higher on the greenstone ridge overlooking the old town. It was on this very crest that the community erected a fine school in 1878, a monument to their faith in education and the future of their children. The school was designed with three stories and its $7,500 cost was considerable for those times. The top floor was used as a hall for town meetings, social events and the arts, while the lower two floors were divided into four rooms for the grade school. During the height of the mining operation, over 200 children attended classes in the new school. Although nothing remains of the large structure, I like to think that the mental ripples created by teachers and pupils here years ago still emanate outward in the lives of their descendants and that perhaps my own modest scholarly achievements had their origin in a kerosene-lit school in Central Mine.

One building stands out among all the somber weathered houses at Central: the old Methodist Church. The Cornish were serious about their religion — John Wesley saw to that during his many crusades in Cornwall — and the miners built a very sturdy church in 1868. The well-kept frame building sits on a stone foundation which extends out from a sloping hillside; its simple square steeple is shaped like the crown of Henry VIII. Since 1907, the church has served as the site of an annual reunion of the descendants of the original residents of Central. During the bicentennial year, I attended the 70th annual reunion service at the old church as a 5th generation descendant of a Cornish copper miner. Here are the observations I scribbled on the back of the church program:

> Still 30 minutes before the service is scheduled to begin and the church is already filled; must be at least 180 people inside and from where I sit by the window I can see at least thirty more sitting on benches outside. The Central Mine church is very simple in the Methodist tradition: narrow wooden pews; tall, unadorned window; oil lamp chandeliers; freshly painted white walls; plain pine floors worn smooth by footsteps for over a century. A sign placed near the pulpit says, "God bless our school."

> Most of the congregation has graying hair . . . but, oh, the singing. My grandmother told me that the Cornish were renowned for their hymn singing and it is still true. It reminds me of the Dick Buller legends, the local equivalent of the Paul Bunyan logging tall tales.

Dick Buller, the story goes, was a Cousin Jack miner at Central whose powerful bass voice could penetrate 10 levels in the deep shafts; and he could be heard at least 10 miles on the surface.

The ties to Cornwall are still strong. An identical service is being held at a Methodist chapel in St. Austell today. I feel like I am standing in the living past.

The program states that nineteen ministers occupied the pulpit during the active lifetime of the church, beginning with Reverend J.H. Cornalia in 1868 and ending with Reverend Guy V. Hoad in 1899.

After a brief service the members of the congregation strolled about the old town, inspecting the few weathered homes which remain standing or poking among the ruins of the mining structures. Many had brought large baskets of food and proceeded to picnic on the lawn near the church or on the sunny slopes of the greenstone ridge overlooking the village.

These old abandoned towns are priceless remnants of our pioneer heritage, they are monuments to the courage and tenacity of our ancestors. It seems to me that we should set aside and preserve a ghost town like Central so that future generations can see where a daring group of miners carved a heritage from solid rock.* Already the Central Mine Methodist Church is listed in the National Register of Historic Places. In 1975, it was included in the Historic American Building Survey, which is conducted by the National Park Service under permanent agreement with the American Institute of Architects and the Library of Congress. Its purpose is to preserve for all time accurate records of the building surveyed through scale drawings, measurements, pictures and verbal descriptions. But other remnants of Central and all the other ghost towns of the Copper Country are vulnerable to vandals and souvenir seekers and must be protected. Places like Central are nonrenewable sources of inspiration as well as windows to our past.

Someone was listening: The new Keweenaw National Historical Park has been created to protect and interpret the invaluable historic treasures of the Copper Country.

T H E   L U R E   O F   O L D
W O O D S   R O A D S

They sprout like tag alders in all directions, beckoning invitations to exploration, luring the adventurer away from well-established thoroughfares deeper and deeper into the remote interior of the Peninsula. Like dark mysterious rivers, old woods roads flow quietly and gently through the forests taking the hiker back through time to a calmer, more restful era. Following these wild pathways whither they may wander is frankly addictive and I confess I'm hopelessly entrapped by their charms. I know, though, that even with unusual persistence I'll never be able to explore adequately even a fraction of the many ancient trails which wind enticingly through my home region. It is not with sadness that I say this; indeed I smile a bit contemplating the prospect of following country roads even into eternity. Granted, I could accelerate my investigations with a suitable vehicle and my neighbors think it odd that I prefer to walk instead of ride. I could cover more territory but I would miss too much and, by adopting a modern pace, destroy the unique aura these pathways offer. No, there is only one proper way to savor old woods roads: on foot, slowly.

The Superior Peninsula is stitched with old tote paths, fire lanes, logging roads and railroad spurs. The forest has reclaimed many and some ancient trails can be discerned only in late fall or winter when the underbrush and trees are bare of leaves. Their original purpose long forgotten, most of the old roads simply meander through the forest; some terminate in a maze of small logging skidways, a mine test pit, a dark pond or small stream. Now they offer an avenue of escape, an opportunity to explore and be on a more intimate level with nature and with the rich pioneer history of the Peninsula.

Although I stumble on more old roads to investigate each year, I find myself drawn to a few favorites close to town. Less than three miles west of my home near the Carp

River are remnants of an old tote path over which raw iron ore was transported in horse-drawn carts from the mines in Negaunee to the harbor in Marquette. An abundance of vegetation — birches, sugar maples and small hemlocks — crowds the path for much of its ten miles, but there are long stretches where it is surprisingly open and in these places the roadbed is still hardpacked. It must have taken an enormous amount of effort to carve this path through the wilderness in the mid 1800s; deep pits can still be seen on each side of the trail where crews of workmen dug out earth and rock to build up the bed of the road. Numerous short spurs sprout from the tote path. Most of them lead to shallow adits where the early miners probed for iron and copper ore they were certain underlay all the granite outcroppings in the region. In the very low spots, near where the path parallels Morgan Creek, stout oak and ironwood timbers which the builders used to corduroy the roadway can still be found.

An abandoned railroad right of way in the Hiawatha National Forest is another woodland pathway to which I return each year. The railroad bed cuts a narrow swath through a sandy jack pine plain. Here I find abundant blueberries, an occasional sharptail grouse, and if I am lucky, a glimpse of a sandhill crane. It is here, too, that I find luxurious expanses of caribou moss which delights my eye and provides a soft carpet upon which to rest. The railway passes through vast stretches of white pine stumps, crumbling reminders of the logging era. Some of the huge old stumps are silvered gray; many are covered with mosses and sprout small trees from their jagged tops; all of them are charred from the immense fires which swept the dry slashings.

But for variety, as well as proximity to town, my all-time favorite is the old logging road which winds through the thick woods and granite knobs near Migisy Lake. Come, let's take an afternoon jaunt on this ancient lane and you will see why I am lured back so often. Wear sturdy shoes and put a snack and raingear in a small pack. We drive only a short distance and then turn off the busy highway. Instant calm and solitude. Parking our car behind a screen of young maples and aspens, we don the packs and our adventure begins. It rained this morning and the sky is still a bit cloudy but the woods smell fresh and inviting; the different hues of green loom even brighter after a rain.

The first and longest part of the road passes through dense stands of maple and yellow birch which intertwine overhead closing out the sunlight; here the pathway is moist and cool even in warm weather. Here, also, we can pause and admire the play of light and shadow where small shafts of sunlight filter through the dense cover of leaves. Although most birds are finished with child-rearing duties and have fallen silent, overhead in the dense canopy we hear the persistent call of the red-eyed vireo. Then, far off in the woods, drifting as if on a summer breeze, comes the lazy drawl of a sleepy peewee — *pee-a-wee*, he says as if trying to make sure that we know his name. Lichens, mosses and ferns grow profusely in this cool, damp sanctuary. The common bracken fern is particularly abundant. In ancient times, during the age of giant land reptiles, ferns were much larger, often growing to heights of 100 feet or more. Let's look underneath a triangular frond. Those brownish spots don't mean disease, they are spore producing cells; ferns reproduce by spores rather than seeds. Botanists estimate that as many as 50 million spores can be formed by a single fern frond. The tiny cells are transported by wind and water. When the spore cells alight on the forest floor, tiny fuzzy rhizoids arise and these serve as anchors; from the rhizoids emerge heart shaped green plants and finally reproduction takes place.

The bracken fern can be found almost everywhere in the Peninsula. It grows densely in poor soil around the edges of fields and in open woods. The leaves are triangular in shape and quite coarse; in some places the plants reach heights of four feet but more commonly grow between two and three feet high. Dark lustrous green in summer, the bracken fern turns a lovely copper-russet speckled with flecks of black and brown in autumn. When the plants emerge in spring, they are curled tightly and are called fiddleheads for their resemblance to the head of a violin. At this time they are quite good to eat either raw or fried in butter.

But just look, don't eat — don't even touch — this bright orange mushroom with white warts on its cap. It's the deadly Fly Amanita. See, over here are several more plants emerging; when they first come up they look like a golf ball on a thick tee and later these, too, will assume the familiar umbrella shape. Although some Amanitas are edible, most of them — Spring Death Cap, Destroying Angel — are as lethal as their names suggest.

We have hiked almost a mile and now the forest is changing. Instead of a thick stand of young trees, we find large oaks, hemlocks, and here and there a colony of moderately sized white pines. To the west is a small cattail marsh; beyond it we can see the thick forest of spruces which guard the outlet of Lake Migisy. In a clearing we come upon a carefully crafted log cabin. It is small, only one room about 12 by 18 feet, but is still in remarkable shape. The square hand-hewn logs have weathered a deep buff color with streaks of dark brown providing an interesting contrast. The logs fit together in carefully crafted dovetails at the corners and even after years of abandonment, there is not an open space between them. Vandals have removed the stove pipe and smashed the glass in the three windows; a dirty grey curtain flutters aimlessly in and out of the larger front window. A dilapidated outbuilding made of crude lumber and tarpaper tilts dangerously nearby and in the knoll behind the cabin we see the remains of a root cellar. Whose cabin was this? When did he live here? What view of life did he have? Did he sit in the cabin door on a summer afternoon and ponder what it all means? Would he be pleased that we admire his handiwork on the cabin and pay our respects to his memory and to an earlier time? As we reflect on these questions, the road opens out suddenly into a second, larger clearing.

The cleared field is at least 40 acres and is slowly being reclaimed by the surrounding forest. Hawthornes, birch and young pines grow in small clumps. Wildflowers of late summer — fireweed, butter and eggs and pearly everlasting — carpet the clearing. Near one edge is a gigantic pile of rocks which an industrious pioneer plucked from the soil; close by we find the remains of a wooden stoneboat. As we wander along the far edge of the field we discover a rusty Chevrolet truck sitting on its rims in a clutter of old parts, discarded farm machinery and baling wire. Its age is indeterminate but it is probably several decades old. Compulsively I lift the rusty hood and check the oil; although the lubricant has long since congealed, the block is still full. We lean against the wood truckbed and contemplate the enormous energy it must have taken to till the soil in this remote rocky land.

A rasping squeal . . . keerrrrrr! . . . interrupts our reverie. Overhead a lone red-tailed hawk makes slow lazy circles; he seems to be protesting our intrusion upon his hunting territory. We watch him for a few moments marveling at how he rides the warm currents with only an occasional flap of his broad wings. Slowly the hawk moves off toward the west and slants downward. Following the larger raptor, we see three squat structures almost hidden in a copse of birches at the far edge of the field.

Coming closer we see that we've discovered the remains of three old charcoal kilns. Made from crude stone, these dome-shaped structures were once 25 feet in diameter at the base and extended upward to 20 feet. All that is left now are the bases of the kilns; one is almost six feet high at the back and the other two have tumbled into disarray over the many years of disuse. The inside of the stones are coated thickly with charcoal. Several birches from thirty to fifty years old have taken root within the floor of the kilns or close nearby; they seem sleek and very white in contrast to the dark stone. Close behind the remnants of the charcoal kilns is a steep bank; from this hill the kiln watcher dumped green hardwood cut in four foot lengths into the top of the domed structures leaving the central core open for the fire. About 40 cords of wood were needed to fill one kiln. After a fire was well-started in the structure, the kiln was sealed and allowed to burn slowly or char for over a week. When the charring finished, the kiln was opened and the charcoal removed in scuttle baskets to be transported to the forges. The inveterate woods road explorer can find many such kilns; they are reminders of the ore smelting era of the 1850s to 1880s.

The roadway now becomes more wild and rugged as it climbs gradually up the shoulder of a steep hill. Before ascending the hill, let's stop by this small stream; for much of its length it has flowed underground but here, just beside the old road, it emerges and drains down through a narrow heavily wooded valley. As we pause quietly and listen to the gentle music of the brook, we see a flash of white among the aspens and tag alders. A large whitetail doe, resplendent in her summer coat of red, steps from the underbrush and looks squarely at us. Although intensely cautious she is also curious; she needs to investigate this intrusion in her forest. The wind is in our favor and she moves slowly toward us and stops, alert, one foreleg raised. In an attempt to get us to react, she stamps the ground hard. Again she stamps. Now the doe has had enough uncertainty and, snorting loudly, she bounds away gracefully, her large white tail marking her flight down the valley.

The old logging road ends just over the crest of the hill. Scrambling up a granite outcropping we find a perfect spot to rest while we eat a snack and absorb what we have seen on our afternoon ramble. At the very top of the hill is a grove of ten large hemlocks the loggers apparently decided were too difficult to remove, or maybe they also enjoyed sitting on the soft carpet of needles in the cool stillness of the large trees. No doubt they also admired, as we did while finishing our food and packing to return, the rich smell of resin which emanates from the thick duff at every movement upon it.

The afternoon has passed swiftly and we must now retrace our path to the car. Although we carry nothing home in the way of material goods, and some people would accuse us of indolence, we do have rich memories of a splendid summer afternoon. The play of sunlight filtering through the canopy of leaves, a legion of ferns, a superbly crafted old cabin, remnants of a homestead and farm, a red-tailed hawk circling in a clearing, a curious whitetail deer, the redolence of thousands of hemlock needles — all these images have nourished our spirits.

As we near the parked car we resolve to return again to this old logging road and to seek out other ancient paths to explore. It occurs to us, too, that some old woods roads should be preserved as monuments to our pioneer heritage before they are further obliterated by motorized traffic. These old roads are like folk tales and when we traverse them they speak to us faintly of discovery, dreams, persistence, misery . . . and the indomitable human spirit.

GRANITE CLUMPS

*D*eep in the forest near the Middle Branch of the Escanaba River is a quiet mysterious spot which I visit once a year during the deer hunting season. Here are five immense granite boulders which form a crude circle resembling the megalithic stone tombs found along the coast of the British Isles, Brittany and other rocky headlands in the Old World. The boulders are tall, well over eight feet, and fit snugly together except for one small opening where it is possible to squeeze between two of the giants. The small sanctuary inside the ring of granite is cool and the forest floor is covered with a thick carpet of pine needles accumulated over many years. Two large white pines stand guard on the east side of the circle; their lower branches form an aromatic roof for the sanctuary. Clumps of red maple and birch surround the boulders on the other three sides. The large rocks bear numerous signs of weathering; kelly green moss grows in most of the fissures and cracks and on the southern portion of the ring there is an abundant growth of rock tripe, a large flaky form of lichen.

This ring of granite boulders is, as far as I can tell, my very private hideaway. Unloading my gun, I slide into the circle, recline upon the soft bed of needles with my back against one of the gigantic stones, and muse. How did these huge stones get placed into such a symmetrical pattern? Did a wandering band of Druids prepare the circle of granite as a burial site for a departed companion? Or is this unusual clump of boulders a result of capricious spalling as the last glacier retreated northward?

The Superior Peninsula, particularly in the central western portions, is granite country. Almost everywhere one looks are rugged cliffs, weathered knobs and long shelves deeply grooved by glacial striations and gigantic boulders of the ancient rock. Granite is often found in association with water: Inland lakes, particularly in the

Michigamme Highlands, are often surrounded by sheer cliffs and flat slabs of it; most streams in the area tumble through or over it; most of the majestic Lake Superior shore-line is composed of it. It is this particular blend of rock, water and pines which gives the Peninsula its unique charm, its heroic proportions and enduring character.

The granite of this region is pre-Cambrian in origin. In technical terms it is classi-fied as the Southern Province of the Great Canadian or Laurentian Shield and is thought to be at least 3 1/2 billion years old. Hidden beneath the schists, granites and gneisses which comprise the Shield is another substance — an element which had, and is still having, a profound impact on the development of the area. During gestation of the earth mass, vast deposits of iron were laid down as chemical precipitates in the shallow waters of the bays and arms of the immense seas which covered this region in pre-Cambrian times. Since iron and oxygen commonly unite to form iron oxides, most of the iron was deposited as the mineral hematite, magnetite and goethite. The Marquette Iron Range was discovered quite by accident one day in the early fall of 1844 and the tide of specu-lators and miners pouring in to retrieve the treasure altered the Peninsula forever.

On September 19, 1844, William A. Burt and his party of surveyors were running a section line in the vicinity of Teal Lake when they noticed that their compass was fluctu-ating wildly. Puzzled when the compass refused to point true, the men split up and looked about; to their amazement, they found outcroppings of raw iron ore in every direction. Less than a year later, in June of 1845, Philo Everett and a group of businessmen from Jackson, Michigan, arrived in Marquette to search for the fabulous lode of iron ore. Their original intention had been to explore for copper in the Keweenaw Peninsula but while resting at L'Anse they heard Louis Nolan, a part-Indian guide who had been with the Burt surveying party, talk about the mountain of iron ore in what is now the town of Negaunee.

At the mouth of the Carp River, near where the Marquette State Prison now stands, the party met a young Chippewa woman, *Tip-Kesa*, who said that her uncle, a local chief-tain, would show the men the site of the ore outcroppings. With *Tip-Kesa* as their guide, Everett and the Jackson party hiked up the Carp River Valley and found *Marji-Gesick* (Chippewa for "Moving Day") encamped at Teal Lake. The Chippewa were frightened of the mountain of ore; its light reflected across the waters of the lake like a mirror and they referred to the area as the "mirrored wall of evil spirits." In spite of the superstition, *Marji-Gesick* led the Jackson party to an outcropping of iron ore under the roots of a fallen pine tree. A month later the Jackson Mining Company was formed. To secure their claim the young company built six log houses and a barn, and this marked the beginning of Negaunee, which appropriately means "pioneer."

When news of the discovery of rich iron ore deposits spread across the country, hundreds of speculators rushed to the area; within one year more than a hundred mining companies were formed. Unprepared for the rigors of the north, ill-equipped and under-financed, most of the boom companies failed in the first year or two. But the Jackson Mine persisted and grew. At the outset, extraction of the ore was done in open pits carved into the hills where the iron was discovered; the drilling was accomplished by hand, using chisels and sledge hammers. The raw iron ore was laboriously carted by mule teams down to Marquette harbor over a plank road. By 1857, railroads had been built for transporting the heavy ore. Some effort was made to process the ore into iron "blooms" (bars of pig iron, 2 feet long and 4 inches thick) near the mine sites. The Jackson forge was built in 1846 but the effort and expense (enormous quantities of charcoal were needed) to make the blooms was too costly. It became easier to ship the ore in bulk lake freighters to the furnaces of Gary, Cleveland and Pittsburgh where coal deposits were close at hand. Within a few years the outcroppings of iron were depleted and the hard rock miners followed the veins of metal deep into the earth. By the autumn of 1975, *one billion* long tons of iron ore had been shipped from the granite hills of Marquette County.

Mining is now the giant among industries in the Peninsula. Elaborate mechanization has replaced hand labor and the next billion tons of the red metal will, at the present rate of extraction, be mined and shipped in a much shorter time than the first. The Mather B Mine in Negaunee, the largest underground mine in the nation, produces more iron ore in one year than the Jackson pit did in forty years. However, the bulk of mining is now being done in open pits and the impact on this beautiful land is becoming ever more obvious: immense open pits and giant piles of discarded rock; diversion of vast acreage for tailings basins; use of free flowing rivers as a source of water for processing the low grade ore; the need for immense quantities of electrical energy, which in turn results in giant coal piles, increased air pollution, thermal discharges of water into Lake Superior and tall smoke stacks which dominate the shoreline. The rapid expansion of iron ore mining has also had a significant impact on the people, the value of their property and their way of life.

Many residents of the Upper Peninsula are ambivalent toward the iron ore mining expansion; the company is resented for its omnipresence and dominance of the region, yet it is needed for the multi-million dollar payroll and its contributions to charities and community groups. The company is viewed as a benevolent big brother by those who will gain by rapid economic expansion. But the image is not completely in focus: the mining company does not exist simply to provide jobs to the local populace. The officers and stockholders of Cleveland, Ohio, see the purpose of the company as mining the available ore as quickly as possible, converting the ore bodies to cash, stock and dividends. The history of copper and iron ore mining in the Peninsula has been to leave when operations are no longer highly profitable, without a backward glance at the people who have become dependent upon the one industry payroll. No one can say if history will be repeated in 50 years — it is clear that a slower rate of extraction would postpone the inevitable bust for perhaps 200 years, but at lower profits in Cleveland. One way to insure that local people are not left with only empty memories and crumbling buildings is to alter the current tax structure. The ore is, after all, a natural resource, belonging to us all.

Prior to 1951, the mining industry paid property taxes on their land and equipment just as do all homeowners and businessmen. As value grew more money was available to the local communities to provide the services needed by the company and its workers. In 1951, the State Legislature enacted the Iron Ore Specific Tax which removed the mines from the property tax rolls and taxes them instead on their production — currently 38¢ per ton. The purpose of the specific ore tax was to provide an incentive to the companies to develop a process (taconite) that would make mining low grade iron ore profitable. The tax worked. The process is immensely profitable; many now feel it's time for the industry to pay their share again.

Yet it still takes more temerity than good sense to criticize the mining industry — growth, no matter how swift, no matter how many negative spin-offs, is still a central value in our society. Somehow the concept of progress became linked with expansion. Larger, faster, exceed the old record — we seem to be caught in a self-destructive cycle that is taking us farther and farther from the natural world. The iron ore which lies beneath the granite hills of the Superior Peninsula has been there for eons — why the rush to exhaust the deposits now? Why not monitor growth carefully and limit expansion to those levels that can be managed, before the natural attractions which make this region so distinct are lost? The stakes are high: what kind of a place will we and our children have to live in when the mining industry is through with the land?

Another use for the granite of the Laurentian Shield was promulgated by the Navy: the construction of a giant antenna to communicate with submerged submarines via extremely low frequencies. The communication is often referred to as a "doomsday" message because its major use would be a one-time directive to fire missiles at pre-determined targets. The ELF (extremely low frequency) Project was born as "Sanguine" but the name was quickly changed when it was discovered that Sanguine could mean not only *optimistic* but also *bloody*. The ELF antenna has two parts: steel cables strung overhead for 56 miles through the forest, and the natural conductivity of the granite formations underlying the soil.

The opposition to erecting the grid in the Peninsula was strong: every referendum held in eight counties resulted in a 2 to 1 or higher vote against the system. Opponents of the system cited the fear of becoming a nuclear target; the acceleration of the arms race, potentially fatal shock near cable breaks, the uncertainties of the effectiveness of the system. The health risks of extremely low frequency networks have been a matter of real concern; there is some evidence that serum triglycerides are elevated in humans exposed to the current. High levels of serum triglycerides are associated with high blood pressure, stroke and heart attacks. Similar research pointed toward a possibility of reduced human capacity to solve simple mathematical problems after long exposures to the low frequency currents. But it is the environmentally-oriented opponents who came in for the most attack by supporters of ELF because they emphasized that the grid would create havoc with huge tracts of wild land and would require additional power in a power-scarce region to activate the antenna.

The supporters of the system were members of the Navy League, American Legion, engineers, local chambers of commerce and those involved in electrical sales and construction along with some ultra-conservative residents who questioned the patriotism of the critics. They made the point that the Navy is the only source of expert information; they overlooked that the Navy had an antenna to grind, and a multi-million dollar program to perpetuate.

Although the U.S. Senate voted in 1995 to eliminate the doomsday antenna as part of the post-Cold War cost cutting, the funding — to the tune of 14 million dollars — was restored. The cable towers still march through the woods not too far from my circle of stones.

I am not advocating the extreme position that all of the Superior Peninsula should be wilderness primeval, that the residents should lock up the treasures of the region and worship in poverty and hunger at altars of granite. My own maternal ancestors were copper miners and I am well aware of my family's debt to the metals deposited in these flinty hills. Yet even the early miners, using primitive hand labor, soon exhausted the ore. The potential for rapid exploitation is now so much greater.

I am saying this: Let us treat the land gently, let us husband the finite resources available instead of extracting them and converting them all to cash in our lifetime. Just because we can, shall we blast and level the granite cliffs, bury cables in them, shove it aside to have at all the iron ore now? Or can we be far-sighted, humble enough to accept a slower pace of development, a reasoned judgment of the best course in which our land and our living can both survive?

A raven, its wings sawing the air noisily, flew low over the granite redoubt and interrupted my long reverie. It landed nearby and uttered a soft "tok"; another raven responded across the Escanaba River. Energized as I always am after a visit in the granite circle, I arose and made my way through the darkening forest to my truck.

PHOTO BY LON EMERICK

A U T U M N

Seasons in the Upper Peninsula of Michigan

"Scarlet skies in the morning"

"Fall storms on Lake Superior"

PHOTOS BY LON EMERICK

- - ◄◄ • ►► - -

A U T U M N

utumn in the north country is a many splendored season for the senses — rich, earthy odors, incredibly beautiful displays of color, and the compelling cacophony of the harvest and annual migration. Fair warning: I am prejudiced, unashamedly so, since fall is for me a very special time of year. All year long I hunger for the stunning array of red and yellow leaves, the crisp nights, the cold dews and sense of ripeness, the tingling suspense of the hunt. So as August wanes and the days grow shorter, I watch impatiently for that first subtle sign of the autumnal transformation — the softening of the dense green foliage of the aspens and maples. And then one day as I take my walk in the woods near home, a single yellow leaf drifts down slowly, a provocative and colorful intruder on the dull grey-brown of the forest floor.

Now the signs of fall burgeon forth in rapid profusion: the clovers and grasses in open fields grow brittle and take on a copper hue; birds, gregarious now that the mating season is ended, begin to flock in the meadows and along the roadsides; the bracken fern turn a pale yellow with mottled spots of brown; flights of geese beat southward against a backdrop of fluffy clouds laced with delicate pink and buff; Lake Superior sends huge rolling waves dashing upon the granite shores. Soon the Peninsula is changed to a scarlet and golden fantasy land as the year draws to a quixotic end in a fleeting profusion of brilliant hues.

And I, too, am transformed, for the liturgy of Autumn alters human minds and moods as well as leaves, ferns and geese. My pace quickens, my spirits expand, I am exhilarated — it is more delightful than ever to be alive. Yet often there is a subtle melancholy, a lingering reverie of long summer days and carefree vacation memories, an awareness of the white winter landscape to come. Turgenev in the *Annals of a Sportsman* describes it best: "You breathe tranquility; but there is a strange tremor in the soul." Indeed, autumn is a precious season for the soul.

THE FRAGRANCES OF AUTUMN

Anyone who has ever watched a trained bird dog tracing the erratic path of a ruffed grouse in an aspen stand on a moist October morning realizes that humans are denied a whole world of sensations. What a myriad of fragrances we miss with our paltry sense of smell! When compared to canine species with 100 times the olfactory power humans possess, we are practically smell-blind. Ironically, our inferior noses are further assailed by polluted air and jaded by the efforts of the cosmetic industry to eliminate or mask all natural odors with sprays, perfumes and deodorants.

Yet we can enlarge our awareness, we can train our olfactory system to tune in to the nuances of nature's rich smells. One of the best ways I have found to accomplish this is to visit an autumn forest before dawn; by temporarily eliminating vision, I can concentrate on the many fragrances of fall. The most compelling odor, certainly the most ubiquitous here in the north country, is the smell of newly-fallen leaves.

The smell of freshly-fallen leaves was especially pervasive the other morning when I woke before daylight and hiked into the woods near my home. It rose like a soothing balm all about me as I picked my way slowly through the darkened forest to an oak-covered ridge where I would keep a silent vigil. The path was moist and soft underfoot, silencing my footfalls, and I could detect the furtive rustling sounds of small nighttime creatures. The silence was punctuated intermittently by the noisy descent of ripe acorns as they caromed off branches before finally hitting the forest floor with a solid thump. Sitting down under a giant oak tree, I leaned back and deeply drew in the heady fragrance of fallen leaves.

For me, this musty herbal odor of downed leaves is the very essence of autumn. The smell is particularly rich and persistent in the moist dawn air and as I sat sniffing, my mind was flooded with memories of other falls, of hunting and hiking on frosty mornings, of harvesting hazel nuts and apples, of gathering and splitting the winter's supply of firewood. I searched for the right words to describe this unique smell of fall. Pungent? Yes, in part, though that term doesn't quite fit the primal, organic essence of moist new humus. Aromatic? The forest floor is certainly aromatic in autumn, especially during a soft rain when the aroma of leafy decay is heavy in the air. I finally settled on ambrosial — to me the fragrance is altogether a divine sensation and I begin to long for it in late summer. In early September I detect its first nuances in groves of young aspen; the odor at that point is elusive and I must search out damp areas to find the heady fragrance. Then by the middle of October, the northern woods are an olfactory paradise.

Now the first gray light of dawn filtered down through the trees on the ridge where I sat. How sweet it is to listen and watch the forest come alive at daybreak! No other time is quite so magical as the birth of a new day; the moments then are fresh, vital and not yet used by others. Closing my eyes, I listened intently: migrating birds, probably white-throated sparrows, rustled among the leaves; a gray squirrel scolded from the top of a nearby oak;  acorns clattered down and thudded on an old burnt stump behind me. The ridge runs east and west and from where I sat facing south I could see down the steep slope; far below in the narrow valley a thick shroud of fog hugged the tops of a dense copse of quaking aspen. Turning slightly to scan the ridge, I was startled to see a four-point whitetail buck, sleek now in his gray-brown winter coat, feeding on the mast; the dawn was so quiet that I could hear the crunching of acorns. The deer ignored the intermittent noise of falling nuts but was instantly alert when I changed position to obtain a better view and scraped my sleeve on the rough bark of the red oak tree. He froze for a moment and then vanished in the underbrush as only a cautious whitetail deer can.

It was time for me too, to leave the ridge but I prolonged my early morning sojourn by taking the longer, more scenic route home. Autumn is a season for wandering, for floating along like leaves in the air. Under the oaks I inspected the place where the deer had pawed among the leaves for acorns. In fall, whitetail deer prepare for the long winter and uncertain food supply by building up a thick layer of fat; mast is a prime source of such nourishment. Descending the steep slope I shuffled through the carpet of maple and birch leaves to raise the delightful odor. In a low spot near the edge of the aspen thicket, I bent down and charged my senses deeply. Looking closely, I noticed that small beads of water, condensed from the morning fog, shimmered like spots of mercury on the undersides of downed and blackened aspen leaves, while those lying face-up were slick and brilliant yellow with moisture. The lowly aspen or "popple" has the most extensive range and is the most prolific of any tree in the north. In fall it is one of my favorites — it's here in groves of young popple trees that the tang and ferment of fallen leaves is strongest.

Plucking a small aspen twig, I moved up the valley to an open field which once served as a pasture for a long forgotten dairy farmer. Row upon row of goldenrod, now a uniform light gray, guard the edge of the field; a score of milkweeds, their fluffy open pods rotating gently in the morning breeze, line an ancient farm lane. I sniffed each deeply but could detect no odor. Nearby I picked one frost-blackened aster and crushed its brittle petals in my palm. When I bent closely its delicate perfume could still be discerned. But it was the fragrance of aspen leaves which lingered in my memory as I hurried home and prepared for my morning classes. The small aspen twig rode in my coat lapel all day and reminded me of the dawn vigil on the oak ridge.

There are, of course, many other fragrances associated with autumn. In early fall I seek out the farming regions near town to soak in the aroma of the moist dark earth lying open in new furrows. Often I stop and chat with one particular old farmer, a gentleman of Finnish heritage with a thick melodious accent. We talk about the rich fecund smell of newly plowed land and I note with some envy his serene expression as he gazes over his fields. During our autumn conversations, the farmer often stoops and picks up a handful of soil; as he sifts it through his fingers, his touch is affectionate, almost reverent. I try to time my visit to coincide with the onion harvest, for after the mechanical picker has completed its raucous circuit, I am often invited to glean a portion of the fields. On a warm afternoon in late September there is nothing more odoriferous than a newly harvested onion field.

Fall also means the delicious fruity fragrance of ripe apples. Whenever I smell them I recall vividly the cooling shed at an orchard my parents visited frequently in the autumns of my youth. Here were stored dozens of peck and bushel baskets of Jonathans and Winesaps ready for sale or shipping. It was dark in the shed — only a single large light bulb illuminated the spacious room — but despite the gloom and cold I would sit quietly watching the orchard workers sorting and assembling the apples. My patience was often rewarded with a cold firm Jonathan; savoring the tart juicy fruit, I inhaled the pleasant aroma of hundreds of apples.

Both taste and smell are chemical senses and, in fact, are closely related; in the absence of smell, food is bland and tasteless. A tankard of cider fresh from the press is a treat not only for the tastebuds but also has a delightful aroma. Although I like cider at room temperature — when it is chilled the savory nuances are dulled — my favorite preparation is spiced and mulled. Take a large container of about nine cups. To the cider add a handful of brown sugar, a pinch of cloves and one or two sticks of cinnamon. Heat, but do not boil, over a low flame, stirring occasionally. The result is a delicious, spicy-smelling, very tasty warming drink. On all my fall excursions to collect winter firewood I carry a thermos of hot cider and enjoy the treat while resting from sawing and chopping.

Far from being a chore, gathering firewood in the fall is an annual labor of love, and one I prefer to do with simple hand tools. It is incredibly satisfying for someone who spends his days in a sedentary profession, who deals hourly with imponderables and probabilities, to use his muscles for a direct simple task. I like the solid sound and feel when a log splits correctly with a single blow; it is fulfilling to see the woodpile grow and know it is a product of my own labor. Most of all I admire the sharp smell of resin from the fresh cuts and the growing pile of sawdust.

The pines, particularly jackpine, have an aromatic resin which fills my senses at each pull of the saw. Maple and birch split cleanly and exude a subtle fragrance which reminds me of sunshine and warm summer rain. My favorite, though only fair as fire-place fuel, is balsam poplar which I prefer to call by its alias, Balm-of-Gilead. The young leaves and large buds of the Balm-of-Gilead are saturated with a fragrant sticky wax which is alleged to have healing properties; honey bees use it in sealing their hives. One fall while backpacking on a long and arduous trail, I made a small sachet of buds taken from a Balm-of-Gilead and kept its soothing smell near my pillow each night. The aroma released when it is sawed and chopped is the same as the herbal essence of downed leaves. There is even a hint of that leafy odor when the split logs burn in the fireplace.

An open fire is a delight to all the senses: the crackling and soft guttering, the dancing red and orange flames, the glowing warmth it spreads, and the bouquet of smells which are released as the wood ignites. Sunshine accumulated for years in the wood fibers is released in an open fire. Despite all our technological sophistication and several generations of urban living, we are still drawn to an open hearth. In order to concentrate on the unique smell of wood smoke, I take long walks on autumn evenings and thus enjoy my neighbors' wood-gathering labors as well as my own.

Fall is also the time of the hunting season and the smells of preparation have worn deep grooves in my memory: the odor of warm bear grease being applied to leather boots, red and black buffalo plaid wool clothing smelling of the cedar chest and moth balls, the sharp acrid aroma of Hoppe's Number Nine nitro solvent as the guns are cleaned and placed back in the rack, bacon frying and coffee perking in the dim frosty mornings as the hunters hurry to prepare for opening day. I remember the fragrance of soups and stews drifting out of the cabin as tired hunters return from the snowy woods and the per-vasive odor of my grandfather's black briar pipe. He smoked his own blend of two com-mon brands of tobacco. Once years later while waiting for a flight in a large air terminal, that same unique smell drifted to where I sat reading and in an instant I was mentally transported back to the Old Man's simple log cabin.

Odors evoke ancient memories and stir long-forgotten images because the olfactory is perhaps the oldest of our five senses. Tiny receptors located in the nose report their messages to the olfactory lobe in the most primitive portion of the brain, the hippo-campus; the latter area is responsible for the storage of memories, particularly those associated with emotional satisfaction. Merchants know that a pleasant smell, even though it may be consciously detected, will bias a person's judgment. Sales of lingerie are facilitated by subtle perfume, and used cars are purchased more swiftly when the interiors are sprayed with "new car" smell.

Similarly the natural odors of each season, because they are so closely associated with our heritage and with centuries of primitive existence, evoke powerful responses in us. The fragrances of autumn, particularly those of downed leaves, may produce rest-lessness, melancholy, even exhilaration. The essence affects me in three interrelated ways. First, it means *fulfillment,* an outward and visible signal that the ever-repeating, never-ending cycle of natural events which commenced with the first blush of green in spring is moving forward according to ancient natural rhythms. In the second place, the smell of fresh decaying leaves offers a *promise* of a new season, it conveys to all creatures the eternal vow that the earth shall rise again, that the links between the seasons are secure. It is an ending and a new beginning. Finally, the fragrances of autumn teach me again the lesson that "to everything there is a season, and a time to every purpose under heaven," and gives me a *reminder* that I, too, am an integral part of the natural order. A fall morning is a good time to hold communion with nature and to offer a personal tithing to the passing of the seasons.

When I was younger I sought some method of preserving the smell of fall so that I might experience it in all seasons. I tried to capture the herbal essence in candles and incense but both ventures failed. Now that I am older and have put away such childish thoughts, I am glad that I failed for I might have surfeited my sense of smell and lost the special delight that each new autumn brings. The fragrance remains poised in my soul, ready to remind me of an oak ridge at dawn, a misty aspen thicket and a quilt of scarlet and gold thrown carelessly upon the forest floor. The sad-sweet woodland perfume! It wafts upward even now in my imagination, laden with memories and evoking that strange mixture of nostalgia and joy which is the very essence of autumn.

C A N O E   O N   T H E   D E A D

Spellbound by the beauty, we sat poised in the canoe reluctant to dip our paddles into the water and disturb the illusion. Mirrored in the translucent surface of the dark rivers were flaming maples, golden birches and dark pines, all framed by a cobalt blue October sky. For a moment — one of those cameo moments in nature — it was impossible to distinguish whether we were seeing the scene reflected in the water or the real trees and sky overhead. We felt as if we were suspended between water and sky. Not one ripple wrinkled the glassy surface. Fog hung just above the water in the distance. The sensation was eerie. It was unsettling and yet terribly moving. We realized once again that there is no better way to celebrate the brief tenure of the autumn color display than an early morning water excursion in a canoe.

The autumn leaf colors in the Peninsula are so intense, so spectacular and compelling that even after three decades of observing I must each year acclimate myself to their gaudy charm. The forest stands poised, ready to slide off the high point of fall into winter darkness; all in nature seems tuned to a fine equilibrium and, in an exuberant last hurrah, the growing season comes to an end in a chromatic extravaganza. I echo Thoreau: "It is too fair to be believed especially seen against the light." Pictures — even my own photographs — do not portray the impact of acres upon acres of birches, maples and aspens in their brilliant fall garments. There is no understatement in a north country autumn; all flags are flying at journey's end. The message is shouted out: summer is dead, winter is coming.

I know, of course, that the startling hues of fall have been residing dormant all along, hidden by the green of chlorophyll during the growing season. Then as days grow shorter and colder, the tree shuts off the water supply to the leaves and the deep green foliage fades, exposing the myriad shades of red and yellow. Many trees turn exactly the same color each year. Sugar maples seem to favor shades of yellow although I have seen them dressed in orange, peach, even bright red. On my favorite hiking path, two elderly maples grow side by side. Each fall one turns bright yellow and its neighbor always assumes a red-orange hue. The inveterate leaf-looker can depend upon red maples, though, to put on a prodigious scarlet show; fortunately there are many of them in the Peninsula.

If days are sunny and the nights chill (temperatures below 45 degrees slow down the removal of sugar from a leaf), the leaves of some species go on making sugar until all the chlorophyll is gone. Young oaks often do this and the resultant extra sugars reacts with the minerals to create deep carmine and purple. The autumn forest appears to have been painted with bold broad strokes by an artist whose brush has run wild in bright and startling colors.

Although the visitor can behold the annual charms of an Upper Peninsula autumn in any portion of the region when every lonely backwoods road becomes a fantasy land, we find ourselves returning again and again to areas where we can see the colorful leaves against a backdrop of water. The rolling expanse of flinty hills surrounding Lake of the Clouds in the Porcupine Mountains, the vista from Brockway Mountain in the Copper Country, even the small reflecting pools at the foot of Alder Falls near Big Bay — all have a special place in our memories.

Our all time favorite way to witness the leaf display is by canoe and one of the best vantage points is the wide dark ribbon of water which forms the northwestern boundary of town. The Chippewa name for the river was *"Djibis-Manitou-Sibi,"* the "River of Dead Spirits" because the spray in the rocky gorges of the river seemed to resemble ascending spirits of the departed. John Burt's survey map in the 1840s designated the river as *"Ne-Kom-a-non,"* the "River of Deaths" either because of lives lost in the white water or the fact that the Indians buried their dead near the encampment at the river's mouth. The French explorers called it "Riviere des Morts" and today it is called simply the Dead River.

In earlier times the Dead River was very lively indeed when it flowed from its origins in the Michigamme Highlands through jumbled granite defiles in wild cascades and white water rapids. Now the river is tamed by a series of dams creating large placid basins which supply water for several electric generating plants. All about the basins are high heavily timbered ridges which pulsate with colors in fall.

We had put in our canoe at dawn on the Forestville Basin and paddled slowly downstream with the slight current. A canoe is an ideal craft for establishing rapport with an autumn morning: it is simple, quiet and goes straight into the heart of the season without intruding. A wood and canvas canoe like ours is especially appropriate since, unlike many modern mass-produced canoes of plastic or aluminum, the Old Town model was made slowly and lovingly of natural materials forty years ago by craftsmen still at work in Maine. It is whisper-quiet as it moves through the water putting us on a intimate level with the river, as if we were on nature's center stage. We recalled a line from Longfellow's Hiawatha, "I a light canoe will build me, build a swift cheeman for sailing, that shall float upon the river like a yellow leaf."

The magical moment when the autumn hues reflected so clearly in the river awed us still as we glided silently down the wide reservoir. The Forestville Basin is large, at least a half-mile across at its widest point, but we paddled close to the many small bays on the south shore to look for wildlife. And almost every bay harbored a raft of ducks which took flight only after we drifted close to them. Mallards, pintails and diminutive green-winged teals predominated. Where a small creek flows into the river we flushed a pair of wood ducks and marveled at their distinctive plumage which rivals the display of colorful leaves. The migration had just begun; soon scores of ducks and geese would seek temporary residence on the Dead River.

As we drifted around the edge of a small rocky point, we surprised a permanent dweller of the forested hills which line the basin. A beautiful whitetail doe stood at rigid attention on the river bank; one foreleg was raised as she poised, ready to flee. We moved so close to the shore that we could see her nostrils winnowing the morning air and discern drops of moisture on her muzzle. Suddenly, she caught a faint drift of our scent, snorted once, and bounded up the hillside in long graceful strides.

Beaching the canoe on a narrow strip of sand, we put on our daypacks and clambered to the top of a nearby ridge. We estimated that over a quarter of the leaves had fallen; the forest floor was littered with red and yellow and the woods had that open illuminated appearance so characteristic of autumn. Near the crest of the ridge a carpet of blueberry bushes, now in deep red fall costume, grew among the granite knobs and stunted jackpine. Selecting a rocky promontory which faced the northwest, we sat and gazed at the breathtaking scene. Far below the wide river, now a dark blue, shimmered in the early morning sun while above and beyond it proceeded ridge after ridge of radiance. In seemingly endless ranks, the waves of gold and red marched off toward the horizon, a resplendent parade feting the arrival of autumn. Now I understood what Sigurd Olson meant when he wrote so poetically of "fall's vivid banners against the sky."

The impact of so much astounding splendor is overwhelming; even though I want to continue looking, to absorb the hues into my very synapses, I must glance away. It's a little like eating too much of a favorite dessert; the overindulgence of the second or third

helping reduces the special value of the treat. We descended slowly from the ridge through the forest attempting now to note the more somber colors of fall. The plentiful bracken fern had turned a soft bronze but soon the frosts would shrivel the leaves to a dull brown; oak leaves had assumed a dignified brown and many of them would hold tenaciously to the branches throughout the late fall and winter. Even white pines choose fall to replace a large supply of their shiny green needles — we discovered under one large tree a ring of pale yellow where the needles had showered down.

Further downstream in a low muskeg area which borders the river, we discovered a stand of tamarack, the one "evergreen" which does in fact shed all its needles in fall. This ancient, slow-growing species — the only deciduous conifer — prefers cold deep swampy areas. The trees sported clusters of bright yellow needles; later in the fall they would become a tarnished dusty gold — Aldo Leopold called it smoky gold — before falling.

Tamaracks (or larches) often grow in old beaver meadows so we looked closely for signs of the large rodent which inadvertently had such a profound influence on the political and cultural destiny of the north country.

Near the huge concrete dam which holds back the water of the Forestville Basin, we spotted a dark head moving slowly in the water, trailing a v-shaped wake. As we turned and paddled toward it, the beaver saw the canoe, slapped the surface of the water with a loud whack and dove deeply toward the river bank. Edging close to the bank, we looked down into the clear water and saw the beaver's cache of aspen branches, the first portion of this winter food supply, carefully forced into the mud. An adult beaver consumes over two pounds of bark each day during the cold weather; before the ice formed his larder would have to be expanded.

On large bodies of water such as the impoundments of the Dead River, beavers often live in burrows located high in the bank with the entrance generally situated underwater. Although we did not find any that morning, beavers also have several escape tunnels, called plunge holes, into which they can slip to the safety of the river if a predator confronts them on land. We did find a mud patty, a beaver "sign post" on the river bank, where the creature deposits liberal quantities of its unique scent, castoreum, on short mud pedestals to alert others that the territory is taken.

Probably no other wild creature, with the possible exception of the bison, has had such an important impact on the land and the people dwelling on it. Not only did the beaver alter the topography of the streams and forests by his relentless damming, the luxurious quality of his fur set in motion conflicts between nations, resulted in exploration of the wilderness and damaged irrevocably a native culture which had existed in harmony with nature for centuries. It is fitting that at least one small village in the Peninsula is named Ahmeek in honor of the beaver (the Chippewa word for beaver is "ahmik").

We stopped for a mid-morning snack in a stand of aspen and watched the play of sunlight on the golden leaves. All the forest has a special luminous quality in autumn, an open resplendent character which contrasts sharply with the deep cool shadows of summer. The woods are lit up by the reflections of light from the thousands of brilliant yellow and red torches, those still decorating the trees and those now strewn carelessly on the ground. Even on somber days in early fall the gloriously colored leaves emit a pulsating glow which seems to flood the thickest glade and deepest valley; countless times during a soft rain I have stood under a huge maple and marveled at the lustrous stream of light emanating from the wet leaves. "Like fires just kindled . . .," wrote Thoreau,

" . . . a general conflagration fairly underway, soon to envelop every tree." In groves of aspens there is a particularly delicate and less garish light. I call it the aspen amber glow. Sunlight is suffused gently through and around hundreds of small golden leaves which flutter at the slightest breeze and reflect beams of light in a thousand different directions.

The wind became stronger and scores of leaves fluttered down where we sat finishing our snack. Remembering an old legend — that a person will have one month of good luck in the new year for each leaf caught in mid-air as it falls — we ran from place to place with outstretched hands until we had a year's supply of good fortune in the form of leafy bits of sunshine gold.

You can collect leaves, press them, photograph or paint them, but you cannot capture them. In the end you must simply experience them — to expand beauty in your soul and to be reminded that all things renew themselves in nature. And that it is better, as Jack London observed, to burn out than to rust out. Autumn is so short and yet so enthusiastic, so spectacular and so important to the endless circle of the season in the north country.

B A L L E T   I N   A N   A S P E N   S W A L E

ess than an hour of daylight remained as I gained the top of a grassy knoll at the end of a long open field; the sun was behind the spruces at the far edge of the meadow and already deep purple shadows reached out from the woods. Below me, my hunting companion and his dog were preparing to make one last swoop down the field. Fascinated, my own search for game forgotten, I knelt and watched Brad and his black labrador, Angus, reconnoiter a stand of aspen near the border of the dense evergreen forest. In a symphony of harmonious movement almost like a choreographed ballet, man and dog undulated along the valence of the popple swale. Suddenly, a ruffed grouse exploded from the aspens and winged for heavy cover. Brad swiftly raised his shotgun, fired once and soon Angus reappeared from the gathering gloom to lay the bird at his master's feet.

As I watched the consummation of this ancient act of cooperation between man and dog, I recalled a favorite verse from Proverbs 30: 18-19:

> *There are three things which are too wonderful for me, yea, four*
> *which I know not: the way of an eagle in the air; the way of a serpent*
> *upon a rock; the way of a ship in the midst of the sea; and the way*
> *of a man with a maid.*

And a fifth wonder for me: the way of a hunter and his dog in an autumn forest. Joining Brad, I sensed that he too was deeply moved, not by the bagging of a grouse in an aspen copse, but by the timeless nature of the event in which he and the black labrador had participated deep in an October evening. It is not easy to describe the mixed feeling of remorse and elation which follows hunting success; it is more visceral than cortical and relates to a time when searching for game was a preoccupation shared by *all* people who lived close to the earth. We were modern actors in an ancient drama, a real life play which links us all to our roots in time past. In hushed tones we chatted while examining the rich plumage of the bird — I could see it was a male by the continuous black band visible when Brad fanned the tail feathers.

"Hens are lighter, trimmer too," observed Brad. "And if you look closely at the tips of the small feathers at the base of a bird's tail, the male should have two or more ivory-colored, heart-shaped dots. Females have only one dot."

Angus whined impatiently, reminding us that other ruffed grouse awaited our pursuit and that not even a modern nimrod abandons the forest while twilight remains.

Autumn is hunting time in Superiorland. Not just any kind of hunting, though. People in the north country are obsessed with bird hunting. And not just any kind of bird, but the elusive ruffed grouse. The ruffed grouse is not large as game birds go, barely a foot and a half long from the tip of his crested head to his feathered feet and weighing between 16 and 20 ounces, but *Bonasa umbellus* is unrivaled king of the upland game species. He holds court daily in the forests of the north from mid-September until late fall. In no other quest do so many hunters walk so many miles and fire so many shots with so little tangible result.

Locally the ruffed grouse is often called partridge or, more simply and affectionately "pat," but taxonomists insist it is not a true partridge. By any name His Majesty is a beautiful bird with warm earth-toned feathers in gray (there is also a rufous phase) mottled with white and black; when he struts about with his tail fanned, his crest erect and his iridescent black and bronze neck feathers ruffled he is regal indeed. He fits right into the north country: he is tough, resourceful and a lover of wild forests. The haunts of the ruffed grouse are dense thickets of mixed cover, never far from small streams and favorite foods — hazelnuts, beechnuts, buds and leaves of all sorts. In fall I often find him in tangles of flaming blackberry canes, in abandoned orchards or along the edges of cedar swamps. His Royal Highness loves solitude as much as I do.

Each morning in late April and May the male ruffed grouse displays another unique talent: he is an accomplished drummer. Mounting a fallen tree — each drummer has a favorite moss covered log — he turns the spring forest into a reverberating echo chamber, proclaiming his territory and enticing a queen to share his throne. Standing almost erect and seeming to lean back on his tail, the ruffed grouse creates a drum roll by beating his wings. Beginning with a slow thump, the movement speeds up until it sounds almost like someone starting an outboard motor. On occasion I have heard the characteristic drum roll in October; even a monarch can make mistakes.

The King, as befits his royal status, doesn't simply flush like other game birds. He explodes — a feathered rocket with wings whirring, hurtling noisily through the trees and dense underbrush. He *always* catches the hunter by surprise. The bird is especially adept at taking wing when the hunter is entangled in brush, when he is shifting his gun from one hand to the other or when he is otherwise unprepared. It has an uncanny way of doing unusual, unexpected things — like flying right at the hunting party — which keep grouse-seekers in a state of apprehension . . . and joy. May His Excellency reign forever in the forests of the north!

If the ruffed grouse is the king of the upland game birds, then surely the woodcock is the clown prince. He certainly cuts a comic figure with his ridiculous physiognomy: chunky neckless body, short legs, long bill (four inches!), and protruding eyes set high, almost on top of his head. Biologists believe that *Philohela minor* represents a link between upland and shore birds. I am thankful that this particular link is not missing.

I first met the court jester while hunting grouse. Along a wet stream bed in a cover of young aspen, a leafy-brown long-billed bird flushed almost at my feet. With whistling wings and dipsydoodle flight, he zipped across the stream. Absorbed in this new sight I did not even hear my partner's impatient command to shoot. Then one spring evening I was introduced to the woodcock's amorous spring display. On moonlit nights in April, the male struts about in a sort of comic little dance. Accompanying his woodland two-step is a low nasal call not unlike a nighthawk, which is quite a different bird. The woodcock then launches on a long upward spiral and plummets down, emitting an eerie whistling twitter with his wings. Although I become renewed in spirit through seeking the elusive ruffed grouse in the fall woods, the woodcock, with his humorous appearance and habits, reminds me to stop taking life quite so seriously.

I count it as an extraordinary boon that the annual bird hunting season coincides with the autumn color show. After nearly four decades of searching for ruffed grouse and woodcock in the painted forests, my container of fond memories is more than filled. Bird hunting means many things: a cold shotgun on a frosty morning; fighting through a tangle of alders and willows along the bank of some small nameless creek; resting on a golden hillside; the rich earthy smell of aspen swales; sore muscles but a calm spirit and clear head at the end of the day. It also means the friendship of some very special companions. A good hunting partner who enjoys the endless talk and preparation as much as the actual hunt, a person who doesn't need to bag his limit to enjoy himself, an individual who doesn't get upset when temporarily lost in a cedar swamp, or has wet feet or cold hands, is hard to find and much appreciated. The most reliable grouse-seeking partner is a man's best friend, a canine companion.

Not just any dog will do, it must be a bird dog. And not just any bird dog, but one that shares an obsession with ruffed grouse and woodcock. It is possible to hunt without a dog, of course, but there is a special thrill in watching a pointer, setter or spaniel work an aspen swale. Good hunting dogs, particularly for grouse and woodcock, are not common; many animals have the right instinct, even a good nose but cannot learn to match their own enthusiastic pace to the slower stalk of the human hunter. Many are called to hunt but few dogs are really chosen natural hunters.

My Grandfather had an exceptional bird dog, a Springer spaniel named Sampson. Sam was an elderly canine of nine years when first I hunted over him. He was a real gentleman and a scholar of ruffed grouse. He was also a one man dog. Although he would permit me to pet his head and scratch behind his silky ears, he made it clear that he was only indulging my whims. When Sam needed any real affection he sought out my grandfather. The old man was very sparing in his overt display of affection; he believed that many good hunting dogs are spoiled by making house pets of them. He snorted contemptuously when he saw well-meaning but misguided owners indulging and hovering over their pets.

"Dogs can't be people," Grandfather would snap when he spied a poodle in a red weskit or a giant St. Bernard squeezed into a Volkswagen, "but these silly people pamper and spoil their animals until the poor buggers are as neurotic as their owners!"

Sampson suffered no identity crisis — he knew he was meant to sleuth for ruffed grouse and woodcock in the autumn woods. And, oh, how he could hunt! He searched slowly and patiently through all the thick tangles, always anticipating the game's movements and constantly checking to see where the human hunters were. Sometimes he would even come to a rigid point despite the book on spaniels which maintained that pointing was a skill that dogs of his breed do not possess. Grandfather sniffed that old Sam simply had not read the book. Sampson retrieved like a charm. Once when a hunting guest nailed a grouse with a nifty snap-shot in thick cover, Sam appeared to ignore Grandfather's urgent command to fetch the bird. The dog remained seated in the thicket looking expectantly up a nearby tree. Finally the old man entered the swale prepared to chastise Sam for his apparent disobedience. As he followed the dog's gaze upward there, caught by one foot in the crotch of an alder, was the ruffed grouse. Sam appeared to improve with each hunting season.

The years finally caught up with Sampson. His spirit was willing long after his joints weakened, his hearing dimmed and cataracts clouded his vision. The old bird dog would whine insistently until my grandfather relented and took him hunting "just once more" but it became more and more evident that Sampson was suffering terribly. Finally Grandfather decided to take the faithful spaniel to a veterinarian friend and have him put to sleep. Sampson lay quietly on the immaculate tile floor while the doctor explained how easily and swiftly the injection worked; the old dog thumped his tail feebly when Grandfather bent down to pick him up and place him on the table. Suddenly the old man could not go through with it. The fluorescent lights, the stainless steel examining table, the white-coated veterinarian — they were all so foreign to the countless hunting experiences the old man and dog had shared. Grandfather could not bear to have this be the last image of a loyal hunting partner.

The next morning at dawn my grandfather loaded the old dog tenderly into his pickup truck and drove out to a brushy river bottom where they had hunted together for many years. Easing Sampson out of the truck, he half-carried, half-dragged the dog into an aspen swale. The spaniel struggled to his feet and tottered slowly but eagerly into the woods. Fortuitously, Sam pinned down a bird almost immediately. Moving in with his shotgun ready, Grandfather flushed the grouse and then, while the old dog's nose was filled with the scent of game which he had sought for over twelve years, Sampson died with one blast of the shotgun.

Since then I have searched for game with many different dogs but the image of Old Sam still dominates my hunting memories. In fact, I did not realize how much I missed Sampson until recently when it was necessary for me to spend some time in a heavily populated city in the Lower Peninsula. A former teacher and long-time mentor was passing on to me the responsibility for his classic textbook in speech pathology and we were meeting with the publishers to discuss editorial and business arrangements. It was a distinct honor to be selected to continue the text; it was likely to cap my career in the field and provide some degree of financial freedom from my university duties so that I could write about the out-of-doors. It was an exciting, hectic and very rewarding time. Yet after only a day of meetings and city confusion, my nervous system was jangling. In order to reduce the cerebral noise, I took my host's Springer spaniel, who resembled Sampson in almost every feature, for a walk in the empty fields behind the farm home on the outskirts of the city. We moved slowly through the edge of a weed-choked field and I admired how the dog "prospected the air" with his sensitive nose — as Aldo Leopold once observed about another canine hunter. Near an old fence post Hercules came to a rigid point, one foreleg lifted in the classic pose. I moved in and a cock pheasant, cackling raucously, iridescent colors flashing, rose in the early evening sunlight. Almost immediately my senses were washed clean of traffic, smoke and city din and once again I was with Grandfather and old Sam searching for a ruffed grouse in a brilliant fall woodlot.

Hercules was my psychoanalyst that day, he helped to reorient my mind to what is important and lasting. He reminded me of my roots, of my biological heritage as a predator, a heritage I share with many other creatures. It is comforting to remember that I am, after all, part of the natural realm. Even now I smile at the self-important posturing, the intellectual arrogance I display when I forget that, despite all my rationality and civilization, I must inevitably dance to the same piper as do all other living things.

It is so easy to forget. Social philosophers call the tendency to equate our idiosyncratic view of reality as *the* correct view, the "illusion of centrality." It is so seductive — the feeling that our perceptions are unique, special, accurate. This illusion spawns an even more outrageous notion: that humans are the measure of all things. A gentlewoman of my acquaintance was shocked recently to discover that I search for ruffed grouse — and on occasion even manage to shoot a bird — in the autumn forests of the Superior Peninsula. No question about it, there is killing involved in the hunt. But it is done openly, honestly and on a very personal level. The instant reporting of human death in airline crashes, earthquakes, military struggles, the violence on television and in the city streets, all make death and dying impersonal and common. The distortion that humans are not predators is perpetuated by the consumer world of packaged instant manna in supermarkets.

But killing is only part of the autumnal ritual. When hunting is limited to utilitarian matters or reduced to bag counts, then something vital perishes for both men and their quarry. The pursuit is the thing which captures the imagination and nourishes the spirit; done in the freedom of the out-of-doors, both body and soul benefit. An integral aspect of the pursuit in the fall woods is the concordance between man and dog. Surely a ballet in a gold aspen swale is just as much a part of our cultural heritage as classical music, Greek sculpture or tomes of philosophy. The pursuit of game is an integral part of the ceremony of autumn in the Superior Peninsula.

━•❖•━━

F A L L   S T O R M S   O N   L A K E   S U P E R I O R

*I*t was still early morning when a familiar sound seeped through the foggy barrier of sleep and into my consciousness. Raising my head from the pillow, I listened — it sounded like several freight trains moving along at top speed. Instantly I was awake. Only one thing can make a noise like that: the waves of autumn are roaring on Lake Superior.

Impatiently, I awakened the children, made their breakfast, packed lunches for them and hurried them off to meet the school bus. Grabbing a slicker I jumped in the truck, drove through town and then headed down Lakeshore Drive which, as the name suggests, parallels the shoreline. It was a gray, misty morning; clouds hung low over the lake and a fine drizzle spattered the windshield. Huge waves assaulted the long sand beach so popular with summer sun worshippers. Pausing briefly at Shiras Park, I could see gigantic combers surging up and completely over Picnic Rocks, two small granite islands a short distance from shore. Where the road passes very close to the shoreline by the old charcoal plant, city crews had piled rocks and pieces of concrete to buffer storms like this one. The waves were lashing over the makeshift seawall drenching the road and spraying my truck with foam. Finally I came to my very special wave-watching vantage point, Presque Isle, a city park on the high rocky peninsula that is almost an island (and is called "The Island" by local people).

Parking the truck near the breakwater which protects the upper harbor and a large iron ore loading dock, I edged carefully toward the cliff. The long concrete breakwater is a popular place to stroll and fish in spring and summer but no one could stay on it today. Waves ten, fifteen, as high as twenty feet crashed over the barrier again and again. Foam spumed upward in white columns like geysers. Awed and thrilled by the display, I crouched at the very edge of the steep precipice, scrutinizing the waves, feeling their power and immersing myself in their continuous roar. Even in the tumultuous action of the water there is a pattern, a rhythm in the size and progression of the breakers; every seventh wave seemed to be noticeable larger than the preceding six. Is there in the waves of Lake Superior a sympathetic resonance to the pulse of the earth? Then, just for an instant, the clouds parted and a thin shaft of light illuminated the crest of a giant wave just as it landed against the breakwater. As the foam catapulted thirty feet straight into the air it was momentarily backlighted and I saw a multitude of intersecting crescents of shimmering blue, yellow and green. Far out on the lake I could see even larger waves rolling toward shore and I trembled involuntarily at the immense display of nature's strength and vigor.

Lake Superior puts on a spectacular show in October and November. When there are great contrasts between air in the polar region and that near the equator, cold and warm air masses collide in the upper atmosphere and high winds intensify. In fall some readings indicate speeds of up to 300 miles per hour in a narrow band of highest concentration referred to as the jet stream. The most dramatic storms originate when the upper-air patterns fluctuate in such a way that cyclonic systems form in the southwestern part of the country; these often charge pell-mell toward the midwest and northeastern sections of the United States. On days when the winds blow hard, the waters of Lake Superior are driven into a fury. Huge waves lash and pound the beaches and rocky ramparts.

I am not alone in my attraction to the waves of autumn. Many residents plan their day to include a trip to Presque Isle or at least a drive along the shoreline; during a fall blow I see scores of persons watching the water from their parked cars. They seem quiet, subdued, as if mesmerized by the spectacle. Wave-watching can, and often does, become a habit, but a casual glance or a few moments of watching from a warm car will not satiate my needs; I must be on intimate terms with the violent beauty. For me, watching the waves of autumn, far from being a sedentary occupation, is exciting, exhilarating. In the lake's rages I admire the total lack of reason and purpose, the blindness to all but the laws of its own nature. The water seems to have a life of its own even if a life only borrowed from the wind. When Lake Superior roars in fall it awakens some latent passions deep within me — the thunder, the spray, the incessant movement unleashes a torrent of elemental creative urges. At times like these I feel that I am suspended on the very leading edge of one of the most powerful forces in the universe. Anyone who doubts that Lake Superior is a palpable living organism should see it when the fall winds blow.

The Chippewas believed that *Michibizhiu,* the Great Panther Manitou, ruled the waters of the huge inland sea. They offered gifts of tobacco and made animal sacrifices to placate the god when storms occurred. While exploring the region in the early 1800s, Schoolcraft discovered a pictograph of the *Michibizhiu* decorating a cliff on one of the Huron Islands forty miles northwest of Marquette. On our many camping adventures, my small daughters used to try to calm Lake Superior by talking gently to its waters and feeding the waves handfuls of sand. Watching them humor the waves, I remembered an experience which suggested to me that men may have always responded to Lake Superior as a living thing.

On our honeymoon my wife and I rented a small cottage on the lake near Copper Harbor, a village at the very tip of the Keweenaw Peninsula. We searched for agates, hiked along the rocky beach and one warm day in late August I summoned up enough courage to dip into the numbing waters for a brief swim. My hands shrunk almost immediately in the cold water and as I splashed about to impress my bride, my new gold wedding band slipped off my finger and disappeared among the copper-colored rocks on the bottom. Frantically I dove again and again in the frigid water to locate the ring. Slowly at first, then at a quickening pace, the waves became larger, more powerful and I could feel the subtle tug of the current pulling me out; when I surfaced from each dive I was a few yards further from shore. Taking a large breath I made one last deep dive and searched the bottom feverishly. It was then that I felt myself slipping — the water seemed to grasp, almost suck me into a dark green vortex. I found myself mentally slipping, too; it seemed so easy to give up the struggle and ride away with the undertow. Bracing my feet on the bottom, I kicked hard and fought my way to the surface. Frightened, exhausted and emotionally overwrought, I swam slowly toward the shore. Just when I reached the shallow water and stood shakily up to walk ashore, I glanced backward to see a large dark wave cresting over me. In a panic I surged forward and stumbled near the shore as the comber broke over me. Grasping a boulder to prevent myself from being pulled out by the backwash, I felt a peculiar small round object. Looking down, I saw it was my wedding ring.

Lake Superior commands respect and is unforgiving to those who are not wary of its power. It is especially foolish to challenge the waves of autumn. During an educational convention one fall, two young teachers were entranced by the giant waves crashing over the breakwater. Instead of watching from shore they laughed off the cautions of several persons and sauntered out on the concrete barrier into the midst of the slashing foam. Almost instantly they were swept off the breakwater and drowned in the frigid, swirling waves.

The men who go down to Lake Superior in long ships dread the autumnal storms. Since modern times scores of sailors and a great number of vessels, from early wooden schooners to the latest bulk ore carriers, have been lost in the giant fall storms. The gales of November are especially dangerous. During the tremendous storm of November 9-11, 1913, a total of 260 men and 10 million dollars of property were lost on all the Great Lakes. The *Henry B. Smith* went down in Lake Superior with 24 men during that infamous hurricane. The 565 foot steel ore carrier was a new steamer on the lakes when it left Marquette at 6:30 p.m. on November 9, 1913. The skipper, Captain James Owen, was under severe pressure from the owners to speed up the transit time and so he sailed the ship loaded with 11,000 tons of iron ore directly into the face of the storm. When warned about the possible danger, Captain Owen treated it as a joke; his ship was only seven years old and one of the largest bulk carriers on the Great Lakes. The skipper was so confident of the *Smith* that he steamed away from the harbor without properly closing the giant hatches where the ore was stored. The *Henry B. Smith* was never seen again.

Several days later wreckage from the *Smith* washed up on the shoreline near Beaver Lake west of Grand Marais. A ladder-way, a single oar, a portion of the deckhouse and two cabin doors were found; the name of the ship was stenciled on the flotsam. Additional wreckage was found near Shot Point a few miles east of Marquette. Two weeks after the ship disappeared, the body of the second cook, Henry Askin, was discovered floating in a life jacket west of Whitefish Point. Six months later, on May 9, 1914, the remains of the *Smith's* chief engineer was found by two Indians on Michipicoten Island in the eastern part of Lake Superior. The ore carrier and the bodies of 22 other crewmen lie somewhere on the bottom of the lake.

Exactly 62 years later on November 10, 1975, another larger and more modern ore ship was lost when the gales of November were lashing. Downbound from Superior, Wisconsin, loaded with 26,000 tons of taconite pellets, the 720 foot *Edmund Fitzgerald* encountered a furious storm. The huge vessel was lost and Captain E.R. McSorley and all 28 crewmen perished in Lake Superior's icy waters.

The *Fitzgerald* steamed out of the Wisconsin port on November 9 with its heavy cargo of iron ore pellets. The freighter soon encountered a terrific storm with winds of 50 to 60 knots and waves as high as thirty feet. Because of the heavy weather, the ship altered its normal course and hugged the north shore of Lake Superior. Then, at its appointed time with fate, the *Fitzgerald* swung down towards Whitefish Bay for the approach to Sault Ste. Marie. Captain McSorley reported by radio on the afternoon of November 10 that the storm had torn down the ship's deck fences, damaged a vent, and caused the freighter to take on some water. According to the skipper of the *Arthur M. Anderson*, Captain J.B. Cooper, who was 10 miles away and in constant contact with the *Fitzgerald*, McSorley was not alarmed. Suddenly radio transmission ceased and the *Edmund Fitzgerald* vanished beneath the heavy seas.

What happened to the large ore ship? Did the gale winds blow off a hatch cover and swamp the vessel? Or did it strike some rocky shoal off the Canadian shore? No bodies have been recovered, only a lifeboat and some lifejackets. Sonar surveys later revealed that the *Fitzgerald* had split in two and underwater photography provided close-ups of the stricken vessel. The pictures show rips and tears in the ship's sides and deck where it split; the ship's two sections lie at angles to each other with wreckage and debris scattered in between. The rudder and hull show no evidence that the *Fitzgerald* struck a shoal. But the vessel did sustain massive flooding, probably sank very swiftly and then broke apart when it crashed onto the bottom of Lake Superior.

Man can control so many things in today's technologically oriented world; his ideas and his machines have rearranged and reshaped rivers, plains and entire mountain ranges to serve his purpose or meet his needs — often with little thought for the interrelated purposes served by the original terrain. The oceans and Great Lakes are still beyond man's control. Our use of them as shipping lanes, pleasure ways and transportation is almost completely dependent on the wind, weather and waves. Loss of life is tragic, yet our powerlessness humbles us to respect, as the Chippewa did, forces we cannot control. After the storm passes on its own timetable, indifferent to our plans and wishes, Lake Superior again appears benign. Ripples lap at pebbled shorelines, sandy bays are washed clean and smooth water sparkles far out to the horizon. The storm is over, the illusion of calm returns — for a time — to the largest and most unpredictable of the inland seas.

A   C O R N I S H   C O A C H

One cold November morning, quite a few years ago, I followed the dim figure of my Grandfather through a gloomy cedar swamp trying desperately to imitate his springy woodsman's walk. His toes came down gently exploring the trail and then his heel followed; despite his stealth, I had to hurry to keep up. We proceeded silently in the frosty dawn until a dry twig exploded violently beneath my inexperienced feet. Grandfather turned gravely and cast a long withering stare in my direction. I can still feel his despairing gaze even unto this day when I stub my size 12 clodhoppers in the woods. Perhaps because he served as my first mentor and model, his influence nearly fifty years later is still fresh and pervasive. Through the lens of his unique experience and personality, I came to see clearly the outdoor world. I wish that every boy could have a coach with my Grandfather's vision.

His eyes were the brightest bits of blue I have ever seen, rivaling even Lake Superior on a sun-drenched autumn day. An aquiline nose dominated his rugged face. Although not a large man, he was lean and hard in both body and spirit. We never discussed it, for Grandfather disliked speaking of himself, but I came to know that independence and self-reliance were not only central facets of his personal creed, they literally supported his flinty exterior.

My Grandfather was a man of great native intelligence, industry and impatience. Born in St. Austell, Cornwall, England, to a family of miners and quarrymen, in which male children were expected, indeed pushed, to make their own way in the world, he migrated at age 16 to Michigan's Upper Peninsula. He labored long hours first handling a drill and later as a mining captain in several deep shafts which probed the famous Keweenaw copper lode. What free time he had was devoted to exploring the rocks, hills and forests of his newly adopted land, and he swiftly became a skilled woodsman and hunter.

The old man taught me much and in my mind's eye I can still hear his distinctive Cornish brogue with its unusual cadence and the omitting and adding of "h"s. Generally he had little difficulty but once he experienced a communication breakdown that sorely frayed his awesome temper. He had taken a sample of milk for analysis and the clerk was filling out a routine form. "Name?" "Hay 'Arris," Grandfather said. The clerk blinked and replied, "Now, sir, that's Hay, spelled H-A-Y and Arris . . .?" "No, 'Hay,' 'Hay,' the 'Hay' stands for 'Halford,'" said Grandfather, becoming annoyed at the delay. "Halford 'Arris," he added tersely. "Okay, that is H-A-L . . ." responded the clerk querulously. "'ere, let me write it, you bloody hidiot," ejaculated Grandfather, spelling out 'A. Harris' on the form.

He knew nothing of child psychology and probably would have dismissed the whole works as a bunch of bloody nonsense (his vocabulary was more colorful). His approach was more direct. "That's not right, no, dammit," he would snap out of one corner of his mouth and then squirt a stream of well-chewed Peerless from the other side for emphasis. Woe be unto the person who did not heed the first such admonition.

The images of my preadolescent summers on my Grandfather's hardscrabble farm in the north country are still vivid after five decades. Life then, as I look back from the present hectic vantage point, was more whole and organic; our daily tasks, although long and arduous, were simple and directly related to warmth, food and shelter. My Grandfather was a taciturn man and for me, a stutterer, he provided an island of silent safety in a frighteningly verbal world. The interests we shared could be enjoyed without words. We did many timeless and simple things together quietly, but most of all I remember the silent ritual performed each evening behind his cabin. Sitting side by side on a crude bench he had made with his own hands, we watched the sun slowly make its descent behind the trees and wash the pines with fingers of pale gold. He neither tolerated or desired chatter and all others were banished from this evening rite.

I also remember the weekly visits to Kahn's General Store in the small forest village a few miles from the farm. Kahn's Store was a veritable treasure house of food stuffs, clothes and hardware. The clerks always greeted my Grandfather warmly and then slipped me a piece of licorice or a jaw breaker; even a nine-year-old boy had status in Kahn's. I would stand close to my grandfather while he chatted with the owners, an obligation if not a delight in those less hurried and more personal days. It would have been rude to simply buy something and leave. My Grandfather would nod and then I was released to wander and examine the wares through wondering eyes.

The smells, however, are what I remember best: The sharp clean odor of leather harnesses, the acrid smell of Hoppe's Number Nine in the gun section, the virile odor of wool shirts and red mackinaws, the pungent smell of the thick rounds of cheddar cheese and summer sausage hung from the rafters. But I always gravitated to the hardware section of the mammoth old store for there on the top shelf of a large glass counter resided the most longed-for item, a shiny jackknife.

It had four nickel-plated blades including a long serrated one with a fishhook degorger on the end; the handle was a beautiful mother-of-pearl that shimmered alluringly. Each visit I looked at the knife and fantasized owning it. Diligently I saved the meagre few pennies I earned each summer hauling water to the men in the field during haying time. But I told no one of my desire for the shiny jackknife; even a lad knew that money had to be put away for livestock feed and seed for the next summer.

It was late August of my third and final summer on the farm when we made one last trip to the country store. But when I approached the big glass showcase, my heart stopped for a moment: the jackknife was gone. Eyes blurred with tears, I fled from the store and sat sobbing on the running board of Grandfather's '41 Ford. When he returned from the store with his purchases, I quickly dried my eyes and slipped into the worn mohair seat beside him. As he dug for the car key in his pocket, he pulled out the shiny jackknife instead and placed it gently in my hand. "'ere, Lad," he said, slipping into his Cornish brogue, "'Old this for me will ye, while I find the bloody keys."

Now as he reached the appointed spot by a small creek in the dense cedar swamp, Grandfather motioned me to hunker down beside a gnarled burnt stump. My inexperienced eyes detected nothing unusual about the place but I knew the old man must have picked it carefully. "This is it, Lad," he whispered, "The big buck will come along that faint trail on your right." He started to leave and then turned back. "Stay put, now," he admonished, and then placed a twig of cedar in the band of my red hunting cap. His eyes twinkled and then without a sound he vanished among the trees.

I sat back against the stump and remembered: so Grandfather had known after all that I had gotten lost during last year's deer season. At age 14 it had been my very first deer hunt and I found it next to impossible to control my itchy feet. Wandering away from my assigned stand I soon became hopelessly lost in a jackpine barren. Blindly and in near panic, I had bulled my way through the dense forest for most of the day. Finally, exhausted and near tears, I had leaned against a tree to rest and discovered I was back to my original blind! The Old Man had never said a word about my disobedience.

Any transgression in safety, though, was swiftly and determinedly punished. Once when the son of Grandfather's favorite hunting partner absentmindedly waved his (empty) gun barrel in the old man's direction, he banished the young man from the woods. For forgetting the unspoken rule of safety, the lad had to spend the entire day sitting in the car.

But with all his severity, Grandfather had a zany sense of humor. He eschewed the usual hunting camp tricks — short sheeting, sewing long underwear pants closed, doctoring the stew with laxative — for elaborate practical jokes. For example, one of his hunting cronies would drink only one brand of beer and he hoarded his supply while in camp. Grandfather stayed up all one night carefully withdrawing the contents of an entire six pack by inserting a huge hypodermic needle he had borrowed from a veterinarian friend. He refilled the cans with water and soldered over the small hole. The shocked look on the beer lover's face when he punched the can open and tasted the water drove Grandfather out into the snowdrifts where he rolled in uncontrolled mirth.

But his best joke of all time was when he cured a hunting crony who habitually slept while waiting in a blind. This habit had annoyed Grandfather for some time and he was determined to cure his partner of this lack of vigilance. One mild afternoon when the sun was warming the hillside where his partner's blind was situated, Grandfather crept up quietly and listened; loud snoring emanated from the blind. Encouraged, the Old Man walked slowly up to the blind, carefully removed his partner's gun and quickly retraced his steps. By that time we were all gathered at the bottom of the hill to watch the show. Grandfather touched off a shot from his rifle. We all looked toward the blind. Ed emerged and raced around the structure looking and poking at every branch. Then he began to dismantle the blind, frantically tossing limbs and hemlock boughs in every direction. By the time we all reached the scene, Ed was on his hands and knees digging in the snow in a frenzied effort to find his rifle. He did not speak to my Grandfather for three deer seasons but, as far as I know, he remained alert on his deer stand.

I almost laughed aloud remembering Ed's education as I sat waiting in the cedar swamp for the big buck the Old Man had assured me would come along. Glancing around the faint trail, I spotted a movement. Instantly alert, I carefully shifted position so that I could shoot swiftly. A huge buck bounded into view and cleared a windfall at the edge of the woods in one gigantic leap. It is amazing how many things you see in one single moment of excitement. The buck was very large and heavy; his muscles bulged under his chocolate brown coat when he sprang forward. The main beams of his antlers were thick and the spread was abnormally wide; the individual tines, ten in all, jutted upward like huge ivory exclamation marks. At each bound a ring of frosted breath puffed from his distended nostrils.

As if in a dream I noticed that my rifle came up, the hammer was cocked and the sudden blast shattered the quiet of the swamp. The magnificent buck lay almost at my feet, sleek and dignified even in death. I must have been overcome with excitement for the next thing I remember my Grandfather was there kneeling beside the big whitetail, a sad smile playing at the corners of his mouth and his eyes moist with tears.

"Got something in my eye," he said gruffly, "'ere, lad, take my knife now and do a good job like I showed you." Later he pounded me on the back and did a little Cornish jig around the big deer.

I killed that big swamp buck almost half a century ago but the event is still crystal clear in my memory. It was a shock when Grandfather announced one fall that he would not hunt any more. From now on he would tend the fire in camp and make sure that the stew was ready for hungry hunters. Despite his protests I bought a license for him and then cajoled and badgered him into sitting beside his favorite runway once more. But all during the early morning hours I worried about the Old Man. Abandoning my stand I retraced my steps to his blind. He was gone and his faltering steps led back to the old log cabin we used as a deer hunting camp. I ran all the way. There he was, sitting quietly, a blanket over his shoulders, smoking his favorite pipe and watching the flames in the stone fireplace. Moving gently toward him I thought desperately for the right words to console the old hunter, but before I could speak he produced that very same knife with which I had field dressed the big swamp buck. His eyes twinkled in amusement as he said: "Be a good lad, will ye, and dress out that deer in back; it's a nice fat spike. 'e was standing by the privy when 'hi' got back to camp."

THE OLD ONE

Somewhere in the lonely dense alder thickets shrouding the narrow Sullivan Creek near Big Bay lives a majestic whitetail buck, an old hermit with a crown of thick stubby antlers worn proudly as if to celebrate his long life and unique wisdom. His muzzle is grey with years and his neck and flanks are scarred from many battles. His fluid grace is marred by a decided limp in his right front leg, perhaps a souvenir of some past hunting season.

I first met the Old One during a sudden wet spring snowfall which sometimes surprises the north country on the opening day of trout season. Instead of following a logging trail down to the main river, I cut through a dense stand of young jackpines, intending to fish my favorite pool below the rapids. As I rounded a blowdown, a huge dark form loomed out of the driving snow. The deer paused just an instant. In that moment I noted his tremendous size, the grey around his mouth and nose, the battle scars and the large gnarled bosses where his antlers were beginning to bud. Just a flash, and then like an apparition he disappeared into the white storm. I glanced down to make certain I had really seen the animal and found his fresh tracks; I knelt to examine the pronounced drag mark in the white mantle following his right front hoof mark. The magnificent old buck was real — and so was my resolve to see him again.

It was almost the end of May before I saw the Old One again. Early one morning as I drove slowly down the Murphy Trail listening for warblers and other late spring migrants, the huge dark whitetail with the characteristic limp crossed the road near Dutch John's cabin. I stopped the car and checked his tracks, huge imprints in the moist sand. Filling my black briar pipe and touching a match to the bowl, I traced the Old One's trail up the faint, weedchoked path leading to the abandoned homestead.

The Old One

Sometime early in the century, the sturdy German immigrant, jaded with city life, fled to this remote corner of the Upper Peninsula, built a log cabin and eked out a living trapping beaver and growing potatoes. Over the years he managed to clear a few acres for his modest crops but the aspens and alders have already reclaimed the land. The cabin stands brooding in a small clearing as if awaiting Dutch John's return. The cracked enamel washbasin, an ancient rusty straight razor and a homemade dust pan are placed carefully near a crude bench within the one-room log shelter. But the independent home-steader died several years ago and will not return. I sat on a stump and tried to imagine what life had been like here — the endless battle with the encroaching forest, the numbing six-month winters and the hordes of mosquitoes and other insects in the spring. There must have been good times, too — the smell of woodsmoke on a frosty morning, the riot of colors in the fall and the peace of mind that comes when you drive life into a corner and reduce it to its simplest terms. A blue jay screamed from a nearby jackpine and roused me from my reverie. Abandoning the Old One's trail through the dew-damp-ened grass, I retraced my steps to the car and laid out careful plans for the summer.

Every moment I could afford away from the summer session at the University was spent scouring the area, building blinds in likely places and, most of all, looking for some sign of the big buck. But I did not see his tracks again until just before school started in mid-September. Most of the deer in this region, especially the big old bucks, spend the warm months in the Huron Mountains where the breezes keep the insects away.

The trophy deer in the Upper Peninsula typically come from three areas: the Porcupine Mountains in the west, the Stonington Peninsula in the south and the Huron Mountains in the north, either at Skanee on the western slopes or near Big Bay on the eastern grade. The soil in these regions, biologists claim, contains unique concentrations of minerals. Deer browsing on the foliage growing in these areas produce large antlers year after year.

The Huron Mountains area is perhaps the wildest and most extensive of the three regions: over 30 miles across, it contains rugged slopes, dense stands of pine and hard-wood, and many lakes and streams. Although much of the area belongs to the Huron Mountain Club, a group of wealthy summer dwellers, other large tracts of timberland are open to the public. Parts of the region have never been fully explored. An attempt was made to re-introduce the Eastern Timber Wolf into the Huron Mountains; although the attempt failed, largely due to the intolerance of some members of the human species out-side of the Huron Mountains area, it is still an excellent wild hunting ground large enough for both wolves and people.

I am often asked why I hunt. Partners never ask because they know the answer, but probably every sportsman has been challenged to respond to the (usually) hostile rhetorical query, "But why do you want to harm wild animals?" Unless the interrogator is a nonviolent vegetarian, the obvious reply is, "Why do you, by your purchase of meat, sanction the killing of domestic creatures?" "Well, that's different," goes the rejoiner. "Farm animals are raised for food and besides, we don't do the killing." But do the sheep and the steer realize that? It must be comforting to the Hereford or Shropshire to know as it is herded to slaughter that it was raised for the noble purpose of human consumption.

Furthermore, to excuse oneself from an animal's death by disclaiming personal involvement is, of course, simply ignoring the point; it is still killing even though the consumer is somewhat removed from the act. Logically, the detractors of hunting should not slap mosquitoes, spray flies or even trap mice. Isn't that killing? At least the hunter will readily admit that he seeks to slay a wild creature by his own hand (although most will also admit that the seeking, the chase is what hunting is all about).

For several years I examined my personal rationale for hunting deer with a bow and arrow but nobody asked to hear my philosophy. Quite unexpectedly, during a neighborhood dinner party, I mentioned the large old deer I had admired near the Huron Mountains. A highly verbal woman who champions various popular causes challenged me to justify my devotion to archery hunting. There was a long pregnant pause while the other guests sat with forks at parade rest silently awaiting my typical inarticulate and often testy defense. Despite the nervous high signs from my wife to let the issue drop, I picked up the lady's velvet gauntlet. As far as I can recall, the dialogue went something like this:

"Well, Mrs. Dilworth, although there are a few boneheads in our ranks who act as if getting a deer every year was part of the Bill of Rights, most sportsmen, and in particular bow hunters, are interested in the chase. Robert Service spoke for most archers when he wrote: 'Yet it isn't the deer that I'm wanting, so much as just finding the deer.' Killing, apart from the chase, is simply not what most hunting is about."

"My word! I had no idea that people who hunt could be so literate. But tell me, if the seeking and not the killing is so important, then why don't you go hunting with a camera?"

"I didn't say that killing wasn't a part of hunting. It certainly is. When I stalk in the forest with a weapon, I become part of nature. Life is not, after all, a mere spectator sport. Humans, too, are part of the food chain which binds all living creatures together. Even though I do not need the meat in order to survive, I do need to be reminded that instead of being apart from or above nature, I am a *participant*."

"Yes, but hunting is so . . . so . . . barbarian!"

"I agree. So are pleasant activities like watching waves, staring into forest fires and attending barbecues. For eons man lived close to the natural world and a few centuries of concrete and cars cannot erase those primitive stirrings, that ancient heritage we all carry deep in our racial memory. You see, death is an essential part of life and when I hunt, I am merely fulfilling an ancient natural urge. We would not be in a critical environmental crisis today, I submit, if more persons kept in touch with their origins as part of the natural order. Hunting reminds me that I am a part of that order."

Mrs. Dilworth paused a moment and speared a lone pea on her plate before continuing her attack.

"Now be consistent! You talk about the natural order: don't those wild animals have a right to live and die without human impact? Won't we have more endangered species with more hunting?"

"You mean, I think, isn't a natural death better? Have you ever visited a deer yard in March when the animals have stripped the trees of food as far as they can reach and are dying of starvation? It's not a sight that's easy to forget. Their coats are ragged, their eyes dull and abdomens bloated. Without killing of some animals, particularly deer, the population eat themselves out of house and food. It is more cruel to overprotect deer. The crucial fact is that nature 'builds in' an oversupply; more rabbits, grouse, deer, etc., are born each year than can find food and hiding places. This surplus — sometimes as high as 30% — will die anyway. Actually, then, the controlling factor for game is habitat, not hunting seasons. There has never been an open season on bluebirds, yet their numbers have declined quite dramatically because of an absence of nesting sites. The creation of shopping malls, freeways and suburban sprawl has probably had more negative impact than hunting. In fact, more deer are killed on Michigan highways every year than by licensed bowhunters. Shall we ban cars?"

The other dinner guests had remained unusually silent during the extended dialogue. But now Mr. Dilworth came to his wife's defense.

"It sounds as though you've done your homework, Professor. But is it not true that everyone has a right to enjoy wild creatures, and doesn't the annual waterfowl season, for example, interfere with *my* chances of seeing migrating ducks and geese?"

"That's probably true, although there are special places — refuges — and all the rest of the year to see birds. You know, though, I'm glad you brought that up: sportsmen, through their license dollars and federal excise taxes, have done more for game species — for all wildlife — than all the bird watchers, mushroom collectors and latter day ecologists combined. Hunting license fees amount to over one hundred million dollars annually, and each year about $50 million is collected by the federal excise tax on sporting goods. This money goes into conservation projects, the refuge system and land on which, by the way, you can hike, photograph and so forth. The hunter is paying the bills for everyone!"

At this point, the hostess broke in announcing dessert and with a sigh of relief, the table talk moved on to other topics. But I felt that I had scored some points and that perhaps the Dilworths, as well as the others present, had some food for thought with their dinner.

It was the second weekend in September and the first red and yellow leaves were showing in the hardwoods when I found the Old One's tracks crossing the woods road near Dutch John's cabin. He was back in his fall territory.

Despite the fact that Marquette, where I live, is only 30 miles from Big Bay, my wife and I spent several weekends camped near Dutch John's in our pickup camper. Even with all our intensive hunting, we failed to see the Old One. I passed up several shots at does and small bucks, holding out for a chance at the big whitetail. By the end of the season, we had located his main hide-out, a 40-acre plot of mixed hardwoods and hemlock near the homestead. It was bounded on one edge by a county blacktop road and bordered by a wet marshy beaver pond which featured a few hummocks with three or four feathery tamarack trees growing from each mound. The only logical escape route was to cross the Sullivan Trail near the homestead and gain the safety of an extensive cedar swamp. We laid our plans. Two hunting buddies would slowly move through the area while I posted near the escape route; we suspended brightly colored balloons from low branches near the blacktop road. Dancing and tossing in the wind, they would turn the Old One back and channel him toward my ambush. The plan drew a blank; we tried it again on the next morning, the last day of the archery season — still without success.

I traced and retraced the area and finally, just as the sun was setting and lighting the pines with pale gold, I discovered the trick. I had paused to rest on the edge of the beaver meadow when the Old One stood up on one of the small tamarack-covered hummocks, took one gigantic leap and disappeared into the hemlocks. Instead of crossing by

Dutch John's cabin, the wise old whitetail had sloshed out to a hummock in the pond and curled up tight. When danger passed, he simply bounded back into his territory.

Alas, my time was gone and in ten days, the regular gun season would open. The Old One might not survive the red-coated army. It was an agonizing ten days. Several times, I took down my dusty rifle and contemplated a return to gun hunting after so long an absence. Did I want to get the Old One this way? I vacillated back and forth but finally on opening morning of the rifle season, I parked my car and headed toward the ambush site. I walked briskly through the dim dawn light, past the marshy pond and then quietly doubled back and hid behind a large burnt stub. In less than ten minutes of breathless waiting, the Old One eased out of the tamarack swamp and stood broadside not more than 60 yards away. His massive gnarled antlers seemed to glow faintly from the rose and pink sunrise; he was a dark brown color — the deep hue of a swamp buck. Easing back the hammer, I slowly raised the rifle and lined up the peep sight on his thick neck. At that instant he turned suddenly and looked directly at me. My finger tightened on the trigger — and then I lowered the gun.

"Get down in the thick swamp," I shouted, and the majestic old whitetail bounded away in long leaps.

This winter, when the winds from Lake Superior drive the swirling blankets of snow into a thick mantle around Dutch John's abandoned cabin, when the aspens explode during the frigid nights, when the Northern Lights dance along the horizon, the Old One will bed down in the dense thickets close to the tall hemlocks. Perhaps I shall see him next year.

⊶⊷⊷⊶

S N O W   B U N T I N G S

Now it is late autumn and nature's tints grow darker, duller, as if a vast stage were being prepared for the long harsh drama of winter. The gay colored leaves have shriveled and lie in somber brown piles mixed with the decaying residue of other years. Only the tough foliage of the oak and beech persist; on my hikes I hear their dry leaves rattling in the breeze, a dirge which accents the final days of the dying season. The secrets which the trees have guarded so well all summer are now disclosed. Among the bare branches the artfully constructed nests of birds stand out starkly, abandoned and dormant now, their purpose served. The small nest of the red-eyed vireo, made from plant fibers and lined with fine grasses, hangs below the fork of a maple sapling almost at eye level — how did I miss it in my summer rambles? The nest of the Baltimore oriole swings from the drooping branches of a large cottonwood; this most elusive nest in summer is outlined clearly now against the November sky.

The sky is a sullen lead gray. The clouds hang low and the air is cool and moist with a hint of snow; a few white crystals float past me. The woods are quiet, expectant, waiting. The dried bracken ferns are dark brown and have fallen in crazy patterns. Once again the only touch of color in the forest is the soft green of a mossy log. Looking back down a long, open field, an ancient pasture near my home, I remember the lines from Thomas Hood's poem of late autumn:

> I saw old Autumn in the misty morn
> Stand shadowless like silence, listening
> to silence.

And then, quite unexpectedly, a flock of birds flashing white despite the dull morning light, fluttered in on a fresh breeze and began to search for weed seeds. I walked toward them and they launched upward like reversible snowflakes, the only bit of color on the dead landscape. "Thanks a lot, snow buntings," I murmured to myself, "I needed that."

I had almost forgotten the singular delight in late fall, when, after all the summer residents have fled, the snow buntings arrive from the far north. Unlike other migrants who merely pass through the region, this small, restless bird remains in the Peninsula, basking in the comparative "warmth" of our winter. The origin and nature of bird migration remains mysterious although ornithologists have studied and speculated about it for years. Early observers thought the cyclic seasonal movement was based on a northern ancestral home; when the birds were forced southward by the glaciers which retreated during the warm season, the pattern of seasonal movements was set in motion. Others postulated a southern home theory. In this concept, birds originated in more southern climes but were forced to move northward each nesting season in order to find a suitable territory. Now most scientists explain the seasonal migration on the basis of photoperiodism — days get longer, sex glands begin to enlarge and most avian species then move northward to mate and raise offspring. The process is reversed in autumn.

Although the Peninsula is not located on a major north-south flyway, we do observe considerable numbers of fall migrants. The first birds to assemble in preparation for the annual migration are the *Icteridae* and *Hirundinidae*, the several species of blackbirds and swallows. In fact, one of the earliest signs of autumn, generally in late August and early September, is the flocking of the swallows, grackles and bobolinks. In the fields, on telephone wires, in the tops of dead elms in the small villages, they can be seen gathering for the annual *hegira*. Like restless children they move, not just one alone, but all together from place to place in large flocks. Another dark bird, the starling, also gathers in large flocks even though most members of this vulgar tribe are permanent residents here. Fall conventions of starlings, unlike those of the lovely snow buntings, tend to lead one to wish a pox upon Eugene Schiefflin who, in the last part of the 19th century, fulfilled his strange ambition of importing all the species of birds mentioned in Shakespeare's plays and thus introduced *Sturnus vulgaris vulgaris* to North America.

In mid-September scores of flickers gather in remote meadows and hardwood forests. This handsome woodpecker whose ringing call helped to usher in spring, and who searched for ants all summer in my backyard, now flushes wildly in fields and along old woods roads. His deeply undulating flight and white rump are unmistakable even in dense brush.

Around the end of September, the seasonal migration takes a great leap forward. Traveling on isotherms of weather, flocks of warblers, vireos and thrushes arrive. The thrushes in particular seem to like our overgrown yard, for they linger several days, resting before the next surge in their journey south. The first to arrive is the Swainson's thrush, looking wide-eyed and slightly disoriented with his buff eye ring (do birds experience time-lag like jet travelers?). Then one morning a gray-cheeked thrush appears and sits silently in a frost-blackened aspen tree. He will tarry, too, and if I am fortunate, reward me with a fragment of his ethereal song — oh, what tales of the far north he could tell!

There is no melody quite like the liquid warble of a bluebird on a warm October afternoon; it caresses the listener gently, lovingly. Alas, now that these friendly thrushes have become less common, it is a rare treat to see a flock migrating. Last fall I was waiting in ambush for a whitetail deer on a platform placed high in a red oak tree. Just before sunset five mature birds, three males and two females, flew into the tree and perched less than 18 inches from where I stood concealed in camouflage clothing. They warbled softly for several minutes and the melody seemed to spread soothingly throughout my entire being. Instead of a deer I took home that evening a lasting feeling of beauty.

October in the north country is also the month for the magic of geese. Unlike the soft call of the bluebird, the raucous gabbling of migrating Canada geese stirs the listener, makes him restless, perhaps a little sad and eager to wander. Whenever they appear overhead, I must abandon my work and immerse myself in their wild voices and the splendor of the sun flashing on their wings. They are overhead for only a few short days, out of sight and sound again until early spring, and we must look closer to earth for our other fall birds.

Although the evening grosbeak is a capricious migrant — preferring to move west-to-east rather than in the usual north-south patterns — we will not question his errant habits if only he will visit us each November. With his yellow body, white and black wing patches and loud piping whistle, the grosbeak offers a splash of color and exuberance at the somber brown end of fall.

And then when the annual avian parade seems to be over, when I have resigned myself to the long quiet winter, the final visitor from the far north makes his appearance. Little *Amauligak*, as the Eskimos call the snow bunting, is a consummate resident of the arctic. He nests on bare stony areas or under rocky crevices near snow drifts; he bathes in snow and burrows in it for insulation at night. It amuses me that this little snow sprite of the tundra elects to spend his winter vacation in our icy Superiorland.

He is a handsome fellow with his large white wing patches, brown-salmon collar and streaked back; the overall impression is a tawny and white small bird about the size of a sparrow. My spirits are always lifted by the snow bunting's canary-clear voice — a lilting descending whistle which often ends in a musical gibbering. Little *Amauligak* even bursts into song in flight. When disturbed, he emits a nasal "beez, beez."

Like many creatures which live in the lonely isolation of the arctic, snow buntings are trusting and can be approached more closely than birds which exist near human-impact areas. A flock continues to feed until I edge within a few feet and then the entire group swirls upward like a gust of wind-blown snowflakes only to alight again nearby. I find these ground-loving birds most often in fields and open meadows where they prospect for seeds. But they are pragmatic and will exploit any bounty. On our campus late one summer, a large building was torn down to make room for a new office complex. When they finally hauled away the last brick and graded the hillside, it was early November and too late to begin working on the new structure. To prevent erosion, the groundskeeper sowed the entire open area in rye. Before the seed could germinate, the weather turned cold and one morning a light cover of snow blanketed the campus. That same morning, a large flock of snow buntings discovered the cache of rye and requisitioned the seeds for themselves. Reveling in the wealth of food, they remained within sight of my office window all winter. Instead of taking coffee breaks, I amused myself watching little *Amauligak*.

After several years of observation, it seems to me that snow buntings are very happy little mites. Despite sleet or storm they always seem to be busy, always singing.

Some biologist friends are bemused by my attribution of human qualities to birds and mutter snidely about anthropomorphism. Secretly, though, I think they agree with Francis Bacon that such labels are figleaf words which cover our ignorance of how things really are outside our human sphere.

This I do know: snow buntings remind me of a very important lesson near the end of autumn each year. It is simply to turn a problem to your advantage. Shakespeare said it more poetically, "Sweet are the uses of adversity." With their apparent joy in living under extenuating circumstances, the small arctic dwellers touch me deeply with a new awareness of life. Snow buntings remind me also of a very special mentor, a biology teacher who took the time to share his contagious enthusiasm for nature with his tenth grade pupils.

Hessel Tenhave was much more than an exceptional teacher, he was a great human being. He cared about us and made us care; he built fires *within* rather than *under* his students. A tall angular man, his face always crinkled by a grin, Mr. Tenhave had the ability to be guide, coach, companion and counselor — all at the same time. He taught by example and parable, not precept, and his impact on my life was enormous. Among all the bits of wisdom he shared, three simple lessons in particular are illustrative of Mr. Tenhave's philosophy.

By his own example, Tenhave showed us that happiness depends on what a person has in his head rather than in his pockets. Wealth, he taught, is an intangible asset which is based on our ability to find happiness in everyday events and in the amount of living we can crowd into the time allotted to us.

Secondly, Mr. Tenhave provided a model of how to live in the here and now, not by pursuing the present with baited hooks and nets, as Annie Dillard wrote, but by waiting expectantly and empty-handed. He would tolerate no worrying, no chronic replaying of what might have been.

"Life is not a dress rehearsal," he observed wryly one day as we hiked along an old woods road, "even though we sometimes feel we will have a chance to go back and repeat a particular event or relive a certain day." Long before the popular song proclaimed it, Tenhave taught that today is forever.

Mr. Tenhave's third lesson has meant the most to me over the past four decades. Quoting Voltaire (it was clever, now that I think about it, how he lured us into reading the classics), he maintained that solemnity was a disease and that the only sane posture was to laugh away the wrinkles of doubt and care. Late one afternoon as we returned from a field trip to Jack Miner's Bird Sanctuary in Ontario, Mr. Tenhave became hopelessly enmeshed in a monumental Detroit rush-hour traffic jam. Noticing his grin I asked him what in the world he found humorous about the blare of horns and the noxious exhaust fumes.

"Oh, it can be annoying," he agreed, still smiling, "but only if I choose to be upset and then dwell on my anguish. So, I keep looking for the pony — and there it is!"

He pointed to a sign in a barber shop window that stated: "Five Barbers, No Waiting." Beneath it, a second sign proclaimed: "Television While You Wait." We all laughed and then one student asked Mr. Tenhave what he meant by "looking for the pony." While we waited in the traffic jam, he told the parable of the pony.

There once were twin boys, Moe and Joe. Moe was a gloomy pessimist while Joe always looked on the happy side of everything. Confounded by this unusual dichotomy in identical twins, a group of psychologists decided to conduct a careful study of the youths. The twins were placed in different rooms and after 30 minutes, the research team began to interview the subjects.

The investigators commenced with Moe, the pessimist. In a large room filled with new toys, the boy sat morosely; he sighed heavily when the psychologists entered. After quietly observing for a moment, one member of the team asked Moe how he liked all the new toys. Did he want to play with the baseball or the fielder's glove?

"No," said Moe sadly, "I would probably lose the game."

"How about the boxing gloves?" suggested another psychologist.

"That's out," replied Moe, "I would just hurt myself."

This line of inquiry continued for several minutes. Each toy the researchers enumerated was greeted with the same gloomy prediction of trouble.

Leaving Moe, the psychologists entered the other room to interview Joe. In a large room filled only with manure, the optimistic twin was cavorting about in spasms of glee. Joe was diving headlong into the manure, throwing it in the air, laughing and chortling in happiness. The psychologists were dumfounded.

"Why are you so happy in this smelly, dirty place?" they asked him.

"With all this manure," Joe responded excitedly, "there just has to be a pony in here somewhere!"

My small avian friends from the arctic, the snow buntings, remind me to keep searching for a pony. Looking for these happy migrants in the somber days of late fall can make the transition from the brilliance of autumn a time of new awareness and pleasure.

S C A R L E T   S K I E S   I N   T H E   M O R N I N G

The never-ending cycle of seasons now moves relentlessly toward the win-ter solstice and soon autumn will be only a bright lingering memory. Already a light dusting of snow covers the fields and decorates the pines; a thin sheath of ice forms on the inland lakes and hoarfrost sparkles on the bare branch-es of maples and birches in the river valleys. The sun rises reluctantly and traverses the sky low on the southern horizon. Winter is almost ready to take up its long tenure in the north country.

But there is one final display of color, an extravagant epilogue to fall before the monochromatic snowscape of winter — it is the time of scarlet skies over Lake Superior. Sunrises in early December are eruptions of crimson; albeit brief, the display is incredi-bly intense. Early this morning I stood on a favorite vantage point overlooking the lake and waited for the sun to rise. Slowly the soft doe-gray of dawn gave way to a deep carmine and then the sky turned swiftly to a brilliant blood-red. I was bathed in the eerie scarlet hue and as I looked out over the water, it seemed as though Lake Superior was aflame all the way north to the Canadian shore. A gull called peevishly reminding me that I must leave the lakeshore and hurry to meet my morning classes.

No question about it, Lake Superior is a dominant force in this region. After coming to know and love the lake for even a short time, most residents could not live happily any-where else. It is like a good and constant companion — cold, aloof and capricious, to be sure — and a source of inspiration. We feel the lake's influence on our thoughts, our moods, our entire lives — its presence is commanding. Lake Superior even influences the weather in the area. Near the shoreline where we live, temperatures in winter may be as much as 20 degrees warmer than in the interior; in summer the situation is reversed and the lake acts as a giant air conditioner. It is no wonder that the Indians called it *Gitchie-Gumme*, the *Great-Sea-Shining-Water*, and worshiped the lake as a deity. It is difficult to talk about this clear inland sea except in superlatives.

Consider its vital statistics:

- greatest width from east to west — 350 miles
- greatest width from north to south — 160 miles
- greatest depth — 1,333 feet; average depth — 472 feet
- covers 31,700 square miles — it could hold Rhode Island, Connecticut and three states the size of Massachusetts inside its borders
- has 2,796 miles of shoreline

The dimensions are reason enough for the name "Superior," although according to historians, the appellation was a fortuitous occurrence. When the early French explorers first discovered the huge body of water lying north of Lake Huron, they referred to it as *le lac Superieur*, or "the upper lake," and so labeled it on their maps. At one time the lake was dedicated as Lac Tracy in honor of a French governmental official. However, the nickname "Superior" persisted and now no other name seems appropriate.

All the superlatives about Lake Superior are true. It is the largest, coldest (maintaining an overall temperature of about 42 degrees Farenheit year round), deepest and roughest of the Great Lakes. It is also the cleanest.

One of the very first impressions a new observer acquires about the lake is the incredible clarity of its waters. An early explorer, John Johnston, who sailed upon the lake in 1792, recorded this comment in his diary: "There is nowhere perhaps on the globe a body of water so pure, so light as that of Lake Superior." Fortunately, the statement is still correct — Lake Superior is still the largest body of transparent water in the world.

Yet, despite its immense proportions, its awesome power and pristine clarity, Lake Superior is a fragile jewel. Fragile because it is still very young in a biological sense and its waters drain very slowly; experts estimate it would take at least 500 years for Lake Superior to purge itself of impurities. By comparison, Lake Erie could cleanse itself in 20 years. Fragile because of the outrageous bureaucratic notion that, since the lake is so clean, we can permit pollution up to a certain level, established by monitoring an already dirty body of water in another area. Fragile, and vulnerable, because — and this is the heart of it — the idea still prevails that our natural resources are inexhaustible.

I am always surprised and offended when I realize that some persons see Lake Superior only as a source of cheap water for industrial purposes, or worse, as a convenient dump for the by-products of iron ore mining. On a field trip with several students, we stopped at a popular restaurant in Munising for a late breakfast. At the next table a party of businessmen were discussing economic issues over coffee. The subject was the Reserve Mining Company, its disposal of taconite tailings in the lake, and the lengthy litigation resulting from the federal government's attempts to enforce clear water standards and stop the dumping.

"Well, let's face it," said one of the men coolly, gesturing toward the lake, "that's a mighty big hole out there!"

The saga of Reserve Mining Company and its use of Lake Superior as a big hole serves as an example of how difficult it is to stop pollution once it is initiated, and why it is important to be vigilant in protection of our precious natural resource. For 32 years, from 1948 to 1980, despite warnings, court trials and timetables for on-land disposal, Reserve dumped *67,000 tons of waste material into Lake Superior every day.*

Reserve, owned jointly by Republic and Armco Steel Companies, had a legal permit to dump into the lake, a permit which most now agree would not have been granted in light of present day knowledge. But times were different in 1948 when the U.S. Corps of Engineers gave their approval to Reserve to dispose of their mine tailings into the lake. The permit was later amended several times to allow for expansion in the quantity of waste materials. The company promised that if the tailings escaped a nine mile zone in the lake or endangered human health or the fish population, the dumping would cease. Asbestos-like fibers from the tailings have long since been found in the Duluth harbor, the waters of Isle Royale National Park and in my home waters of Marquette Bay. Yet no closure occurred.

Throughout the lengthy trials the Company maintained that the tailings were composed of inert metals and sand, materials similar to those which flow naturally into the Lake Superior watershed.

Yet objective analyses of the tailings showed that one day's dumping was adding an astounding quantity of elements to the water: 30 tons of phosphorus, 4-1/2 tons of chromium, 3 tons of copper, 3 tons of lead, one ton each of nickel and zinc and 373 tons of manganese! Unknown at the permit time, trillions of microscopic silicate fibers were also being released. No one really knows what impact these "inert" elements had — or will continue to have — on organisms which exist in the lake or those who draw their drinking water from it.

Residents along Minnesota's north shore and as far east as the Apostle Islands (Lake Superior's current is counter-clockwise) noticed that the normally clear waters were turning cloudy-green. Led by Houghton native Verna Mize, scores of people complained and petitioned the authorities to investigate. In 1971, the Environmental Protection Agency issued a report which erased all doubt. The taconite tailings were polluting the lake far beyond the original dump site. Reserve was advised to develop a plan for on-land disposal. The Company temporized, threatened to close down and brought powerful political pressure to bear.

Eventually the federal government, in conjunction with the states of Michigan and Wisconsin, took Reserve Mining Company to court. When the trial ended in 1974, Reserve was ordered to cease dumping in the lake, select a new site and prepare a timetable for disposal of their mining wastes on land. For six years, the mining company appealed the decision while dumping continued unabated. And each day, trillions of asbestos-like fibers — invisible, odorless, tasteless — invaded the cleanest body of fresh water in the world.

In 1980, Reserve lost final appeals and built an on-land disposal facility. By 1983, the Company requested approval to treat and release water from its tailings pond; the water would eventually flow into Lake Superior. Once again citizens raised a storm of protest. Finally, in the mid-1980s, citing reduced demand for iron ore (the plant was operating at 25% capacity), Reserve closed its facility at Silver Bay.

Today, the issues raised by the long Reserve Mining Company story are dormant. But there are still dangers to the pristine jewel that is Lake Superior. Municipalities still discharge waste water, gold mines on the north shore release mercury and cyanide, and a number of pulp and paper mills use the lake water for manufacturing their products. Not all pollution comes from the shores of the lake; some toxins are borne in by winds from sources hundreds of miles distant. For all who love Lake Superior, the pivotal question is this: Is *any* economic gain worth the price we may pay in the decline of water quality? Can we endorse *any* development which results in the warning that children and women of childbearing age should not consume fish from what was once the purest lake? Can we afford to waste a Superior Lake?

My love affair with *Gitche Gumme* is of long duration. As a youngster growing up in a crowded suburb of Detroit, Lake Superior meant wilderness, a portion of North America still almost the way it was when Brule, Radisson, Allouez and other explorers canoed along its shores. I traced an outline of the lake and pasted it on the wall above my desk. Lake Superior is shaped somewhat like a bent bow; the north shore resembles a drawn bowstring and the Keweenaw Peninsula looks like an arrow about to be shot into the heartland of the United States. Someone gave me a copy of Holling C. Holling's book, *Paddle-to-the-Sea*, as a birthday present. Holling pictures Lake Superior's outline as the head of a wolf. Isle Royale is the eye and the Keweenaw Peninsula forms the mouth; the snout faces to the west and Duluth is the tip of the wolf's nose.

During his infrequent trips from the Copper Country, my Cornish grandfather described the Big lake in glowing terms; he called it "the blue profound," a phrase he had read somewhere and admired enough to remember.

"Actually," he added, "it's blue on its way to being purple."

When I finally saw Lake Superior with my own eyes, it was love at first sight: it was late afternoon on the first day of our honeymoon and the great expanse of water shimmered in the slanting rays of the August sun. Someday, I vowed, I would live close enough to see the lake every day. After a lengthy period of graduate work and an exciting four years teaching at a small college in western Minnesota, I found myself at a major crossroad. Two job opportunities presented themselves. The first position was at a large prestigious university where I would work with leaders in my field and have access to a magnificent library and well-equipped research facilities. The other job was at Northern Michigan University located on the south shore of Lake Superior. Most of my colleagues and former teachers advised me to take the assistant professorship in the large university where I could grow professionally.

"Don't go to Northern," a good friend advised. "You will be in a backwater, isolated both geographically and intellectually." For over a week, I vacillated between the two offers. Finally I called an outstanding member of my profession, a man who had helped me untangle my stuttering problem; I knew Dr. Van Riper had grown up in the Upper Peninsula and I trusted his judgment. His response was typical of him: "If you want to be in the forefront of the profession, opt for the job at the Big Ten university . . . but if you want to *live well*, my friend, there's only one choice."

The decision to accept the position at Northern was almost made by the time I drove the 500 miles from Minnesota to Marquette for the initial interview. Weary from hours on the road, synapses eroded by traffic, I came over the crest of a hill just east of the airport and saw Lake Superior framed between rockcuts on either side of the highway, stretching out to the horizon. The blue profound. I knew that regardless of the salary or future professional advancement, this was where I wanted to be. In the three decades since that time, the salary and advancement have taken care of themselves, and the decision has never been regretted. Ironically, I now get sly notes from the same former colleagues who advised against moving to a "backwater" asking if any positions are open at Northern!

The passage of time has only increased my affection for Lake Superior. I have come to admire deeply its many moods, the infinite variety of colors it reflects, the music of its waves upon the shores, and the fresh smell of the north wind blowing over more than a hundred miles of clear open water. Thoreau might have been thinking about Lake Superior when he wrote:

> *A lake is the landscape's most beautiful and expressive feature.*
> *It is the earth's eye, looking into which the beholder measures the*
> *depth of his own nature.*

The opportunity to live, work and find recreation by the Superior Lake, the joy of seeing it each day brings the responsibility of protecting and guarding its health and beauty. If I would earn the right to savor the Superior Peninsula, I must continue to work to save it.

EPILOGUE

The landscape where we reside shapes and defines our lives — the impact of geography is substantial and pervasive. The desert dweller, the prairie resident and the lover of mountain vistas all are influenced and changed by the lands they choose.

Surrounded by the forests and granite hills, living near the myriad streams and lakes of the Superior Peninsula, we feel connected to and in harmony with the earth.

The choice to live in this remote land also brings with it certain hardships — a degree of isolation, harsh weather, and employment uncertainties. Those who have resolved to remain here believe that living with natural beauty creates a special type of people to match a special place.

We are blessed with the opportunity to live in a unique and wondrous land. Surely that is why we are so protective of this native valley.